Environmental Jobs for Scientists and Engineers

Nicholas Basta

John Wiley & Sons, Inc.

New York • Chichester • Brisbane • Toronto • Singapore

Text printed on recycled paper.

In recognition of the importance of preserving what has been written, it is a policy of John Wiley & Sons, Inc., to have books of enduring value published in the United States printed on acid-free paper, and we exert our best efforts to that end.

This publication is designed to provide accurate and authoritative information in regard to the subject matter covered. It is sold with the understanding that the publisher is not engaged in rendering legal, accounting, or other professional service. If legal advice or other expert assistance is required, the services of a competent professional person should be sought. *From a Declaration of Principles jointly adopted by a Committee of the American Bar Association and a Committee of Publishers.*

Library of Congress Cataloging-in-Publication Data

Basta, Nicholas
  Environmental jobs for scientists and engineers / by Nicholas Basta.
    p.   cm.
  Includes index.
  ISBN 0-471-54034-X. — ISBN 0-471-54033-1 (pbk.)
   1. Environmental protection—Vocational guidance. 2. Conservation of natural resources—Vocational guidance. I. Title.
TD170.2.B37 1992
628'.023—dc20   91-34057

Printed in the United States of America

10 9 8 7 6 5 4 3 2 1

Printed and bound by Courier Companies, Inc.

*For two adventurers in the career world,
my sister and brother,
Evelyn and Timothy*

Preface

This book, together with its companion volume *The Environmental Career Guide* (Wiley, 1991), calls attention to an exciting new trend in professional work: the growth of environmental preservation and protection as a field of employment. "Environmentalism" remains a hotly debated philosophy in the halls of government, in corporate boardrooms, in classrooms, and even around the kitchen table. Fewer and fewer people, however, dispute the value of protecting the Earth that we have inherited from unnecessary or unwarranted change or degradation.

The term "green-collar work force" has been coined here to address this growing field of employment. If they put personal feelings about the pros and cons of environmentalism to the side for a moment, great numbers of businesspeople, lawyers, government officials, researchers, and teachers will realize that they are green-collar workers. By one estimate, there are already three-and-a-half *million* such workers today, and the total will at least double by the end of this decade. Other numbers are also impressive: The current bill for pollution abatement and control is pegged at over $115 billion per year, and is expected to rise to almost $200 billion by the year 2000. At that time, pollution abatement and control will be a bigger activity of the United States than is this country's support of the military. Swords into plowshares—into tree seedlings.

The work of environmental protection and preservation has become increasingly professionalized. While there will always be a place for the unstudied nature lover—indeed, a primary reason for preservation is to keep the wild as a place for contemplation, or simply to know that it exists—today's work is highly complex. In a legal context, environmental work is risky and difficult to do correctly. In a business sense, environmental work is chancy as a profitable enterprise. And in a scientific and technological context—the context of this book—environmental work is highly specialized and full of surprise and continual change.

The clamor for the services of scientists or engineers with the right expertise, available at the right moment, can be deafening. To take just one example drawn from recent headlines, when the chemistry of the upper atmosphere over the Antarctic Circle became an important issue, job demand for experts in this heretofore obscure field bloomed. As the concerns over more and more aspects of the Earth's condition grow, the call goes out for more scientific and technological expertise. Some hardened veterans of the previous era of environmental activism—the late 1960s and early 1970s—may feel that an old fad has simply returned for a short run, only to fade again. But there are many signs that, this time around, a permanent change in social, business, and technological policies has occurred.

Chapter 1 provides details on these signs, and lays out the general landscape of green-collar work for scientists and engineers. A guiding principle of this landscape is that in coming years, all scientists and engineers will be able to locate their work in proximity to environmental protection and preservation. They will either be applying technology to solving pressing environmental problems, or they will be changing technology in order to prevent unnecessary damage to the Earth. A broader context of these themes, including career opportunities for nonscientists, is described in *The Environmental Career Guide*; here, the emphasis is on research and technological issues.

Chapter 2 details the professional requirements and green-collar opportunities for scientists. All of the major scientific disciplines are presented in terms of their history, current educational requirements, and typical green-collar work opportunities. One medical profession—environmental medicine—is also described.

Chapter 3 details the same requirements and opportunities for the leading engineering disciplines as well as for computer science. While most scientists are involved in research, most engineers and related technologists are involved in design, production, and preservation. Opportunities both among manufacturing firms, which are currently expanding their environmental protection efforts, and consulting and regulatory organizations that enforce environmental laws are detailed.

Chapter 4 provides a listing of key green-collar occupations for scientists and engineers. Certain of this material reprises what is described in many individual engineering or scientific disciplines in the preceding two chapters. However, it is clear that environmental work is increasingly cross-disciplinary in nature. The number of jobs tied to a single, exclusive academic background is shrinking.

An extensive set of appendices lists important professional and not-for-profit organizations, key publications, and addresses of governmental offices in both the United States and Canada. Also provided is a listing of graduate schools and training organizations with offerings in specific environmental fields.

Science and its sibling profession, engineering, have a true love-hate relationship with environmentalism. For some scientists and engineers, the natural world around us is, in a sense, their professional playing field. It is where they venture out to achieve mighty things, whether the discovery of some new physical or biological principle or the installation of some new device that helps humanity—a bridge that crosses a dangerous chasm or a factory that provides wholesome employment for thousands and a needed product for the marketplace.

Science and engineering are increasingly finding, however, that what they can do professionally is limited by society's desires, as expressed in laws and regulations. Certain types of research have become hampered or outright prohibited. And a great many types of manufacturing, construction, and agricultural activities have become transformed, thwarted, or abandoned. The source of many of these laws and regulations has been the environmentalist community. Individual scientists and engineers, usually a rather dispassionate lot, find their feelings rising into a hot rage over what has occurred.

In truth, we all have ambivalent feelings about the environment and environmentalism. We love nature, but we also love the comforts of civilization. The plight of scientists and engineers is different because the environment, one way or another, is their professional arena. They must be able to probe the universe around them, or build or produce somewhere on the land. As this book shows, society is increasingly depending on them to answer the burning questions about the future fate of the Earth, and to solve the terrible issues of poverty, sickness, and ignorance without destroying all the other inhabitants of this planet.

Contents

CHAPTER FOUR
Green-Collar Professions **155**

CHAPTER ONE

Fixing the Environment

When one thinks about the conjunction of science and technology with the environment, the temptation is to rewrite the 1960s-era slogan, "If you are not part of the solution, you are part of the problem." The revised version would read, "You are part of the problem *and* part of the solution."

The basis for this revision is simple: Many, if not all, of our environmental problems are the result of humanity's application of technology to nature. Air pollution or toxic chemicals in rivers and in the ground are obvious examples. Less obvious—but still the result of technology—is the loss of biological diversity due to the application of pesticides or to the destruction of wetlands. Even in cases where the environmental problem seems to be purely a matter of population pressure—as, for example, tropical forest destruction in South America—one could argue that the population growth would not have occurred without the intercession of modern medical care to save more newborn and to lengthen lifetime on Earth.

In a similar, all-encompassing vein, many, if not all, environmental problems can be addressed or possibly solved through the application of new technology. Soil erosion, ozone-layer depletion, toxic landfills—you name it—are keeping teams of scientists and engineers at work. "The solution to technology is more technology" is a statement of belief to which many technologists adhere. A sizable segment of modern Western society would prefer otherwise—to turn back the clock to an earlier, supposedly more innocent time when technology had not wreaked so much damage on the environment. More will be said about this philosophy later in this chapter; for the moment, let it be emphatically clear that this book supports those technologists who are looking for technological solutions to environmental issues.

"The intersection of technology and environment in a sense has been the blind spot in our system of knowledge, and this gap is at the root of today's environmental crisis," noted Robert White, president of the National Academy of Engineering, in a 1989 report entitled *Technology and Environment* [1]. It is doubtful that anyone outside the scientific and engineering communities could fill in this gap; it remains the responsibility of these communities to develop solutions to the problems they helped create.

Economics and the Environment

Fixing the environment is today a big business, especially in the United States. According to a 1991 estimate from the U.S. Environmental Protection Agency (EPA), $115 billion were expended in 1990. This figure represents just over 2 percent of the U.S. gross national product (GNP) and is also somewhat less than half the size of the U.S. defense budget. By the turn of the century, predicts EPA [2], the dollar figure will rise to nearly $200 billion, representing 60 percent of the military budget and about 2.8 percent of GNP. These figures include spending only for direct control of pollution; wildlife preservation, agricultural conservation, and environmental medicine would add billions of dollars more.

Management Information Services, Inc., a Washington, D.C., consulting firm, has looked at these and other figures and concluded that some 3.5 million workers are directly employed by government and industry to spend this money. Relative to other sectors of the U.S. economy, the work force of the environmental field is highly educated and professionalized. Scientific training is the core knowledge in this business.

The rapid growth that the environmental field is enjoying today has led to dramatic pressures to fill the ranks of these workers with scientists holding the highest academic degrees. Just as the computer revolution that gained force in the late 1970s and the biotech revolution that came to the fore in the 1980s, so today high-tech environmental businesses have become the target of venture capitalists and the Wall Street investment community. These are heady days for environmental technology.

American society has put the environment in this limelight before—in fact, over this century, the issue has cropped up roughly every 30 years or so. At the turn of the century, as the American frontier was officially declared closed, a backlash against the rapid exploitation of western resources led to the founding of the National Parks Service, the first federal water pollution laws, and the creation of the Sierra Club and other naturalist organizations. In the 1930s, under the gathering clouds of the Depression, the fear that national resources were being lost or wasted led to federal efforts to conserve soil, the great dam-building projects of the West, and, in 1935, the founding of the Wilderness Society. (The U.S. Fish and Wildlife Service followed close by, having been formed in 1940.) In the early 1960s, a backlash again developed, but this time against the rapid dominance of the automobile on the national landscape, and federal "beautification" programs appeared. Simultaneously, the publication of Rachel Carson's book *Silent Spring* alerted the populace to the wanton destruction of wildlife through the use of pesticides. The drumbeat grew throughout the 1960s, culminating in the formation of the U.S. Environmental Protection Administration (later, Agency) in 1970, passage of a host of environmentally related laws, and the first Earth Day (also in 1970).

Now, in the 1990s, there is talk of upgrading EPA to a cabinet-level department. The number of laws regulating industrial pollution is in the dozens. Environmentalism has also, finally, become an international cause, as exemplified by the precedent-setting Montreal Protocol governing the abandonment of chlorofluorocarbon (CFC) chemicals because of their effects on the Earth's ozone layer.

The preceding discussion is one reading of recent environmental history. Another parallel structure could be constructed around the milestones of new, science-based professional societies that were involved in the environment and public and occupational health. In the 1870s, a "Sanitarian Movement" took hold in the larger American cities, leading to improvements in municipal waste and sewage removal. The 1920s saw the growth of a tremendous number of water-treatment and transportation systems and greater regulation of urban air quality. The 1950s saw the first strong wave of concern over occupational safety and increased regulation of air pollutants. The American Public Health Association was formed in 1872. The American Society of Agronomy was founded in 1907, the same year as the Air and Waste Management Association (then named the International Association for the Prevention of Smoke); the American Ecological Society, in 1915; the precursor of the Water Pollution Control Federation, in 1928; the American Nuclear Society, in 1954; the American Academy of Environmental Engineers, in 1967; the National Association of Environmental Professionals, in 1975; and the National Association of Environmental Managers, in 1990.

Both of these readings might seem to indicate that the environment as an area of professional involvement has undergone steady, inexorable growth for over a century. In a historical or sociological sense, this is true; however, there have been many lulls or downturns. The environmental job market is booming today—will it last?

The Step Change

Mathematicians speak of a "step change" when, because a critical threshold has been reached, the values of an equation jump up to a higher plateau. Such a step change has indeed occurred over the past ten years, and there will be no turning back to a time when environmental issues are of minor importance. This step change has led to the genesis of a body of knowledge of the environment—still in a state of rapid evolution—and a group of professions that can be labeled the "green-collar work force." Today, most of the professions inside or outside of commerce are being affected by the new environmental agenda.

The justification for these claims proceeds from two pieces of evidence: the theoretical and the practical. The theoretical evidence is all around us, in the mountains of garbage our cities produce, in the durable synthetic compounds now floating in the stratosphere and in underground lakes, in the disappearing species and forests. During this decade, the world population will pass 6 billion; in 1960, it was half that total. The longer-term projection is for population to bulge to 8.5 billion by 2025. The phrase "carrying capacity" became prominent during the 1960s, when an initial wave of concern over world population appeared. The phrase was used to argue that the Earth's carrying capacity for humanity would soon be exceeded, causing a disastrous readjustment when the population could no longer be supported.

Subsequent analysis showed that carrying capacity is a rather elastic concept; as population pressure rises, new forms of agriculture, industrial production, and social mores arise. A disaster that seemed to be looming in plain sight has receded to a distant horizon. The debate over the carrying capacity of the Earth is still very much open; what gets lost in highly charged discussions is the fact that, with each ratcheting upward of population and economic production, the need grows for society—its political leaders, business executives, and technologists—to manage human affairs. Food distribution becomes more critical. Managing floods, droughts, and other natural disasters becomes less an issue of cursing the fates than of cursing the short-sightedness of governments. The need for energy and other natural resources drives industry deeper and deeper into the wilderness, making the chances for an Exxon Valdez type of disaster more proba-ble. In each of these cases, the call goes out for technological exper-tise to plan for, handle, or make amends for humanity's effects on the Earth. Whether or not Wall Street capitalists will fund the growth of new environmental firms, society will be spending more for analyzing the environment, changing harmful industrial activities, or correct-ing previous insults.

"It took some 50,000 years for human numbers to reach 2.5 billion in 1950, but only 37 years to double to 5 billion. It will likely double again in the lifetime of today's children," said Gus Speth, president of the World Resources Institute, Washington, D.C., in a late-1990 speech.

The practical evidence for the step change in environmental professionalism is best summed up by a look at Figure 1, which is simply a plot of the number of federal environmental laws over time. While some of these laws are simple legalistic modifications of existing rules, others represent fundamental changes in how American soci-ety functions. Banking, insurance, advertising, marketing, and other business activities that might at first glance appear far removed from toxic landfills or vanishing wildlife have now been drawn into a regulatory net. While it has been traditional for manufacturing leaders to bemoan the increase in paperwork and diverted resources to deal with all of these rules, more farsighted industrialists have decided to take advantage of the situation. To cite just one example, Du Pont Co., high on any environmentalist's list of polluting com-panies, now plans to grow a $1-billion division to handle others' environmental problems—for a profit.

Washington is by no means the only government deciding envi-ronmental issues in the United States. Borrowing a page from the guidebook for the antinuclear protests of the 1970s, many states,

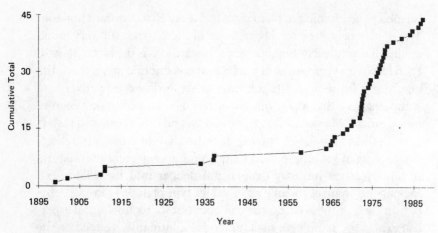

1899 River and Harbors Act (RHA)
1902 Reclamation Act (RA)
1910 Insecticide Act (IA)
1911 Weeks Law (WL)
1934 Taylor Graring Act (TGA)
1937 Flood Control Act (FCA)
1937 Wildlife Restoration Act (WRA)
1958 Fish and Wildlife Coordination
     Act (FWCA)
1964 Wilderness Act (WA)
1965 Solid Waste Disposal Act (SWDA)
1965 Water Resources Planning Act
     (WRPA)
1966 National Historic Preservation Act
     (NHPA)
1968 Wild and Scenic Rivers Act
     (WSRA)
1969 National Environmental Policy Act
     (NEPA)
1970 Clean Air Act (CAA)
1970 Occupational Safety and Health
     Act (OSHA)
1972 Water Pollution Control Act
     (WPCA)
1972 Marine Protection, Research and
     Sanctuaries Act (MPRSA)
1972 Coastal Zone Management Act
     (CZMA)
1972 Home Control Act (HCA)
1972 Federal Insecticide, Fungicide and
     Rodenticide Act (FIFRA)
1972 Parks and Waterways Safety Act
     (PWSA)
1972 Marine Mammal Protection Act
     (MMPA)

1973 Endangered Species Act (ESA)
1974 Deepwater Port Act (DPA)
1974 Safe Drinking Water Act (SDWA)
1974 Energy Supply and Environmental
     Coordination Act (ESECA)
1976 Toxic Substances Control Act
     (TSCA)
1976 Federal Land Policy and Manage-
     ment Act (FLPMA)
1976 Resource Conservation and Re-
     covery Act (RCRA)
1977 Clean Air Act Amendments
     (CAAA)
1977 Clean Water Act (CWA)
1977 Surface Mining Control and Recla-
     mation Act (SMCRA)
1977 Soil and Water Resources Con-
     servation Act (SWRCA)
1978 Endangered Species Act Amend-
     ments (ESAA)
1978 Environmental Education Act
     (EEA)
1980 Comprehensive Environmental
     Response Compensation and
     Liability Act (CERCLA)
1982 Nuclear Waste Policy Act (NWPA)
1984 Resource Conservation and Re-
     covery Act Amendments (RCRAA)
1984 Environmental Programs and
     Assistance Act (EPAA)
1986 Safe Drinking Water Act Amend-
     ments (SDWAA)
1986 Superfund Amendments and Re-
     organization Act (SARA)

FIGURE 1 **The Rising Tide of Environmental Legislation**
(*Source:* Adapted from Yeager, K. E., and Baruch, S. B., "Environmental
Issues Affecting Coal Technology." *Annual Reviews of Energy,* 1987, Vol.
12, pp. 471–502).

counties, and cities have been instituting environmental bans or restrictions affecting a host of manufactured products, ranging from cash deposits on recyclable beverage containers to bans on chloro-fluorocarbons. Through the intercession of the federal community right-to-know rules (passed in 1986), each locality now gets annual data on the volume of toxic chemicals being released by industries in their area. Hundreds of local laws mirror or anticipate federal laws.

The financial and legal liabilities that these laws entail are having a real effect on how products are designed, manufactured, and disposed of today. These effects are changing the practice of engineering regardless of what types of raw materials are exploited or what types of products are manufactured. And the technology these engineers apply, in turn, depends on basic and applied research conducted by scientists. Consider the following two examples:

- "Job opportunities expand as scientists from many disciplines join forces to preserve a multitude of plant and animal species," read the subhead of a 1991 article in *The Scientist* [3]. The article went on to say that "scientists from many fields—museum curators, conservationists, field biologists, even mathematical modelers—are being swept up" in a tide of attention on addressing the biodiversity issue.

- "The same space mission that sent men to the moon launched a series of satellites that provided the first real glimpses of now-pressing environmental issues," noted a 1989 article in *Business Week*, "The Next Giant Leap for Mankind May Be Saving Planet Earth" [4]. While most scientists' eyes have been focused outward, toward the stars and planets, during the reign of the National Aeronautics and Space Administration, at least a few have begun looking back from space, to the mother planet. In the absence of a national commitment to other forms of space exploration, NASA has recently latched onto the environment as a cause for sustaining its mission (and budgets). What does planetary and space research have to do with the Earth's environment? Plenty—the satellites just alluded to (specifically, *Nimbus-7*) were among the instruments that confirmed the growth of an ozone hole above the Antarctic. The article quotes one NASA scientist as saying that "subliminally . . . those of us who were looking outward to other planets were always searching for some social and economic relevance to our work."

It can be asserted, axiomatically, that in the coming years, all scientists at work in the United States, regardless of their specialty, will be able to locate their work in proximity to environmental protection and preservation. Indeed, many scientists will be forced to perform this calibration simply as a matter of professional survival.

Traditionally, scientists drew a line in the sand between "pure" and "applied" research, and, if pure research remained today what it has been in earlier generations, pure-research scientists could argue that their work has little or no relationship to environmental issues. Currently, however, the distinction is more sharply defined between what might be called "commercial" and "noncommercial" research. With the great debates engaged in during the past decade in the United States over national economic competitiveness, the funding of research with commercial potential has taken a dramatic upswing. University professors now regularly find themselves in tangled discussions with their administrators over the patentability of their research, and they just as regularly fend off enticing job offers from the business sector.

The point here is not to debate the pros and cons of the commercialization of pure research. But the point must be made that, while pure research will undoubtedly continue in some form, the momentum (read, money) is with those scientists who can tie their research into the social issues of the day. The environment is simply too tempting an opportunity and too important to ignore. Over time, research with a strong environmental component will dominate research that lacks such a component. The article in *The Scientist* cited earlier goes on to note that "the irony is that a highly academic, highly esoteric activity [i.e., biodiversity research] is becoming a commercial activity. . . . " But where is the irony? Is not this situation rather a confirmation of the value of "pure" research?

The Antitechnology Rap

A generation ago, when graduates of some of the finest schooling the country could offer chucked it all to live on communes in the wilderness, seeking to subsist in a model pre-nineteenth-century culture, there was an intense antitechnology mindset in much of the intelligentsia. The thought was to somehow revert back to a more innocent, preindustrial form of life. By demonstrating the success of this life-style in communes, these radical thinkers believed they could turn the tide of civilization.

The commune dwellers did not spring out of the 1960s as a uniquely new idea. Communes were the most radical demonstration of a powerful back-to-nature movement, which itself was something of a generational reaction to the quiet, comfortable 1950s. In the intellectual arenas, a profound distrust of the powerful success of science and technology over the past 25 years also helped create the logic for communes. Writers such as Lewis Mumford, Jacques Ellul, and Theodore Roszak depicted the concept of technology as a mindless force raping the natural world. The greatest fear was that technology had been released from human control and would soon destroy humanity as it already seemed to be doing to the environment.

For better or worse, practically all of these communes failed, most of them quickly. Either they could not sustain themselves economically without periodic infusions of cash from outside sources, or their members lost interest and moved on. Such utopian experiments have a long-standing tradition in the United States; indeed, parts of the country settled by Europeans were themselves utopian communities of one sort or another. And, with profound religious orientations, such as those of the Amish and Mennonite communities scattered through the American Midwest, preindustrial communes have been demonstrated to be viable, at least for the believers.

Over the same period of time, the intellectual animus against technology has abated, if not disappeared. The forms and directions of technological development, as well as its consequences on society and the environment, are studied and debated intensely. But the designation of technology *itself* as the root cause of social and environmental problems is not today in the mainstream of critical thinking. In a word, the scientist or engineer can be the hero of an environmental story, as well as the villain.

In fact, it is remarkable how often an environmental issue seems to be born out of a new advance in scientific knowledge, particularly one that involves instrumentation. The controversy over the effect of chlorofluorocarbons on the stratosphere was kicked off when James Lovelock, a British chemist, developed a type of chromatograph that detected the compounds in the atmosphere in part-per-trillion concentrations.

The consensus seems to be that, in order to provide for 5 billion people, *some* accommodation with *some* level of technology is necessary. Technologists of all stripes now debate where to draw the line. During the 1970s, this debate centered around the philosophy of "appropriate technology" (i.e., technology that could be deployed and maintained with minimal advanced training and that could solve many economic problems for underdeveloped nations). More recently, this school of thought is expressed as "sustainable development." Broadly defined, this concept admits any technologies that do not consume irreplaceable resources and that do not create a net increase in pollution.

Irrational fear of technology has not disappeared—witness the prevalence of the so-called NIMBY syndrome, an acronym for "not in my back yard." NIMBY appeared in the early 1980s as the monumental problems of industrial-waste dumps encroached upon neighborhoods. This conflict between industrialism and environmentalism appeared in starkest form in Niagara Falls, New York, at Love Canal. Love Canal, originally a real estate development, became an industrial dump for local manufacturers in the 1940s and early 1950s. By the end of that decade, it had reached capacity, was capped over with earth, and deeded to the city. The city, in turn, authorized development of the area, going so far as to build a public school directly over the dump. Health problems and birth defects began to appear among residents of the area. Soon, the mismanagement of the site was compounded by an inability of the city, state, or federal government to make amends. The toxic wastes seeping from under the ground clearly were not an immediate hazard, such as a fire or an explosion, nor were they a natural hazard, such as a flood or an earthquake. Both immediate and natural calamities had well-defined governmental responses; a suspected industrial dump did not.

An activist movement by residents of the area finally brought the issue to a head, and, in 1979, President Jimmy Carter proclaimed a federal emergency for the area, authorizing evacuation of part of it and reimbursement for lost real estate values. Even so, a neighborhood had been destroyed.

NIMBY soon became the rallying cry for property owners, community groups, and environmentalists across the nation. The various new laws and regulations that had been spawned by Love Canal created the need for new disposal facilities, but getting permission for siting these facilities has proved next to impossible in many areas. State and federal governments are in agreement with industry that some type of disposal capacity is necessary in each state, but getting agreement from communities for building and operating the facilities is a daunting task. NIMBY has come to be applied against municipal waste incinerators and against many types of manufacturing, especially any having the potential for air or water pollution. Occasionally, NIMBY's scope enlarges to NOMP, for "not on my planet."

Some of the impetus for NIMBY is a very rational economic calculation; for example, the property next to an industrial development will decline in value, and unless the siting process for a facility takes this decline into account, the property owner has a legitimate concern. But some of the impetus is not rational; the fear of any chemical or any type of waste—what the chemical industry likes to call "chemophobia"—is not justified. More scientific knowledge, as well as the communication of this knowledge in a form that the layperson can understand, can ameliorate the situation. The knowledge can take two forms: (1) the development of ways of eliminating the hazard that people fear, which is emphatically not always possible; and (2) the more definite assessment of what hazards do exist and what countermeasures can be taken against them.

The communication process is vital in either case. The lay public is demanding a greater say in technological decisions. In some cases, this say is authorized by the rule of law, and a lengthy series of public hearings is often required before a construction project or environmental cleanup takes place. The dialogue between experts and the public often results in an improvement in the overall design of a project.

The Relevance of Science and Engineering

In the two chapters that follow, the current conditions affecting the professional lives and interests of scientists and engineers will be reviewed. Today's environmental work has descended on these professions in a new, unpredictable fashion. Who could have foreseen, for example, that the debate over the supersonic transport in the 1960s would ultimately have resolved into an international ban on chlorofluorocarbon refrigerants? Or that the techniques that mining engineers have evolved to handle the disposal of acidic mine wastes would become important in the design and remediation of municipal garbage landfills?

It is for this reason that a brief examination of the history of the various science and engineering professions is in order, along with an assessment of current environmental activities. Everyone agrees that the environmental projects of the future must be interdisciplinary in nature. Who, then, can predict from what profession or from what field of academic study breakthrough solutions to pressing environmental problems may come? A profession such as agricultural engineering, to cite just one case, has traditionally been most closely associated with the development of farm machinery, irrigation systems, and the like. But today, with a dramatic push for "organic" farming, agricultural engineering may have positive contributions to make in new farming techniques.

These historical perspectives will also aim more at the employment patterns and main research and development directions of the various professions rather than at a decade-by-decade examination of the many directions in which science and engineering professions have evolved. Historians of science and technology may find these perspectives woefully understated, but in a book about current employment prospects, this information is the most pertinent.

A similar qualification should be stated concerning the North American orientation of this book. It is hardly the intent here to minimize the environmental consequences of issues such as tropical deforestation, African desertification, or the overpopulation of the Third World. Indeed, some of these issues will be addressed.

However, the underlying theme of this book is how science and engineering educations can be applied to environmental issues in the U.S. job market. Many such jobs are defined by federal or state legislation, much of which does not exist (or functions in radically different form) in other parts of the world. In addition, many, if not most, environmental issues are the result of industrialization as practiced in market economies, of which the United States is an example *par excellence*. Finally, while there are plenty of opportunities for U.S. scientists and engineers to do research or fieldwork abroad (indeed, for many environmental issues, it is practically essential), the job or employer is usually based in the United States. There is lamentably little international transfer of environmental expertise, but, as will be seen, this trend is changing in a positive fashion. To put the point in ecological sloganeering terms, the environmentalist's credo of "Think globally, act locally" might be restated as "Think globally, seek a job locally."

Readers, who might be studying for or who already have earned a degree in one or another of these science or engineering disciplines, will find information on what coworkers in the profession are doing. Ideally, however, they should look at the *combination* of various disciplines during their education (either after taking an undergraduate degree in one specialty and a graduate degree in another or while setting up a major/minor program for an undergraduate degree).

Another, much larger issue has to do with the relevance of these professions to environmental work. Many environmental activists, especially the more radical ones, would say that professions like civil engineering (the builders of dams) or nuclear physics (the inventors of nuclear bombs) have been the causes of many of the environmental problems we face today rather than a resource for their resolution. At some point early in this century, many of the benefits of new discoveries in science and engineering were successfully applied in curing diseases or in developing new machines, to the acclaim of all around. While many scientists enjoyed this celebrity, they were usually quick to assert that they developed "pure" science only for the inherent value in new knowledge and emphatically not with any commercial or even socially valuable purpose in mind. As far as they were concerned, science and technology just happen; it is the decisions (and responsibility) of business people and government leaders as to what ends the knowledge might be put. The British mathematician G. H. Hardy, in a celebrated (and possibly apocryphal) after-dinner toast, may have put it best: "To pure mathematics; may it never be of use to anyone" [5].

By the 1930s, some scientists, especially those in Great Britain, began to question the "sinister implications of politically subservient science," according to John Young in his recent book *Sustaining the Earth* [6]. And World War II, with its revelations of concentration camps run by Germany (in which medical "experiments" were conducted) and the detonation of atomic bombs by the United States, blew the lid off the supposed intellectual neutrality of science. While there are many who would still defend the social purposelessness of science, the great weight of intellectual discourse in the postwar years has been a succession of revelations about the inherent biases of scientists toward what they choose to study (and, often more significantly, what they choose *not* to study).

For the past ten years at least, the U.S. scientific and engineering communities have moved—and been pulled by government and commerce—in the direction of developing knowledge to make the U.S. economy more competitive in the world arena. The key component in this campaign is, simply, money. The federal government (through such agencies as the National Institutes of Health, the National Science Foundation, and the Department of Energy) as well as most of the leading manufacturing enterprises have supported a growing portion of the money that academic scientists spend. Both government and industry employ large numbers of scientists and engineers and fund expensive research in corporate laboratories. The chase for funding grants and laboratory expansions has grown intense, even as some science leaders decry the growing competition and insist that society must commit more funds to this applied research and development. Leon Lederman, president of the American Association for the Advancement of Science, issued a call at the beginning of 1991 for an across-the-board doubling of funds for research in the United States [7]. In an environment like this, hardly anyone is toasting the "uselessness" of science.

This leads to an important point about the relevance of the science and engineering professions to solving environmental problems today. If, as few would dispute, the direction of science and technology can be pointed toward desirable social goals, then, in many cases, scientists and engineers can be foremost in leading this effort. It is a question of how committed the individual scientist or engineer is to preserving and improving the environment; it is not a question of the validity of one or another type of study.

This is the philosophical perspective, if you will. A more practical perspective is simply put: If scientists and engineers do not solve environmental problems, then who will? Who will develop plans to clean up an abandoned hazardous-waste dump, and who will do the actual cleanup? If global warming is the issue, who will either confirm its existence or confirm that the Earth's temperature rise can be attributed to some other cause? Scientists and engineers will not be the solitary resource for curing environmental ills; the political, economic, and social dimensions of environmental protection are becoming clearer with each passing year. But when an environmental problem is postulated, no activist-group study and no government legislation will cure the problem. Scientists and engineers will have to provide the necessary information to identify the parameters of the problem, and they will carry out the changes in manufacturing, agricultural, or transportation practices or find the means of correcting a festering pollution problem.

Recent History

Imagine a scientist of a century ago who is contemplating the environment of greatest interest at the moment, the American West. Such a scientist might have an interest in geology and earth science and would study the gigantic folding strata of the Rocky Mountains or the ancient record written in the walls of the Grand Canyon. Or imagine a biologist who is contemplating the dizzying array of native species that had received only cursory attention until then or who is beginning to get excited about the unprecedented richness of fossils that were just becoming known. What would be the outlook of such a scientist? His (nearly all scientists of the time were men) *weltanschauung*?

We can imagine (and that is all this is, a thought exercise) that this scientist is in awe of the mighty forces that had pushed up the mountains or carved the canyons. We can also imagine the biologist's fascination with the unknown purposes and interrelationships of plant and life forms that are now being studied and with the miraculous dinosaur fossils now being discovered. Nature would be seen as a majestic, omnipotent force that, if the scientist were skillful enough, could be enticed to surrender some secrets. Nature would also remain as something of an enemy—with its harsh, bone-dry deserts; freezing winters; and untamed, dangerous rivers.

Next, imagine a scientist—a physicist, say, or an electrical engineer—of 50 years ago, when the Depression was winding down as the next world war was gearing up. This scientist might be studying the growing body of knowledge about electromagnetics and atomic theory, the hottest topics of the moment. If he were sufficiently plugged in to the right grapevine, the whispers about Einstein's unbelievable prediction that the power of the atom could be tamed and put to military use might have been heard. To this scientist, nature would be like a flower just opening up for observation and enjoyment. He might also take comradely pride in the accomplishments of his peers, who built the great bridges and dams of the West, who designed more and more powerful airplanes that were crisscrossing the sky, and who discovered exciting, new chemical agents that could counter infections and save lives. The world was full of threats, but the worst ones seemed manmade; it also seemed that new scientific tools offered means to defend against these threats.

Now, move to the present—look in a mirror and consider today's scientific worldview. What do we contemplate? The destruction of rain forests and the corresponding loss of biodiversity? The maddeningly knotted problem of providing low-cost energy while ending our addiction to crude oil? The disappearing ozone layer that protects us from harmful solar radiation? The growing inability of the planet to sustain a human population of more than 5 billion, even as this population races toward 6 billion?

Today there is little dispute that nature has been transformed from an omnipotent force into one that is being injured by human activities. For many scientists and engineers, the conflict between nature and technology has been changed into a race to find technologies that can preserve or resuscitate natural systems before they are lost forever. At the same time, the traditional purpose of technology as a tool for improving humans' living conditions is changing into a rancorous fight over dwindling resources. Not coincidentally, the body of scientific knowledge has grown immense during these times, with projects such as supercolliders for subatomic research, and the reading of the human genome, moving well within reach. Here, too, the challenges turn more directly on where the financial resources will be found for these projects than on the technical questions of how to accomplish them.

It is true both that human deprivation has existed since the beginning of recorded history, and that scientific research has been resource-limited for centuries. What is different today is the power of science and technology to alter the human condition and to solve pressing environmental problems. The stakes are rising, and the challenge for today's scientists and engineers is to transform the threat of technology into solutions for the benefit of the Earth and, ultimately, of humanity itself.

CHAPTER TWO

Scientists and the Environment

Science, by many accounts, is the single most important accomplishment of Western civilization. Coming out of the darkened Middle Ages, natural philosophers and Roman Catholic monks laid the initial philosophical foundations of inductive reasoning. Scholastic learning that was derived from the ancient Greek philosophers as well as Arabic mathematicians and astronomers provided some fundamental tools for viewing the outside world.

Many historians of science attribute the next key step to René Descartes, the French mathematician/philosopher whose principle of *cogito, ergo sum* opened the way to inductive reasoning and the scientific method of deriving fundamental truths from experimentation. At the same time, his philosophy created the mind/body dichotomy that separates the thinker from the environment. This is arguably the most basic distinction of Western science from that of any other part of the world, especially the philosophies of the East. It is also the seed of the alienation from one's environment that has come to dominate the debate of environmentalist philosophers and that could be the blame for the sorry damage that Western-style industrialism has caused.

What does this 500-year-old philosophizing have to do with modern science and with the potential for employment of scientists on environmental problems? The scientist who seeks to apply the scientific method to solving environmental problems will be challenged at almost every turn to demonstrate the validity of how a scientific question is addressed. Saying that such a question can be evaluated only by rational, inductive logic is no longer acceptable.

Examples of the difficulties that modern science has with environmental issues abound. One of the most controversial—at least in terms of how professional scientists and nonscientific environmentalists confront each other—is the famed "Gaia hypothesis," formulated by the British chemist James Lovelock. Having examined the remarkable ability of Earth to maintain chemical and physical conditions so that life can be supported, Lovelock postulated, in 1972, that the Earth itself was alive and that living creatures, from oceanic protozoa to corporate executives, were but cells in a giant organism that maintained itself by adjusting atmospheric chemistry, for example, to keep the planet's temperature in a suitable range.

The Gaia hypothesis is such a powerful metaphor for the connectedness of all living things—indeed, the Earth itself—that it has become almost an article of religious belief among many environmental activists. Many scientists, while admiring the clarity of the metaphor, scoff at it as a serious scientific principle. "I just haven't paid all that much attention," says Stephen Gould, a Harvard evolutionary biologist, in a 1991 article in *Science* magazine. "Gaia's a pretty metaphor, and not much more. I can't say I've lost sleep over it" [1]. But other scientists, such as Lynn Margulis, a botanist at the University of Massachusetts, see the Gaia hypothesis as a revolutionary new perspective on all of biology, one that will blow away Darwinist evolutionary theory and radically change our perspectives on biodiversity, and the very concept of individual species.

In a normal debate over such a new theory, proponents and opponents will conduct experiments, present results, and draw conclusions. But in the charged atmosphere between thoroughgoing environmentalism and conventional national industrialism, the proprieties of scientific discourse are simply one other debating point. In truth, science is not value-free knowledge. Scientific research into an environmental problem will suggest scientific solutions. As one contemplates scientists and engineers digging up hazardous wastes that were dumped under the guidance of scientists and engineers a generation ago, only to take these recovered wastes across the countryside to another dump and bury them in the Earth again, one can readily question "scientific" solutions.

The historian John Young, in his book *Sustaining the Earth* [2], describes the process by which his school, the University of Adelaide, Australia, began a program in environmental science in 1970 in its Faculty of Agricultural Science (which is as good a place as any, although at other schools such programs began in biology depart-ments or engineering departments or in general sciences). As the professors grappled with course descriptions, they realized that the department would need courses in a variety of sciences to accommo-date the "interdisciplinary" aspect of environmental science that is widely accepted today. Within a year, however, as the course planning took shape, the teachers realized that political, sociological, and historical issues were also critical to the subject, and thus the depart-ment's name was changed to the Interfaculty Committee in Environ-mental *Studies* (author's emphasis).

"Environmental *science* was the product of a state of mind which proposed a range of technological remedies for a problem of human, and therefore historical, origin," writes Young. "Environ-mental *studies* implied the insight that [environmental] problems were symptomatic of an underlying problem. . . . It implied recogni-tion of the need to understand the nature and cause of the disease before prescription, that is, for the causes of environmental problems to be understood in historical and social as well as scientific terms as a prerequisite for the prescription of the appropriate remedies."

All of this is emphatically not to say that scientists are unneces-sary to addressing environmental issues of the day—far from it. "Science is our most reliable compass," William Reilly, administrator of EPA, has said on numerous occasions in discussing the environ-mental decision making that the nation faces.

As the following sections will show, scientists across the board are deeply involved in identifying, characterizing, and offering solu-tions for these issues. But the situation calls for considerably more than undiluted scientific brainpower. Scientists contemplating envi-ronmental work today need to be aware of the historical context of the problems they are studying. They need to be able to translate their science into terms that are meaningful to the layperson. Most of all, they need to challenge accepted dogmas, especially those of the science they are studying or practicing.

Demographics and Dynamics of the Scientific Job Market

To read the scientific literature, it is the best of times and the worst of times to be a scientist. The science professions are enjoying a rising tide of prestige as blue-ribbon presidential panels send out a call for more science and for more science funding and express the extreme importance of scientific work to both the nation's industrial might and to the great problems faced across the country. At the same time, individual scientists decry the low pay, uncertain job security, and cutthroat competition among themselves to win university appointments and to gather grants from the National Science Foundation or from corporate sponsors.

"In academia, administrators and investigators [i.e., research scientists] alike are hounded by money shortages. In industry, vice presidents of R&D are bemoaning the sluggish economy, which they blame for holding down research budgets. Policy gurus in government are anguishing over where the next generation of scientists will come from. . . . And nearly everyone connected to science fears for the morale and motivation of young investigators." That is how *Science*, the leading journal of scientific research in the United States, summed up the situation in a 1991 report [3].

In truth, the gloom is more reflective of the particular condition of academic science, which is still adjusting to monumental changes in the past 25 years, when all of academia grew tremendously and then began to shrink due to the smaller number of college-age students in the country. Between 1985 and 1995, this number will have dropped by some 25 percent. More students are choosing college after high school (which helps keep the overall enrollments up), but proportionately fewer of them are choosing science or engineering programs to study. At the same time, the closer ties to industry have brought some marketplace-style competition into the ivory towers of academe, and this strong gust of reality from the business world can chill the outlook of many academics more accustomed to a quieter era with less of the hurly-burly commercial world.

Figure 2 shows the growth in R&D spending by "performer," the type of organization where the research is being conducted. (The *performer* is to be distinguished from the *source* of the funds. For example, the federal government budgeted about $72 billion for R&D in 1991, but only $17.5 billion of this total was spent in government labs; the rest was "extramural" research carried out in industry or at universities.) This data series is published annually by Battelle Memorial Institute, an international, private research organization headquartered in Columbus, Ohio [4]. Based on other data from the federal government and other private organizations, the Battelle R&D Forecast is an authoritative summary of U.S. research trends.

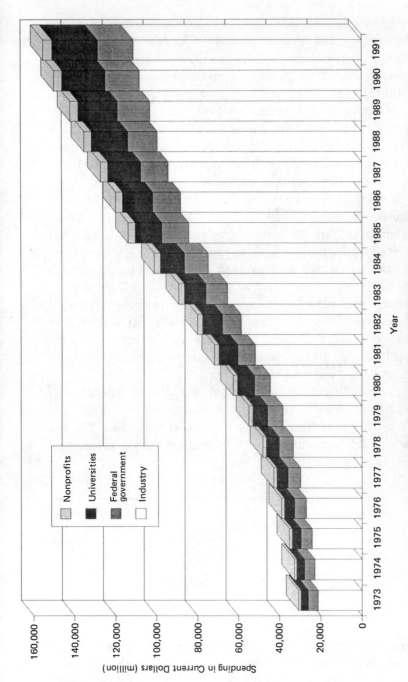

FIGURE 2 The Growth in R&D Spending by Performer (*Source:* All data to 1990 from National Science Foundation; 1991 data from Battelle estimate)

Figure 2 presents R&D spending in current dollars. Note the steady upward climb, slow in the early 1970s, very fast during the mid-1980s, and then slow—but still growing—in the late 1980s. Over this period of time, the U.S. economy underwent a period of "stagflation" (in the early 1970s) and then dramatic inflation (in the late 1970s), a bitter recession (in the early 1980s), and an economic boom (recently). Yet the R&D totals show a steady climb. Even when the data are converted to constant dollars, the series shows a near-doubling between the early 1970s and the late 1980s. Few things in the realm of economics maintain such steady upward progress.

About 4.1 million natural science, engineering, and computer specialists were employed in the United States in the mid-1980s, according to the National Science Board's annual publication *Science & Engineering Indicators* [5]. (This total excludes psychologists and social scientists as well as individuals with science or engineering degrees who are not employed as such.) About 1 million of these scientists were employed primarily in R&D; this total roughly equaled *all* the scientists, engineers, and computer specialists in the rest of the industrialized world put together! The U.S. research establishment is huge and growing, regardless of how much gloom this establishment feels.

The Battelle data series divided according to performer is also noteworthy because it gives a rough estimate of where the research jobs are and the dollars available to support these jobs. For the predicted R&D performance in 1991, the proportion among performers is as follows:

Sector Performing Research	Total (Billion $)	Percentage of Total
Federal government	17.5	11.28
Industry	111	71.54
Colleges/universities	22.35	14.41
Other nonprofits	4.3	2.77

No directly comparable breakout of employment of scientists and engineers is available according to these four sectors. But other data published by the National Science Foundation (NSF) give some indications. The most general breakout is as shown in Table 1 (note that these

Table 1 Scientific and Engineering Employment

Type of Employer	Percentage of Distribution
Industry	67.8
Educational institutions	13.6
Nonprofit organizations	3.6
Federal government	8.3
State, local, other government	5.0
Other	1.6

Source: National Science Foundation, 1987.

data are for the year 1986). A further breakout of these data according to type of science or engineering discipline is shown in Table 2.

The preceding data relate to all degree levels (bachelor, master's, doctoral). In the eyes of many employers (and many workers as well), a "scientist" is someone with a doctoral degree. Their employment trends are somewhat different. According to NSF data, there were 419,000 total scientists and engineers with Ph.D.s in 1987 [6]. Of these, over 209,000, or 53 percent of the total, were employed in academia. The totals for various science and engineering disciplines are shown in Table 3.

Finally, even within academia, a number of trends of work activity occur. Not all scientists and engineers employed by colleges and universities teach; in fact, only about half do so exclusively. Many of the others are involved in research or in the administration of R&D programs. These proportions vary according to the type of academic discipline and are also shown in Table 3.

It is noteworthy that the data in Table 3, when compared with data from previous years, show a growth in the number of academics devoted to R&D and a stable or declining total devoted to teaching. Looking at the overall job market, there has also been a trend among Ph.D. scientists and engineers toward working in industry and a corresponding decline to their working in academia. Ph.D. scientists and engineers can work (whether in industry or in academia) on either basic or applied research. NSF data indicate that there was a crossover in the mid-1980s, with the number of applied researchers exceeding the number of basic researchers.

The grand summation of these trends is that the scientific

Table 2 Employment by Type of Science or Engineering

Science or Field of Engineering	Industry	Educational Institutions	Nonprofit Organizations	Federal Government	State, Local, Other Government	Other
			Percentage of Distribution			
Life scientists	37.2	35.9	7.0	10.7	7.7	1.5
Computer specialists	78.2	6.7	2.5	7.3	3.7	1.6
Physical scientists	56.8	24.7	3.3	10.6	2.9	1.7
Environmental scientists	58.5	16.4	1.2	17.1	5.3	1.5
Mathematical scientists	41.8	44.8	2.1	8.9	1.7	0.8
All engineers	79.5	4.1	1.5	8.4	4.9	1.7
Total distribution	67.8	13.6	3.6	8.3	5.0	1.6

Source: Adapted from U.S. Bureau of the Census, *Statistical Abstract of the United States, 1990* (Washington, D.C.: Government Printing Office, 1990), table no. 999, p. 589.

Table 3   Doctoral Scientists and Engineers, 1987

	Number	Number in Academia	Number in Academia Teaching	Number in Academia Doing R&D
Total scientists and engineers	419,118	209,384	101,835	73,227
Total scientists*	351,350	185,746	90,370	65,439
Physical scientists	68,647	28,729	13,535	11,931
Mathematical scientists	16,699	13,031	8,735	2,983
Computer specialists	18,571	5,439	2,681	1,501
Environmental scientists	17,811	7,375	3,256	3,259
Life scientists	107,378	64,738	19,883	34,059
Total engineers	67,768	23,638	11,465	7,788
Astronautical/aeronautical	5,005			
Chemical	6,923			
Civil	6,479			
Electrical/electronics	12,601			
Mechanical	6,711			
Other	30,049			

Source: National Science Foundation, 1987.
*Total includes scientists not listed below.

enterprise is becoming increasingly interwoven with the economic enterprises of the United States. Even within the rarefied atmosphere of Ph.D.-level research, the siren call of applied research for commercial purposes has grown.

There are two ways of looking at this situation. One, the usual response, is that the U.S. scientific enterprise is selling out to commerce, getting big bucks for developing commercial products. Pure research becomes impure research. This attitude harks back to the old days of science, when scientists prided themselves on their irrelevance to commerce. "Pure scientists have by and large been dim-witted about engineers and applied science," wrote C. P. Snow, a British scientist, in the 1950s [7]. "We prided ourselves that the science we were doing could not, in any conceivable circumstances, have any practical use. The more firmly one could make that claim, the more superior one felt." It is also something of an ideological conceit, in the sense that, since corporations are usually the ones to commercialize new products, scientists have become the servants of corporate capitalists when they devote their efforts to applied research rather than to knowledge for its own sake.

But there is another interpretation, one that, may it be submitted, is equally valid: The pace of transforming science into socially useful products or knowledge has quickened dramatically. It is a cliché to say that scientific knowledge has exploded in this century. This knowledge includes a better understanding of the process of commercializing technology itself. A good example has been the crash program to develop a test to identify viruses that can be transmitted through blood, such as the AIDS virus. The worldwide blood supply network could have come to a crashing halt, resulting in many more AIDS victims, had a test not been developed. Yet the technology required first to identify the virus itself and second to develop a test had appeared only a few short years before the crisis loomed. A close reading of the history of science, in fact, reveals many examples in which pure science was "created" by virtue of meeting a social need, from Archimedes' "eureka-in-the-bathtub" in ancient Greece to Claude Shannon's development of information theory so necessary for telecommunications and information theory in this century. When the tools to commercialize science are readily available, one can be sure that someone is striving to do just that—and fast.

Lord Snow made this statement in his often-cited book *The Two Cultures*, an examination (and criticism) of the distance separating the scientific culture from the literary one. Within the scientific culture, however, a second dichotomy exists between pure science and its application. Snow felt that civilization has been going through a scientific revolution in this century on a par with the previous agricultural and mechanical ones. "Why aren't we coping with the scientific revolution?" [8] he asked, addressing the question to his countrymen who were failing to progress in applying science successfully. Snow's essay preceded the current debate over U.S. international "competitiveness" by a full three decades. Instead of lamenting the corruption of pure science by commercially oriented R&D, Snow wished there were more of it.

Job Demand

Like most things in life—the cost of living, our waistlines, and the world population—the job market for scientists continually expands. It does not do this in a continuous process; there are periods of contraction. However, relative to the ups and downs of the total U.S. job market, unemployment in science and engineering is almost laughably small. In the worst times, scientists as a group have an unemployment rate of a few percent, and, most of the time, engineers (especially those with Ph.D.s) are measured in fractions of a percent.

Between 1980 and 1988, the number of people employed in science and engineering jobs in private industry increased at a rate almost twice that of all workers, according to the National Science Board [9]. In fact, overall employment for scientists *doubled*. Sounds too good to be true? Perhaps, although the slightly desperate lamentations from industrial employers over the paucity of suitable job candidates gives credence to this strong job market.

The catch in these low unemployment rates and rising job demand is that there is no guarantee that graduating scientists will get the jobs they want, where they want them, and for the salary they desire. This is especially true in academia, where the number of jobseekers traditionally exceeds the number of openings. Even here, however, the demographic trends are toward a graying academic work force, with the number of retirements likely to rise toward the end of this decade. Not coincidentally, the number of college-age young people will also begin rising then, compounding the shortage that could appear.

How large is the job market for green-collar scientists and engineers? Unfortunately, there is no definitive count. The primary reason for this lack is that it would be very difficult to identify with any rigor which jobs in the science and engineering work force are green-collar ones, and which are not. Perhaps the best indication has been provided by Management Information Services, Inc. (MIS), a Washington, D.C., economic research and consulting firm [10]. Their study, based on an econometric model of the economy, showed that nearly 3.5 million jobs were directly connected to pollution abatement and control in 1991; of this total, some 109,000 were engineering jobs (see Tables 4 and 5). If one assumes that the same ratio exists between these 109,000 engineers and the overall engineering work force (2.44 million strong) as between scientists working on the environment and the total number of scientists (2.19 million), then a reasonable estimate is that there are about 98,000 green-collar scientists. MIS's projection for employment in pollution abatement and

Table 4   PAC Jobs Created in 1991

	Number of Jobs (1,000s)	
Employment Sector	*1991*	*2000*
Manufacturing, total	1,337	1,857
Textiles and apparel	33	36
Chemical and petroleum products	208	319
Fabricated metal products	67	79
Machinery	182	254
Transportation equipment	94	137
Other manufacturing	748	1,032
Agriculture, forestry, and fisheries	87	109
Mining	226	308
Construction	130	197
Transportation, communications, and utilities	563	898
Finance, insurance, and real estate	84	130
Services	396	632
Government (federal, state, local)	385	591
Total in all sectors	3,469	5,107

Source: Management Information Services, Inc., 1991.

Table 5 *PAC Jobs for Engineers*

Engineering Profession	Number of Jobs	
	1991	2000
Aerospace	3,690	6,020
Chemical	12,144	20,966
Civil	12,572	21,505
Electrical	24,212	40,097
Industrial	16,402	28,002
Mechanical	14,316	24,818
Metallurgical	1,294	2,382
Mining	1,925	3,118
Petroleum	2,650	4,506
Sales	1,672	2,760
Engineers, not elsewhere classified	18,357	32,616
Total of all engineers	109,234	186,790

Source: Management Information Services, Inc., 1991.

control in the year 2000 shows that there will be nearly 187,000 engineers employed in the field. If the number of scientists employed in this way shows the same growth rate, 167,000 will be so employed at the turn of the century.

MIS's analysis is valuable—if only to demonstrate the importance of job creation via environmental regulation—but it is limited. One limitation is that these jobs refer only to "pollution abatement and control," which is only part of the green-collar scene. Such occupations as wildlife preservation, parks management, environmental health (within the context of medical care), and teaching are overlooked. More importantly, identifying pollution abatement and control jobs separately from the general run of scientific and engineering employment draws a false distinction between the two. Science does not fit neatly into econometric pigeonholes. Today's basic research on, say, catalysis could result in tomorrow's production of cleaner-burning fuels for automobiles. At what point does the research stop being "basic" or "commercial," and start being "environmental"? It is worth reiterating a point made earlier in this book: At some time in the near future, *all* scientists and engineers at work in the United States, regardless of their specialty, will be able to locate their work in proximity to environmental protection and preservation.

Another approach to addressing the employment question is to consider the growth rates of individual companies in the environmental business. As shown earlier, many of these companies are showing revenue growth rates of 15 to 20 percent per year, with a corresponding rate of increase among staff. Some now have staffs of thousands. Don Carlton, a chemical engineer and founder of Radian Corporation, a Houston-based environmental services company, says that his company (with some 1,800 employees) is nearly half comprised of professional staff, with over 1,000 technical degrees among them.

Like most large environmental firms, Radian Corporation is expanding abroad, but Carlton says that his firm has a special reason for doing so. "We can't hire enough well-trained scientists and engineers in the United States. By opening offices abroad, we can tap into those job markets to find the people that we need." The company has already opened offices in both the Far East and in Europe and is now looking to expand them.

Looking Ahead. In the sections that follow, the scientific professions of chemistry, biology, the applied sciences, and the earth sciences and geology will be reviewed in detail. Doctoral engineers will be treated as part of the engineering professions, whose descriptions are in Chapter 3. Computer science will be reviewed there as well. Each program description will have data on recent graduating class sizes, drawn from annual summaries published by the National Center for Educational Statistics (a part of the Department of Education). The intent with these data is to show the national trends for growth or shrinkage in class size; when this is compared to the dynamics of the job market, a good sense is obtained of job markets that are over- or undersubscribed. In general, however, nearly all science job markets, as well as engineering ones, demonstrate low unemployment rates and a very bright future. Projections for future employment are drawn from the biennial estimates made by the U.S. Bureau of Labor Statistics.

Chemistry

Overview

Chemistry is one of the central physical sciences and has been studied since the beginning of recorded history. In this century, it has spawned an enormous industry, which the Department of Commerce notes is worth over $300 billion in annual sales and which employs over a million people in 12,000 plants. These plants produce some 50,000 different products. Not much is heard about foreign competition or trade problems from the United States because the industry as a whole runs a $15-billion surplus in chemical trade.

These positive economic facts are overshadowed, in many people's eyes, by the tremendous cost to society and the environment caused by the chemical industry. The chemical industry is the most prominent and highest-volume producer of hazardous wastes. Chemical plants are routinely excoriated by the public when spills, explosions, or other accidents occur, causing the evacuation of entire towns or the shutdown of highways or rail lines. The chemical industry has historically been dangerous to its employees. In recent years, however, it has recorded the best record against accidental injury or death of any employer. A major qualification of this fact is that these accident data do not record the long-term injury to workers caused by exposure to poisonous chemicals in minute amounts over a working lifetime.

Another industrial sector where chemists tend to concentrate is that of the pharmaceuticals. At the outset of the 1990s, the pharmaceutical industry is enjoying a period of robust growth and profitability. Wall Street analysts speak of this industry in the way they regarded the computer and electronics manufacturers in the early 1980s—with a vista of growth and profitability for as far as one can see into the future. Here, too, however, the risks of environmental damage and the heavy regulation of the pharmaceutical industry under such agencies as the U.S. Food and Drug Administration make one cautious in contemplating the industry's place in the world.

Studying chemistry is a gateway to most of the professions tied to the physical sciences. Geologists, physicists, meteorologists, materials scientists, and others all take a series of chemistry courses during college. Most of the life sciences, including biology, environmental sciences, and premedical programs, require chemistry training as well. Many students combine an undergraduate degree in chemistry with training in another science or in engineering as preparation for a career.

History and Current Assessment

Ancient Greeks to Alchemists. Chemistry was one of the favorite topics for philosophizing by the ancient Greeks; in their wide-ranging curiosity about the world around them, they theorized about flavors, colors, fire, and water. Except for metallurgy and some basics of agriculture, little of this philosophizing bore fruit in new knowledge. This inability would remain in civilization for centuries due to the difficulties in analyzing precisely what is reacting in a dish of chemicals or what the end product of this reaction might be.

While other sciences, such as mathematics and, to a certain extent, physics and medicine, showed steady progress over the centuries, the period from the early Roman Empire to the late Renaissance is a great blank for chemistry, in most regards, except for alchemy. Alchemy was a half-scientific, half-mystical body of knowledge, combining astrology with the practical components of metallurgy. We remember alchemy today mostly for the fabled search of a way to transmute base metal into gold. In reality, alchemy involved many other goals, such as the prolongation of life [11]. By the early Renaissance, the revival of writings such as those of Zosimos (Egyptian) and Hermes Trismegistos (Greek), combined with new experimentation, had led to the identification of mineral acids and common materials such as sal ammoniac and saltpeter. In later centuries, alchemy became obsessive hobbies of scientists such as Isaac Newton.

Scholars disagree on whether modern chemistry arose from these semimystical investigations or from advances in medical research that led to the development of medicinal compounds. However, it seems that medical research of the Middle Ages was even more unscientific than alchemical research; at the very least, alchemy created a mode of research—the investigation of reactive chemicals and the analysis of their products.

Phlogiston to Plastics and Polymers. Much of the early modern chemical research was conducted in France in the 1700s. Antoine Lavoisier is generally credited with the discovery of oxygen. Studies of this and other gases led John Dalton, an English chemist, to postulate an atomic theory of matter. Soon, natural philosophers all over the Continent were experimenting with glass beakers containing various gases, reacting the gases with one another and trying to determine fundamental properties. The study of fire was especially critical since it had been postulated for centuries that all matter contained a substance called *phlogiston* that was vaporized in a fire. (A piece of wood, for example, is turned into a smaller mass of ash after it is burned; the "missing" material was thought to be phlogiston.)

Advances in knowledge in this period were retarded by the difficulties of inventing instruments that could accurately weigh amounts or that could measure temperatures or volumes. As these developments progressed during the Industrial Revolution, so did chemical research. In most cases, such research was more closely allied with the industry for which it was performed, such as medicine, textiles, or metallurgy, rather than with a body of knowledge common to all. In the mid- to late 1800s, the focus of chemical research concentrated in Germany and England, where researchers developed an array of valuable dyes from coal chemicals. This is the first modern petrochemical research. The first plastic, called *nitrocellulose*, was derived from treated wood chemicals by an English scientist, Alexander Parkes, according to Peter Spitz's history, *Petrochemicals: The Rise of an Industry* [12]. In the United States in 1868, John and Isaiah Hyatt developed an alternative version of this—to win a prize offered by a billiard ball manufacturer to find an alternative to elephant ivory as a raw material! The Hyatts' product eventually came to be known as *Celluloid*, famous for being the first base material for motion-picture film.

In the late 1800s, British scientists succeeded in spinning liquid cellulose derivatives into fine threads; the product later came to be known as *rayon*, which is still made today as a synthetic fiber. By the early 1900s, manufacturers in Europe and the United States succeeded in reconstituting cellulose in film form (cellophane). At about the same time, another U.S. scientist, Leo Baekeland, developed a hard plastic derived from coal chemicals, which eventually was called *Bakelite*. This product, made from a reaction of phenol and formaldehyde, went into large-scale commercial production and was used for everything from electrical equipment components to phonograph records.

Bakelite is a type of plastic known today as a *thermosetting* one, meaning that once its components are reacted, it cannot be melted back to a liquid before it decomposes. The reaction to make it, once it became known, is fairly simple. The other large class of plastics, known as the *thermoplastics*, can be melted, and they have by and large taken over the industry. (This distinction is important in discussing the environmental implications of plastics recycling.) Thermoplastics are much harder to study because they are formed of long chains of hydrocarbon molecules, called *polymers*, wrapped around one another, cross-linked, or crystallized. By subtly altering the manufacturing conditions, they can be made into a vast array of products. Chemists studying them in the early 1900s were stymied by the great variety of reactions that all ended up with a seemingly similar result— a gooey, resinous mass that defied further study. The invention of X-ray crystallography in the 1920s and 1930s helped chemists begin to analyze these resins, and, in short order, other thermoplastics, such as polyethylene, polyvinyl chloride, and polystyrene, were developed.

In the late 1920s, Du Pont Co., having developed a successful business based on the production of cellulose derivatives, took a bold step in luring a prominent academic chemist, Wallace Carothers, from Harvard to a new laboratory in Wilmington, Delaware. This industrial research laboratory, equipped with the best instrumentation available and given a large budget, became phenomenally successful in turning out an exciting combination of basic research on polymer chemistry, as well as the applied science needed for new commercial products. The most significant of these products were nylon (technically, a "polyamide"), polyester, neoprene rubber, and polyacryonitrile. Du Pont's laboratory and successful commercializations set a pattern that was followed for decades afterward: Industry could benefit substantially by funding basic research and by hiring the best scientific talent. (Unfortunately, the story ended sadly for Carothers, who committed suicide in 1937.)

Post–World War II and Petrochemicals. Although, in the post–World War II era, plastics underwent phenomenal growth, they did not constitute the entirety of chemical research. The success in commercializing these materials in large quantities was dependent on the parallel development of petroleum-based chemistry. Prior to the 1930s, most petrochemicals were derived from coal tar, which was produced in large quantities both for its own sake and as a byproduct of steel production (where coal is purified to "coke") and municipal coal-gasification plants, which were common near many large cities in the early twentieth century. The growth of the automobile during the first 30 years of this century created an intense demand for fuel; in the 1920s, there were a variety of forecasts showing that fuel consumption would soon outstrip oil production. The oil-refining industry underwent a technological push similar to that of the plastics industry during the 1930s, resulting in the development of more efficient, catalyzed refining techniques. Crude oil, as it comes out of the ground, has dozens of components, which need to be separated from one another or reacted with one another to form the desirable fuel-type compounds.

The success of the giant oil companies in finding new sources of oil (the giant fields of the Middle East were found in the 1930s), combined with the success of petroleum chemists in refining crude oil more efficiently, has created a vast, interlocking network of raw materials, semirefined products, and consumer goods. Although, on a volume basis, the energy uses of oil far dominate the derivative uses (such as plastics), both are equally large sectors of the economy in terms of capitalization, and the derivative or, to use the industry parlance, "downstream" industries are larger in terms of employment. This interlocking network has helped make petroleum the key component of industrialized economies and, increasingly over the past 30 years, has shaped international affairs. As petroleum production grew, so did that of natural gas, which is often found in the same places as oil. The two together have cut coal's dominance (known, until World War II, as "King Coal") from the marketplace, except for electrical power production.

Other large petrochemical-based downstream industries include fertilizers and agricultural chemicals (such as pesticides), building materials, paints and coatings, rubbers and elastics, and some components of food processing and pharmaceuticals. As the body of knowledge of how petrochemicals could be manipulated has grown, the applications in commercial products have expanded. Many environmental activists, as well as the average consumer, draw a distinction between "natural" products, derived from plants or animals or from historically common materials such as glass or metal, and "synthetic" products, derived from petrochemicals. But to the chemist, trained in looking at the chemical composition of a material, the two are for most intents and purposes identical: A so-called natural product such as rayon, derived from plant fiber, undergoes extensive chemical manipulation before it is consumed in finished goods; a synthetic such as polyethylene often has fewer production steps than competing materials such as glass or metal.

Since the early 1960s, when the shape of the modern chemistry profession could be said to be set by the industries that use it, chemistry has become integrated in nearly all manufacturing businesses. Even when an industry does not perform chemical manipulations of matter, the need for chemists is ever-present. A good example can be drawn from the fabricated metals business, in which sheet or bar steel is bought and then bent into containers, structural components, or machinery parts. Chemists are used in quality-control laboratories to check the incoming consistency of the raw material and the outgoing quality of the finished product. A vast array of coatings, lubricants, chemical treatments, and similar operations go on, all of which are guided by chemical knowledge. Finally, the most astute manufacturers, following the Du Pont model, employ chemistry researchers to, for example, develop alternative materials or processes for their businesses.

The Academic Front. On the academic front, chemical research can be said to have gone in two directions in recent years, infringing on the traditional turf of two other disciplines—physics and biology. Due to the rise of the electronics industry, which can be traced in its earliest form to the 1900–1910 period, but which really began to grow in the 1950s (see the description of electrical engineering in Chapter 3), the atomic nature of chemicals became critical for industrial applications. This, in turn, spurred research and development in devising chemical methods of producing electronic materials, such as semiconductors. Similarly, the success of the Manhattan Project in the 1940s led to a broadening of atomic research from its traditional base in physics; chemists began looking at the chemical effects of radioactivity and helped devise methods of refining uranium.

The traditional borderline between chemistry and biology—the distinction between living and nonliving matter—began to break down in a significant way once biologists' knowledge expanded beyond the cell, the fundamental unit of living matter, and into the components of cells. In the previous century, the distinction between chemistry and biology was less sharp, as both disciplines struggled with understanding the nature of living matter and the effects of chemicals on life. But as the Industrial Revolution wore on, the two disciplines grew apart.

By the middle of this century, however, the success of biologists in using chemists' tools to develop new medicines and the success of chemists in using knowledge derived from biological research have brought the two disciplines closer together. Biochemistry is now a well-identified specialty within the chemistry profession; conversely, molecular biology is well known in biological circles. The distinction between the two is today more a matter of mindset than of the specifics of training or the topics selected for study. A biochemist will seek to derive knowledge of the chemical reactions going on in living things; a molecular biologist will seek to understand what biological effects occur due to the chemicals present in living things. It is often hard to distinguish a piece of research as coming from one or the other discipline.

Current Employment Trends. The American Chemical Society (ACS), the leading professional organization of chemists, recently conducted a study of the employment trends among its members [13]. These "chemical scientists" (a term used to bring chemical engineering under the ACS umbrella, as well as biological scientists who work in industrial manufacturing) are divided among industry, academia, and government as shown in Table 6.

Another study, by William Bowen at the Mellon Institute, found that "academic" (i.e., university-employed) chemists constituted about 33 percent of all doctoral-level chemists—a percentage that has dropped by about 3 percentage points over the 1977-1987 period. This number is approximately twice the amount indicated in Table 6 (18.6

Table 6 *Where Chemists Are Employed*

	Employment (in 1,000s)		
Sector	Chemical Scientists	Chemists	Chemists as Percentage of Total (Chemists)
Industry	275	134	
Manufacturing	215.5	104	53.7
Nonmanufacturing	59.5	30	15.5
Academia/nonprofit	45	36	18.6
Government	31	23.5	
Federal	21	15.5	8
State and local	10	8	4.1
Total	351	193.5	100

Source: American Chemical Society, based on Kline & Co. study, 1990.

percent). It is well known that college and university employment for academics is by and large restricted to doctoral-level graduates; what is less well known is that even at this level, two out of three work outside academia.

The ACS study went on to forecast growth rates among the broad employment categories of chemical scientists. It predicted that, while industry grew at a 1.6 percent average annual rate between 1988 and 1993, academia would grow at a 2.1 percent average annual rate and government employment would shrink. See Table 7.

Chemists' work can be organized according to the specialty area in which they practice. The most common such categories are as follows.

Agricultural Chemistry

Agricultural chemistry is primarily concerned with fertilizers and pesticides. It also deals with other aspects of the interaction between plants and the nutrients on which they depend.

Analytical Chemistry

Analytical chemistry represents one of the strongest cross-disciplinary specialties among chemists. Analytical chemists develop and operate instruments to perform analysis of chemical materials in laboratories.

Table 7 *Employment Growth among Chemical Scientists*

| | Employment (in 1,000s) | | |
Sector	1988	1993	Average Percentage of Growth per Year
Industry	275	298.1	1.6
Academia	45	50	2.1
Government	31	30.9	−0.1
Total	351	379	1.6

Source: American Chemical Society, based on Kline & Co. study, 1990.

Biochemistry

Biochemistry is the common ground between chemistry and biology. Biochemists conduct research on the chemical aspects of life. With the intense focus of the new biotechnology industries, this field has begun to subdivide into areas such as protein chemistry, carbohydrate chemistry, enzyme chemistry, and others. When researchers specialize in the chemistry of pharmaceuticals, they are often called *medicinal chemists*.

Environmental Chemistry

Environmental chemistry is a relatively new field. It is most closely focused on the "fate and transport" of chemicals released in the environment.

Food Science

Food science chemists are employed by the food-processing industry to monitor the quality of foodstuffs. These chemists also help develop new methods of processing.

Geochemistry

Geochemistry focuses on the chemistry of the Earth, its atmosphere, and oceans. Geochemists work closely with geologists and geophysicists, attempting to understand the nature of the Earth's chemistry.

Materials Science

The field of materials science is something of a crossover with engineering. Its practitioners develop new, commercially useful materials and methods of producing them. Most materials scientists specialize in one or another form of matter, such as ceramics, metals, or plastics.

Organic Chemistry

Organic chemistry is the study of the chemicals based on carbon, which encompasses all petrochemicals and coal-derived substances as well as many biological compounds. A special subset of this field is *polymer chemistry*, which is concentrated in rubber and plastics.

Physical Chemistry

Physical chemistry focuses more on the bulk properties of materials—how they solidify or liquefy, their electrical or magnetic properties, and the like. Like analytical chemistry, physical chemistry crosses the boundaries of most of the other chemistry specialties.

Radiochemistry

Radiochemistry analyzes the effects of radiation and radioactivity on compounds. It is sometimes known as *nuclear chemistry.*

Another ACS survey, published in the summer of 1991 [14], showed that ACS members had a median salary of $52,000 and that the profession had an unemployment rate at the time of 1.6 percent. (At about the same time, the overall U.S. economy had an unemployment rate of 6.8 percent.) At the doctoral level (a level reached by 56 percent of the respondents), median salaries were $58,000; at the bachelor level, they were $40,300. Note that all of the salaries mentioned here are medians over the entire range of work experience; for newly graduated B.S. or B.A. chemists, average salaries are in the $26,000 to $29,000 range, according to various industry surveys. The ACS salary survey also found that 18 percent of the respondents were women and that 10 percent of the total were members of minority groups.

Education

As the data in Table 8 indicate, chemistry as an academic major has been in decline, at least on the undergraduate level. The picture looks even worse if one compares these data with data of earlier years; in 1983, for example, there were 10,796 bachelor graduates. The master's-level and doctoral-level trends are encouraging, except that a large proportion of most graduate-school bodies are made up of foreign nationals, many of whom return to their country of origin upon graduation.

These trends are occurring notwithstanding the generally good job prospects for chemistry graduates. Part of the reason has been a demographic shift that college-age Americans are undergoing cur-

Table 8 *Chemistry Degrees Awarded, 1987–1989*

Degree	1987	1988	1989
Bachelor	9,661	9,025	8,654
Master's	1,738	1,694	1,785
Ph.D.	1,976	1,990	2,034

rently. There are fewer students of college age, and enrollments are beginning to slip at many schools. However, this is not the sole reason for the decline. Along with most of the other professions profiled in this book, chemistry is suffering from a lack of interest—indeed, almost an antipathy—among the young. College students have been abandoning the sciences and engineering for other disciplines, especially business-related ones.

In response, national organizations ranging from the National Science Foundation to the American Chemical Society have been starting new programs to improve how science, technology, and mathematics are taught in grade schools and high schools. Outreach programs for minority groups are included.

As things stand now, most college-level chemistry majors build on the coursework that they performed in high school. The regular schedule includes a general chemistry course, followed by organic and physical chemistry. Some of these are multisemester programs. By the junior year, the chemistry major is expected to have learned a foreign language—preferably French or German (the latter is especially useful for chemists since Germany remains a power in chemical research). Upper-level courses run the gamut of interests in which chemists specialize, from biochemistry to advanced-level organic or physical chemistry. Students can also opt various courses in applications-oriented courses such as environmental studies, petrochemical or chemical engineering, aquatic chemistry, and others. As with most science or technical majors, some facility with computers and programming is often incorporated into the curriculum.

Most programs will have a course entitled "Quantitative Analysis" or something similar; a substantial portion of this course is laboratory work. The student laboratories are a major feature for college administrators to show off to prospective students; the most prestigious programs have richly equipped labs. Whether or not undergraduates get to use all of this expensive equipment is moot; in any case, laboratory work is one of the key distinguishing elements of a chemistry degree. Many students who finish schooling at the undergraduate level will be able to get employment as a result of their laboratory experience.

Chemistry truly shows its gateway nature at the graduate level, from which students can proceed in a diverse range of directions. Some schools have graduate programs oriented around local industry—papermaking or textiles in the South, electronics in the West or Northeast, agribusiness in the Midwest. Alternatively, students can pursue specialized training in one of the theoretical areas of chemistry—catalysis, physical chemistry, biochemistry, radiochemistry, and so on. There are a considerable number of programs in which students can concentrate on environmental issues.

Also, depending on the school and on one's graduate adviser, graduate chemistry students have an opportunity to engage directly in environmental work, through the performance of research grants awarded by governmental agencies or through sponsored research with industry. Some universities have close ties to nature areas and wildlife preserves; students can also study or work at them. (Occasionally, these facilities are also open to undergraduates.)

Environmental Impact

Obviously, chemistry plays a central role in almost any environmental issue. The question that professional chemists must ask themselves is whether they want to work in an area directly relating to environmental problems, such as water conservation, for example, or Superfund cleanups, or in areas that indirectly affect the environment, such as the creation of new manufacturing techniques that are environmentally cleaner. This distinction is quickly fading, however, as both business plans and government regulations "close the loop" between what products are made, how they are made, and what past, present, or future effects they have on the environment.

Chemistry graduates are, in one sense, the foot soldiers of environmental work: The hundreds of laboratories in private industry, government, and consulting organizations need well-trained people to run the sophisticated equipment that determines the contamination of the air, water, and ground. Old-time industrialists often complain that the precision of modern laboratory equipment far exceeds science's or medicine's ability to explain the significance of a measurement. Water quality, for example, is now measured in parts per *trillion*, a fantastically small concentration. (One part per *billion* has been compared with one drop of water in a large swimming pool; a part per *trillion* would be obtained by dividing this drop 1,000 times.) Chemical lab equipment is a booming business these days, and much of this equipment is being purchased by independent laboratories that perform contract analyses under highly specified conditions. (Independent laboratories do not belong to a manufacturer or other corporation, a university, or a government agency.)

"Environmental labs aren't kidding when they say that despite the downward national economic trend, their business is better than ever," writes Susan Hale Abbot, editor of *Environmental Lab*, in a 1991 article [15]. "In fact, one study by Hempstead & Co. estimated that the market for environmental analytical services reached an incredible $1.1 billion last year."

A critical test for manufacturers or landowners with hazardous wastes, called the *toxicity characteristic leaching procedure* (TCLP), was written into law by being published in the Federal Register. TCLP determines whether an undifferentiated sludge or soil sample is a hazardous waste (for which there are strict definitions) or simply a waste or bit of slightly contaminated soil. The difference may seem legalistic, but in terms of the cost of disposal or treatment, it can amount to hundreds of dollars per ton of waste. TCLP requires that the material in question be tested for the presence of dozens of toxic chemicals and metals; the concentration at which they are leached from the sample by passing water through it determines whether it meets hazardous-waste guidelines. In addition, these samples are tested with injections of the toxic chemicals in question to validate the accuracy of the procedure. Finally, it may occasionally occur that these tests need to be audited by a third party to validate the overall testing standards. When one considers that dozens of samples may be taken from a site to be tested and that each of these is tested multiple times, the volume of test work going on today begins to come into focus.

Due to this high volume of analyses, EPA has helped set up an "EPA Contract Laboratory" program, under which EPA certifies the quality of work that the laboratories perform. Informally, it is also a way of disseminating new technology on analyses and instrumentation in the laboratory community. EPA also works with professional organizations like the Association of Official Analytical Chemists to create these test procedures.

The big drawback to laboratory work is that it is often very tedious. It is one thing to be among the first scientists to detect the presence of chlorofluorocarbons above the Antarctic Circle, as British and American scientists did in the early 1980s; it is another thing altogether to have performed the 575th test of a Superfund site's soil and to be getting ready for the 576th. Partly for this reason, analytical work is becoming more and more automated. Another reason for the automation is the strain of keeping up with the number of tests required by environmental work. A stroll through the aisles of the Pittsburgh Conference, an annual meeting and trade show of laboratory equipment, reveals high-powered computers that can collect and process data in milliseconds; there are also robotic systems that will automate some of the preparation and testing steps of samples.

Doing laboratory work could quickly become tedious for the chemist, although the state of the art is continually advancing through new equipment and procedures. Moreover, analytical chemistry retains a proud tradition at the doctoral level as an area of research. For the chemist who intends to become deeply involved in environmental issues over the course of a career, performing laboratory work is an excellent first step.

In industry, chemists perform the same sort of analytical work in quality-control laboratories, often on the factory floor. In addition, chemists work in industrial laboratories where new materials or production techniques are devised. Following the tradition established at the Du Pont laboratories in the 1920s, many of these laboratories are serenely academic centers, with scientists performing research, giving lectures, and writing up results, just as their academic peers would do. (Many academics, too, consult with industrial scientists and sometimes work at their laboratories on a part-time basis.)

Although it is not exclusively so, it is probable that the best chance to do fieldwork in remote areas of the Earth is most readily accomplished through an academic position. Some of the laboratories run by the federal government, such as the National Center for Atmospheric Research, emphasize this feature. Within EPA itself, several laboratories perform research and conduct testing; as yet, relatively little international work is being done, but this may change due to the growing internationalization of environmental issues.

EPA's own agenda for research, published annually as the *EPA Research Program Guide* [16], gives a good sense of what the current areas of chemical research on environmental issues are. Like EPA itself, the research is organized according to "programs," including air, water, solid wastes, toxic substances, pesticides, energy, radiation, and Superfund. A relatively new area—and one that is getting a rapidly increasing level of funding—is known as *multimedia* pollution, whereby a substance that starts out as, say, an industrial raw material becomes an air or water pollutant and then gradually migrates to the soil. This concept had been a blind spot in EPA research and regulations in the past; a waste would be identified as a water pollutant, for example, but once it was removed from water, it slipped out of the regulatory network. Some examples of the chemistry-oriented research being performed are as follows:

■ *Hazardous Waste—Municipal Solid Waste Monitoring*. Support is provided to the Office of Solid Waste (OSW) to improve the siting and monitoring of municipal waste combustion disposal facilities and to identify key groundwater monitoring issues pertaining to municipal waste combustion ash disposal facilities.

. . . Existing data on leachate characteristics and groundwater contamination around types of Subtitle D facilities and municipal waste combustion ash monofills are being collected on a continuous basis and evaluated. Groundwater monitoring parameters for ash landfills will be developed. Potential indicators of biological contamination will be identified.

Wet environments will receive special emphasis with an evaluation of siting practices relative to wet environments.

. . . Monitoring and site characterization guidance and an expert system for permit writers will be developed.

■ *Drinking Water—Groundwater Environmental Processes and Effects*. Groundwater is the major source of drinking water for the nation. This research program provides both technical information and improved methods for predicting contamination movement and transformation. The research focuses on methods development for and studies of subsurface transport and fate processes such as biological transformation, oxidation-reduction, hydrolysis, and ion exchange. Facilitated transport research will address complex mixture processes such as multi-

phase transport and solvent composition effects on sorp-
tion. . . .

Field evaluation of techniques for determining the mechanical integrity and adequacy of construction of injection wells will
occur. Work to develop technological alternatives for regulating
Class V wells will continue. . . .

■ *Air—Scientific Assessment of Indoor Air Pollution.* EPA's indoor air research program is geared to identify, characterize,
and rank indoor air problems and to assess and implement
appropriate mitigation strategies. EPA's research and analytical
activities will pursue both source-specific and generic ap-
proaches to indoor air pollution. From a source-specific stand-
point, the agency will identify high-risk pollutant sources and
characterize the exposures and health risks of various populations to those sources. . . .

Activities in FY91 in the area of scientific assessment include
the continued development of risk characterization methodol-
ogy to assess noncancer health effects; develop and apply
methods to assess exposures to both single compounds and
mixtures; continue comprehensive review of biocontaminants
in indoor air; develop portable, comprehensive test kit for initial
screening of indoor air quality problems; update and publish
Indoor Air Reference Bibliography.

Biology

Overview

If there were not so many colleges with academic programs labeled
"Biology," the term would by and large disappear from the technical
lexicon. The reason for this is not that there is any weakness in the
profession, but that it has become so strong and so specialized or, to
use a catchy biological term, "speciated" that few professionals identify themselves simply as a "biologist." Instead, there are botanists;
physiologists (of both plants and animals); marine, cellular, and molecular biologists; geneticists; ecologists; zoologists; and, last but certainly not least since it is the largest specialty, microbiologists.

Even if the discussion is limited to the animal kingdom, one can
reel out a list of specializations, including entomologist (insects),
ornithologist (birds), lepidopterist (reptiles), paleontologist (dino-

saurs and other extinct species), and ichthyologist (fish), which are the better-known ones. The professional who studies life on other planets (not yet found, but people are still looking) is an exobiologist.

Like the gray area between biology and chemistry that overlaps in biochemistry, there is a gray area between the biological sciences and the medical ones. Specialties of the human body, such as immunology, endocrinology, neurology, and physiology, are often considered part of the medical establishment; nevertheless, some of the practitioners of these specialties may seldom, if ever, see a human patient.

The fable is told by William Beck, in *Modern Science and the Nature of Life* [17], of a biology student who attempted to know—with no uncertainty—how one organism, a simple amoeba, lives. In the process of setting up his experiments, the student first stumbled on the question, How do I know it is an amoeba I am studying? Upon cursory analysis of the samples he received from a supply house, he found that some contained enzyme X, and some enzyme Y, and that some that contained enzyme X also contained enzyme O, but some did not; so, he identified the main group as amoeba, subdivided among strains according to the enzyme they contained. Then, he realized that amoebas were radically different in appearance at different stages of their lives and that to properly identify what made an amoeba live he would have to subdivide the various strains into the parts of their life cycles. At each next step of organizing his experiments, he either had to make further distinctions in his samples or had to compromise the quality of his results. The fable ends with the laboratory burning down due to all the equipment the student used.

Beck's point, besides the obvious one of the difficulties of absolute certainty in biological research, is that each level of understanding about living things stands on a lower level of more details and distinctions. This seemingly endless ladder of subdivisions is one of the reasons that there are so many biological professions. It is also the reason that so many biological scientists go on for graduate degrees; it is very difficult to cram enough learning into the four years of an undergraduate program and provide a professionally useful level of knowledge. Roughly 60 percent of biology students go on to graduate school of some type, according to data from the National Center of Educational Statistics; the average for most other undergraduate disciplines is about 25 percent.

Biological sciences are important to environmental work for two well-established reasons and one emerging reason. The two are (1) the harmful effects of pollution on the lives of individual plants and animals and (2) the harmful effects of pollution on entire ecosystems and classes of life (i.e., the loss of biodiversity). According to many scientists' estimates, more species are becoming extinct now than at any other period in history (this statement is extremely important in its implications; unfortunately, it is next to impossible either to prove or to disprove). The third reason is the effects of biosystems on the environment itself, ranging from the ecosystems of lakes or mountains to all the biota of Earth together (the Gaia hypothesis).

One last point is eminently worth noting before describing the details of biological history and training. It is the incredible progress that has been made in the past 20 years in genetics and molecular biology. Gene splicing and other genetic-manipulation techniques have spawned an entirely new industry called *biotechnology* that is shaking up the old patterns in drug manufacturing and testing, agriculture, and animal husbandry. Over the past ten years in particular, it has become a $4-billion industry, by some estimates, and is growing by 15 to 20 percent per year. Now, with schemes like the Genome Project (a federally funded effort to enumerate all the nucleotides on the human DNA genetic chain), it is poised to create even more dramatic changes in the future. As will be seen, biotechnology has its own environmental aspects, both beneficial and detrimental.

History and Current Assessment

The Origins of Biology. What is life? is one of the fundamental philosophical questions that has puzzled humanity seemingly always. Due to concepts such as spirit or soul being inextricably intertwined with life, many aspects of the subject are impervious to Western-style inductive reasoning.

Most historical accounts of the origins of biology make mention of the ancient civilizations' success with cultivation and animal husbandry and with medicine. Even today, pharmaceutical researchers venture into the Amazon and other parts of the world to learn what plants have medicinal properties of value to the aboriginal cultures. Two ancient Greek concepts of life were that it was inanimate matter infused with water and *physis*, some type of gaslike substance. Anaximander used the term *apeiron*. Hippocrates, the father of medicine, studied the interrelationships between the environment and health, especially climate and the sun. The Hippocratic school formulated a structure of human health involving a balance among its four *humors*: blood, black bile, yellow bile, and phlegm. (The humoric view of health lasted thousands of years and has parallels in certain concepts of Oriental medicine.)

It was Aristotle, the great organizer, who gave biology some central topics aside from health and spiritual questioning. He sought to organize the forms of life he encountered into groups, a subject now called *taxonomy* and very important for everything from evolutionary theory to biodiversity research. Aristotle was also an anatomist and studied embryology.

Roman-era biology in the first few centuries after Christ is remembered primarily for Galen, a Greek who lived in Rome around A.D. 150. Galen was a surgeon at gladiatorial arenas—can a better place for anatomical research be imagined in the ancient world? His studies of human and animal anatomy set the subject for over 1,300 years.

Middle Ages to Modern Day. In the Middle Ages, most ancient Greek and Roman knowledge was retained by the Arabian culture; their maintenance and addition to the historical record was essentially the main resource for the Church philosophers of the twelfth century and after. Nearly all the important figures of Renaissance science—da Vinci, Galileo, Newton, and others—bent their efforts to various avenues of biological research. The figure of Andreas Vesalius, born in Belgium, taught in Paris, and a teacher himself in Italy during the 1500s, looms large, not only for his modernization of Galen's work but also for his skeptical research style, which overcame the scholasticism of the Renaissance. (There is a legendary anecdote about scholasticism—knowledge based purely on the interpretation of ancient texts—which has two learned scholars arguing over how many teeth a horse has, based on Aristotle's writings. It never occurs to either scholar to examine a horse themselves.)

In the 1600s, biology was able to take a giant leap forward with the development of the microscope, a scientific tool that soon spread from Galileo's invention of the telescope to researchers in the Netherlands (Leeuwenhoek) and in England (Robert Hooke, an officer of the Royal Society of London, which was founded in 1662). The microscope enabled scientists to observe bacteria and protozoa directly and to distinguish among human cells.

With naval explorers then traveling all over the world, it was time to reassess Aristotelian taxonomy. The classification systems of Linnaeus (Swedish) and Cuvier (French) provided the structure that remains in use today. Linnaeus also specified the "immutability" of species; contemporaries of his also attempted experiments to either prove or disprove spontaneous generation of life (notwithstanding the awareness of microbial life).

The nineteenth century is something of a climax in the history of biology: Darwin developed his evolutionary theories, overturning Linnaeus and others; Pasteur established microbiology, disproving spontaneous generation and starting the debate on the "germ theory of life," which eventually had a powerful impact on public health and food preservation; and Mendel, an obscure German monk, established genetics as a science. (Mendel's work, performed in the middle of the century, was lost until 1900.)

This cursory overview of the history of biology leaves out many offshoots and sources of knowledge, such as medicine and agriculture, that contributed greatly to the furtherance of the science. By 1900, the shape of biological research was set, with distinctions between it, medicine, and agriculture. The exception to this generalization is the primary biological contribution of the twentieth century—molecular biology and biochemistry, which developed as new knowledge of chemical reactions and the chemicals in living things were revealed by new types of scientific instruments, such as electron microscopes, X-ray crystallography, spectrometers, and others. These devices were critical to the elucidation of deoxyribonucleic acid (DNA)—the very stuff of life—by James Watson and Francis Crick in the 1950s, as well as to the development of new medications. By the 1970s, molecular biology and biochemistry were able to make the great leap to genetic manipulation and the determination of the genetic nature of disease.

Current Employment Trends. Biology today remains difficult to organize succinctly, and the many specializations of it will not be reviewed here. A more helpful structure, perhaps, is by area of employment. The main groupings, according to U.S. Bureau of Labor Statistics data, are federal and state/local government, hospitals and physicians' offices, noncommercial research organizations, the pharmaceutical industry, and education. See Figure 3 for a breakdown of the employment areas. (These proportions do not include agricultural, food, forestry, and conservation scientists, who are discussed later.) Fully 37.5 percent of all biological scientists work for federal and state/local government. Thousands of these scientists alone are employed at the National Institutes of Health, whose total employment is over 13,000. Another 40,000 workers are employed by the U.S. Public Health Service, part of the U.S. Department of Health and Human Services (see Appendix C), which has corresponding agencies at the state and sometimes municipal levels.

Due to its importance in medical research (as distinct from medical practice at hospitals and doctors' offices), the National Institutes of Health is worth reviewing. This agency, with a multibillion-dollar budget, sponsors researchers as employees (intramural research) as well as pays for the research conducted at university- or hospital-based centers (extramural research). The specific institutes are:

National Institute on Aging

National Institute of Arthritis and Musculoskeletal and Skin Diseases

National Institute of Allergy and Infectious Diseases

National Cancer Institute

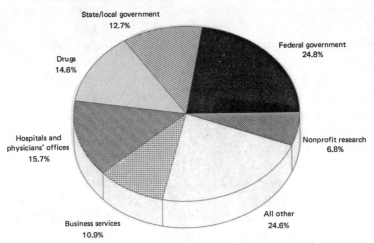

FIGURE 3 **Employment Concentrations of Biological Scientists** (*Source:* U.S. Bureau of Labor Statistics, 1990)

National Institute of Child Health and Human Development

National Institute of Dental Research

National Institute of Diabetes and Digestive and Kidney Diseases

National Institute of Environmental Health Sciences

National Eye Institute

National Institute of General Medical Sciences

National Heart, Lung, and Blood Institute

National Institute of Neurological and Communicative Diseases and Stroke

National Center for Nursing Research

National Library of Medicine

Although the intent of these agencies (except for the National Institute of Environmental Health Sciences) is not directly related to environmental work, the overlaps are many. To take one obvious example, many toxic chemicals are identified by their carcinogenic or teratogenic effects on adults and the young; these topics are researched by the National Cancer Institute and the National Institute of Child Health and Human Development.

Another prominent part of the U.S. Public Health Service is the Centers for Disease Control, which contains the Center for Environmental Health. A newly established (1985) Public Health office is the Agency for Toxic Substances and Disease Registry. This organization seeks to pool all the data coming in on exposure to chemicals in order to draw conclusions on their health effects.

Finally, a very critical role is played by the U.S. Food and Drug Administration (FDA), which is the center for federally sponsored toxicological research and which monitors food safety. One issue of great importance to green marketers is the FDA's current efforts to monitor and regulate "natural" products (i.e., those that are free of pesticides or other synthetic residues).

Biological scientists in industry are concentrated mostly in the pharmaceutical industries (except for agriculture and forestry, as discussed later), where the development of new medications, medical devices, and health-maintenance systems are researched, developed, and manufactured. Prior to the mid-1970s, a test for the medicinal effects of microbes or chemicals that they produce would have required painstaking testing with a few organisms or a few milliliters of chemical. Once the technique of genetic manipulation was devised, however, microbes could be "turned on" to produce a wide variety of compounds, which could be collected by the gallon. Another useful tool of the new biotechnology is the ability to produce monoclonal antibodies, which can be likened to magnets for one specific compound out of the millions that exist inside organisms.

Perhaps the genetic technology farthest along the road to commercialization is the manipulation of plants. Prior to the development of gene splicing, plant scientists grew generation after generation of a plant, seeking to encourage a useful attribute (such as disease resistance) and to discourage detrimental ones (such as small size). With the new biotechnology, a new generation can be grown practically on a daily basis.

A 1991 issue of *Science* magazine [18] identified the leading areas of biological research. They are as follows.

Molecular Biology

Following on their successes in elucidating the molecular structure of genetic materials, molecular biologists are now learning how to cope with the three-dimensional structure of important biochemicals. Unlike simple petrochemicals, each of which by and large has the same structure, enzymes, proteins, and other biologically important compounds have a complex, tangled arrangement. Molecular biologists must deal with not only what atoms and molecules are present in a biochemical but also where they are and what surrounds them. The use of powerful supercomputers is helping this effort.

Genetics

According to one scientist in the field, genetics used to be considered a subspecialty of medicine; now medicine, in a way, can be considered a subset of genetics. Not only has the process of reproduction been much better understood, but also geneticists are now identifying genes that cause medical problems ranging from cystic fibrosis to alcoholism. Next, geneticists will undertake the repair of damaged or malfunctioning genetic material, thereby curing or preventing diseases. Such "gene therapy" is fraught with ethical issues but offers hope to many.

Immunology

The tragedy of the AIDS virus has cast a spotlight on immunology; the AIDS disease itself is a deficiency of the immune system. As the AIDS epidemic draws increasing attention from biologists around the world, the science of immunology is advancing in response. "Immunotherapy," like gene therapy, may offer a new way to fight this and other diseases.

Neuroscience

The biotechnological tools developed in other areas are generating excitement in neuroscience, which more than once has been called the "last frontier" of biology and medicine. The biochemical nature of brain function, communication, and memory is now coming into focus. Results of this research will improve the care of the aged and those with Alzheimer's disease.

These four areas are only the highlights of current biological research. The new biotechnology keeps rebounding into more and more areas of biological research and practice, causing revolutionary changes. The excitement—and the pressure to succeed—is palpable.

Education

Unlike most other sciences, enrollments in the life sciences have held fairly steady, as Table 9 demonstrates. The life sciences also stand out as the largest of the "hard" sciences (i.e., not including psychology and related social sciences).

As anyone in the process of getting a life sciences degree

Table 9 *Life Sciences Degrees Awarded, 1987–1989*

Degree	1987	1988	1989
Bachelor	38,114	36,761	36,079
Master's	4,954	4,769	4,933
Ph.D.	3,423	3,598	3,533

(whether in biology or in one of the closely related disciplines, such as microbiology or biochemistry) knows, there are two types of students—premed students and everyone else. The demands of medical school admissions and the intense competition to win admission greatly color the experiences and outlook of undergraduate students. Not all biology students are premeds; conversely, not all premed students study biology. But nearly all premed students take some biology courses.

For the purposes of this book, life sciences that pertain to human health (and the green-collar types of employment thereof) are described at the end of this chapter. In this section, the "other" life sciences and the "other" students are described. This distinction is important in trying to analyze career trends. As an example, consider the previously cited National Center for Educational Statistics data [19] showing the large proportion of biology students going on to graduate school. According to a follow-up survey of 1986 college graduates, one year after obtaining their B.S. or B.A. degree, only 13 percent of the graduates are pursuing a master's degree, which is a rather low percentage compared with figures for other science disciplines. But fully 28 percent are in the process of obtaining a "first professional" degree—and surely the great majority of these graduates are seeking a medical degree. See Table 10. As this table indicates, biology and other life sciences students love learning or, conversely, are required by their disciplines, such as medicine, to continue schooling.

Biology at the undergraduate level is also one of the few sciences where one can regularly obtain either a Bachelor of Science (B.S.) or Bachelor of Arts (B.A.) degree. The B.S. degree usually allows more room for science courses, at the expense of foreign language and other liberal arts courses that the B.A. student is obliged to take. Getting a B.S. is an obvious first step to graduate school in the life sciences. However, for the green-collar worker who may have other goals in mind in place of becoming a research scientist, the B.A. may be ideal. This is especially so if it is combined with courses in environmental studies, public policy, or business administration.

Roughly 70 percent of the life sciences majors study "General Biology." The graduating class trends are shown in Table 11.

Undergraduate studies in biology sometimes seem to resemble the taxonomy of life itself. Students march through the microbial,

Table 10 Postgraduate Activities of Science and Engineering Students

Status	Biological Sciences (%)	Physical Sciences (%)	Engineering (%)	Social Sciences (%)
No additional education	38	70	72	62
Master's degree	13	16	22	16
Doctoral degree	6	4	1	2
First professional degree	28	4	1	12
Other*	15	6	4	8
Total	100	100	100	100

Source: U.S. Department of Education, based on National Center for Educational Statistics data, 1990.

*Includes other bachelor degrees or other education.

Table 11 *General Biology Degrees Awarded, 1987–1989*

Degree	1987	1988	1989
Bachelor	27,458	26,802	26,251
Master's	2,022	1,977	2,120
Ph.D.	537	582	529

plant, and animal kingdoms, eventually reaching courses in human biology and picking up courses in genetics, physiology, and biochemistry along the way. Mathematics through calculus, introductory chemistry, and physics courses are often required; a foreign language often is not.

Schools that lack formal environmental science programs often provide an environmental biology concentration within the department. Courses in field biology, advanced chemistry, and sometimes geology, along with electives in economics or public policy, are included.

At the master's and doctoral levels, the diverse range of biological studies becomes apparent. The modern list of biological specialties, among others, includes:

Botany

Biochemistry and biophysics

Cell and molecular biology

Microbiology

Biostatistics

Ecology

Nutritional science

Toxicology

Zoology

Pathology

Physiology

Some of these programs are geared primarily toward human health and professional employment in the health care system. Others offer a more research-oriented version of the applied sciences that are economically important, such as wildlife management, veterinary science, pharmacology, agriculture, forestry, and the like. All of them have aspects that make them suitable for green-collar work. It is important to note that nearly all of these specialties can be found at the undergraduate level at some school in the United States; however, the number of graduates recorded by the National Center for Education Statistics on some of these programs is only a few dozen. The exceptions to this are biochemistry and biophysics—1,976 1989 bachelor graduates; cell and molecular biology—693 graduates; microbiology—1,755; and zoology—2,109.

Where in this welter of biorelated topics is ecology? Somewhat surprisingly, it turns out that ecology has remained a very small academic field; it is also true that few employment opportunities are available outside academia, government, and private research organizations. When the novice green-collar aspirant notices how "eco-" is applied to everything from wildlife preserves to disposable diapers, it is a shock to realize that ecology is so small a field.

Ecology formally took shape only in this century; the American Ecological Society was formed in 1915 and enjoyed its greatest breakthroughs during the 1940s, when the concept of energy flows into and out of ecosystems was established. Ecology's definition has come to be understood as the study of the interactions among all forms of life and between organisms and their environment. The profession appears to be hampered by a lack of formal boundaries between it and biological studies of individual genera of plants or animals; an ornithologist, for example, might perform a population survey and dynamics study of the birds of a forest valley just as an ecologist would. At the same time, potential industrial employers, such as agribusinesses, seem more interested in the nurturing of one or a few species of life (wheat, for example, or chickens) than in understanding these forms of life in the context of an ecosystem. The employers would then hire biologists or applied scientists trained in these individual species.

"Long unfamiliar to the public, and relegated to a second-class status by many in the world of science, ecology emerged in the 1960s as one of the most popular and most important aspects of biology" is how one reviewer summed up the status of the profession in that decade [20]. But by 1982, the National Academy of Sciences could write, in a survey study of science and technology, that "because ecological knowledge is a key to solving important environmental problems, ecologists [in the 1960s and 1970s] found themselves thrust into the political arena. Initially, the expectations of the environmentally concerned public and the hopes of many professionals tended to be unrealistically high. Now a pattern is emerging in which the modest but useful contributions of ecologically related sciences are being appropriately applied to solve environmental problems" [21].

The size of the ecology profession may be estimated by the membership of the Ecological Society of America, which was around 6,000 in the late 1980s. At the college level, 418 B.S. degrees and 68 doctoral degrees were awarded in 1989.

In recent years, it seems that ecology is most valuable, and most valued, for its strength in teaching and in setting the debate on many environmental issues. One of the science papers most often cited in the past quarter-century has been the "tragedy of the commons" paper by a University of Santa Barbara ecologist named Garrett Hardin [22]. In it, Hardin pointed out that many of the worst environmental problems—urban air pollution or contaminated rivers and lakes—occur because the pollutants are dumped into a "common" area that is owned by everyone and is therefore the direct responsibility of no one. (Hardin cited specifically the English tradition of a village commons, in which all the village's cattle foraged; all other things being equal, the farmers began to attempt to overuse the commons because there was no additional cost to their doing so. Eventually, the commons was overwhelmed.) In the past few years, the importance of biodiversity and the horrific loss of biologically rich tropical forests have been rightly trumpeted by ecologists.

In coming years, as the great increase in knowledge of the biology of individual species or genera becomes disseminated, there will be a correspondingly greater need for scientists with formal ecology training to synthesize this knowledge into a larger understanding of the environment. For the moment, ecology remains a small, but valuable, biological specialty.

Environmental Impact

While it is certainly true that many people worry about the pollution of the ground, water, or air—all inanimate things—the environmental implications of these forms of pollution are nearly always cast in terms of their impact on living things. Thus, heavy metals in groundwater poison the neural system; pesticides kill birds and insects; tropical deforestation causes the loss of biodiversity.

Thus, it is no surprise that biology and nearly all of its sub-specialties are important to environmental work. Practically all college-trained biologists can consider themselves green-collar workers. An exception to this generalization can be made for human health care workers, but, even there, the medical specialties of environmental medicine, biostatistics, and toxicology give health care workers entree to the green-collar work force.

The picture that most of us have of biologists comes from the many nature programs that are a staple of public television: Biologists are those who are working in the field, in remote, exotic locations. Whether the topic is mountain gorillas in Kenya or white sharks off the Great Barrier Reef near Australia, these biologists always seem to be pursuing topics far removed from everyday life in the United States. The reality, of course, is far different. Biological work is embedded in the products we use in homes; it is also the work performed at factories and offices and, most especially, at parks, wildlife refuges, hunting and fishing reserves, and botanical gardens around the country.

A key function of the professional staffs of parks and wildlife areas is interpretation—the guiding and explaining of what goes on in nature to visitors and young students. Such work at national and state parks is often the first exposure that college students get to fieldwork. Because visitor travel peaks during the summer, this work also fits in nicely with most academic schedules. Interpretation is also an important aspect of zoo-keeping.

Biology graduates perform another very basic, very essential function in the green-collar work force. Like the chemistry graduates that keep laboratories running, biologists work in biological laboratories, gathering data and interpreting the results of experiments and surveys of plant and animal populations. Just as chemical data must be obtained on the environmental quality of, say, a Superfund site, so biologists run tests on native flora and fauna, keeping track of the effects of pollution on indigenous life. The microscope along with a host of new biotechnological tools are the keys to this work. Biology students who have spent much of their undergraduate years tackling laboratory courses will find that this experience is valuable in the job market.

Laboratory work is critical to human health studies as well, particularly in toxicology. Much toxicological work depends first on running extensive tests and then on performing sophisticated biostatistical analyses of the data. Biostatistics is a tremendously useful, but tremendously controversial, field of science today. It is biostatistics from which seemingly endless series of announcements come, such as those saying that eating tomatoes or being exposed to sunlight causes cancer. Biostatisticians were the first to demonstrate conclusively that exposure to asbestos could cause fatal disease and that smoking can kill. The controversy comes in when extremely small exposures or extremely small risks are analyzed, and tremendous economic and social trends are at stake. To put this into perspective, consider that, informally at least, EPA has adopted a one-in-a-million risk of injury or disease as the limit for certain types of exposure to toxic chemicals. But how easy is it to interpret biological test data to distinguish between one in a million (the limit) and two in a million (beyond the limit)?

As it happens, this subject is getting much attention both from biologists who are devising new, more definitive tests and from statisticians who are looking at new ways to analyze data. One intriguing example of the latter is known as *meta-analysis*, by which the partially indicative results of a large number of small studies (small in the sense that only a few data points are obtained) can be amalgamated into one cumulative result, which is more reliable than any of the partial results.

Biologists are by no means limited to the laboratory. Industrial employers depend on biologists for a variety of functions, including production technology. Although the naive observer might believe that anything coming out of a factory is synthetic and therefore not "natural," the reality is that industry depends on many naturally produced materials. A large percentage of pharmaceutical products are derived from plants. Chemical producers depend on wood extracts (turpentine, lignin, cellulose), chemically treated plant extracts (polysaccharides from algae), and biologically driven reactions, such as the production of chemical-grade ethanol from corn via fermentation. The entire food-processing industry, of course, employs the talents of diverse biological scientists to process foodstuffs and to devise more healthful or longer-lasting foods.

Nor is it a rare occurrence that life forms themselves are part of a production process. The most common example of this is wastewater treatment. Sewage (or even the toxics-laden leachate of a chemical dump) is treated in a municipal wastewater plant by exposure to biologically enhanced microbes that can digest the organic content of the waste. Typically, this treatment is carried out *aerobically*, meaning that air is injected into the wastewater to speed up the biological degradation. It is also possible, by changing the processing conditions and the microbes employed, to accomplish this *anaerobically*, meaning without air. The result is methane gas, which can be used as fuel. The term *industrial biotechnology* has come into being to describe biologists who are succeeding in translating the dramatic results of the new biotechnology into production techniques for manufacturers. In general, when a process can be carried out via living microbes rather than through the use of expensive reactants and energy, the process can be more efficient. What is going to be developed in this field is much more exciting than the many concepts that have already been commercialized.

Some of the most exciting work in Superfund remediation projects, as well as the cleanup of accidents like an oil spill, depends on biologists' devising microbial brews that are targeted to digest a specific waste product. As the research results mount up, microbiologists are beginning to realize that many synthetic materials, thought to be impervious to microbial attack, in fact can be destroyed biologically. The implications of this are dramatic: Instead of cleaning up a contaminated underground reservoir by pumping out millions of gallons of water and removing the chemical contaminant, *bioremediation* specialists can inject tailored microbes, along with nutrients and oxygen, into the reservoir; the microbes then destroy the contaminant *in situ*.

Bioremediation was used to help clean up the mess created by the Exxon Valdez tanker spill of 1989. The U.S. Office of Technology Assessment, in reviewing the results obtained, gave a provisional endorsement of the technique [23].

A microbiologist working in bioremediation could be employed in the laboratory, where tests are run to determine what types of microbes work best with what toxic chemicals; in the factory, where a microbe is cultivated for volume sale; and in the field, where at a cleanup site the microbes are put to work.

Another line of biological work that is almost exclusively in the field involves *systemics* and *taxonomy*. These terms refer to the careful, sometimes tedious, process of finding and counting species in tropical forests, in the soil of wetlands or fields, and in coastal estuaries—essentially, wherever there is life. Taxonomy has tended to be overlooked in recent decades as the "action" of biological work shifted to genetic manipulations in the laboratory. However, vitally important questions of species growth or decline, the condition of biodiversity, and the very substance of biological science itself depend on a reliable understanding of just what kinds of life forms exist. Evolutionary biologists are currently in an intense period of reassessment of Darwinian evolutionary theory; weaknesses in the theory have been roundly attacked, and scientists have found that their knowledge of just what species exist is not strong enough to provide definitive answers. At the same time, the passage of the Endangered Species Act in the 1970s has created a demand for biologists who can find rare species in the vicinity of construction projects; the builder is then challenged to prove that the project will not destroy the only known sanctuary of the endangered species.

Another emerging specialty of green-collar biology is the resuscitation of ecosystems. In some cases, this type of work is similar to a Superfund project in that previous environmental damage must be repaired. But in others, it represents a very new and important challenge to biological skill. These biologists can be likened to archaeologists, who not only find ancient cities but also restore their buildings and public works and seek to repopulate them with their original inhabitants.

The Nature Conservancy, for example, is hard at work in the vicinity of Northbrook, Illinois, trying to revive a unique "savanna ecosystem" that once existed in the region. The ecosystem is characterized by grasslands with occasional stands of oak trees [24]. By identifying the appropriate types of plants and insects that would live in this ecosystem and by establishing the necessary soil and irrigation conditions (if they have changed radically since the savanna disappeared), a self-perpetuating colony is set up. Soon, transitory insects and birds appear that complement the plants growing in the area. Besides making a dramatic, pristine wildlife refuge, the restored ecosystems can help in maintaining endangered species.

In sum, biologists perform green-collar work in laboratories for government agencies, pharmaceutical companies, and entrepreneurially minded consulting firms; in industry; and in research functions at universities, private research groups, and nonprofit organizations.

Applied Sciences: Agriculture and Renewable Resources

Overview

The agricultural sciences include agronomy, plant science, animal breeding, and soil science; the renewable resources sciences include forestry, conservation, and wildlife management. Since the Industrial Revolution, and aided in the United States by the land-grant college systems of the Midwest and West, the academic study of these disciplines has become firmly established. These applied sciences, based on biology, helped make America the breadbasket of the world during the first half of the twentieth century. Following the precept of teaching people to fish rather than giving them some, American agricultural sciences helped spawn the "Green Revolution," which refers not to the green products revolution of the 1990s but to an effort to create easy-to-grow strains of rice and wheat that helped the Third World become agriculturally self-sustaining during the 1960s.

In an earlier era, the Green Revolution would have been hailed as a scientific miracle, and its leading proponent, the agricultural scientist Norman Borlaug, would have been a worldwide celebrity. (He was the winner of the 1970 Nobel Peace Prize but has not been widely acclaimed in the United States, his home country.) But the Green Revolution took hold just as scientists and naturalists began to question the benefits of high-yield crops that require aggressive cultivating and liberal doses of fertilizers and pesticides. The Green Revolution was called into question, and while its short-term benefit in pumping up the production of foodstuffs is undeniable (and vital to the hungry of the world), the long-term consequences of an agricultural dependency on chemical fertilizers and on mechanized cultivation are hard to overlook.

"Sustainable" agriculture is the buzzword of the moment. Scientists and farmers are seeking new combinations of seeds and cultivation methods that are less harmful to the environment. A pattern of monoculture farming, through which the repeated planting of one type of crop in a field begins to exhaust its soil, is being superseded by sophisticated crop-rotation techniques. Many farmers, however, are now experimenting with a method that depends on low- or no-tillage crop production. This alternative agriculture is being helped along by a rising demand for certified organically grown produce and animals (*organic* in this sense means the absence of pesticides, synthetic fertilizers and hormones, and other injections for animals).

If alternative agriculture can be called a "low-tech" form of agriculture, then biotechnology can be called a "high-tech" version. Biologists, agronomists, and other plant scientists are becoming adept at using the new genetic manipulations to create crops with resistance to disease or to herbicides. (Having herbicide-resistant plants then enables the farmer to use chemicals that would otherwise harm the plant.) Some biotech companies have developed hormones that increase milk production from cows and synthetic enzymes that help age cheese (these enzymes had previously been harvested from slaughtered animals).

Agriculture, being *the* oldest form of civilized social activity, is deeply intertwined with social and cultural mores, which in turn creates a certain ambivalence toward its "greenness." While farmers are lauded on the one hand for maintaining traditional culture while feeding a nation, they are criticized for polluting rivers with the chemical runoff of their farms, for overgrazing ecologically fragile brushlands, and (especially in tropical regions) for causing deforestation. Like society at large, farmers, animal breeders, and foresters have the potential of helping or hurting the environment. New technology as well as the emergence of new environmental issues create dramatic opportunities for scientists in these professions.

History and Current Assessment

Agriculture, animal breeding, and horticultural and plant sciences are all ancient crafts; out of them came the modern, Western-style sciences of biology, medicine, and veterinary science. As a professional *applied* science, however, these professions awaited the growth of large-scale, industrialized production that came to farms and forests in the wake of the Industrial Revolution.

Ancient Beginnings of Agriculture. Traces of agricultural development have been found around the world as long ago as 7000 B.C. Rather than developing in one place and spreading to other cultures, agriculture seems to have evolved gradually and concurrently on most continents of the Earth. A distinction as valid to make as any other is to identify cultures by the main crop they produced—wheat in the Middle East and the Mediterranean, millet and rice in India and China, beans and maize in the Americas. It is said that the Mesopotamian civilization (in modern Iraq) severely damaged its agricultural capacity by overirrigating with salt water. In Egypt, agriculture became heavily regulated probably because of the discipline imposed by the annual cycle of flooding of the Nile River. The Egyptians were also very successful with animal husbandry. In the Americas, recent research has continued to raise the reputation of Incan and Mayan cultures, which depended heavily on terraced fields along mountainsides and elaborate water-conveying systems for irrigation.

In most of the ancient cultures, agricultural policy and governance were one and the same; the main activity of the citizens was planting and raising crops. Royalty became accustomed to receiving duties in the form of bushels of grain, and armies were only as strong as the agricultural enterprises backing them. Through the Middle Ages, there was steady progress in the types of crops grown and in the development of domesticated animals; little of this was done on a scientific basis, and much of the state of the art depended on passing traditions from generation to generation. The main technological developments of the Middle Ages, at least in Europe, were the development of crop-rotation systems, water irrigation, and new types of plows (to go with the bigger and stronger oxen and horses that were being bred).

Agricultural Improvements in the 1700s and 1800s. By the late 1700s, as national populations grew, agricultural improvement efforts became formalized in royally chartered scientific bodies such as the Royal Society of London. At this time, too, forestry had become a formal science in Germany, where wood was a valuable export product and landowners collectively developed methods to harvest and then regenerate their famed forests.

The introduction of the huge number of totally new plant species from the New World changed many agricultural practices in Europe, especially with regard to the cultivation of corn, the potato, and cocoa. Tea and coffee also came from the Orient.

In the 1800s, the opening up of the New World provided an opportunity for new types of agriculture; however, a pattern of overexploitation quickly became established. Forests did not have to be renewed when the next valley held all the wood one could desire, and soils did not have to be conserved when one could move farther west and start anew. This was particularly true of cotton in the South. Also during this period, the mechanization of agriculture began in earnest, with the McCormick reaper in the 1830s and, later, with steam-powered cultivators and harvesters.

In the United States, agriculture and forestry were given new breadth and depth with the passage of the Morrill Act in 1862, which set up schools of agriculture and mechanical arts in each of the newly established states. Great Plains farmers of the 1800s practiced "dry" farming due to the lack of sufficient irrigation. The development of pumping and drilling techniques for water wells made this practice fade (although now, as the Ogallala Reservoir under most of the Great Plains runs dry, dry farming may eventually come back into fashion).

Forestry, Agronomy, and Soil Science. The great conservationist movements of the turn of the century helped establish forestry, agronomy, and soil science in the United States. One of the giants of the profession, Gifford Pinchot, was trained in France, worked in private parks, and then, having gained the ear of Theodore Roosevelt, helped catapult the Forest Service and the concept of environmental conservation into the public eye. It is important to note that, in its main themes, Pinchot's conservationism did not necessarily imply *preservation* but rather the "efficient" use of natural resources. Out of this philosophy came the concept of multiple use of resources, meaning that a dam, for example, is evaluated for flood control, soil conservation, and recreation as well as for power generation. (Obviously, this type of multiple use negates the original, free-running wild river and the fish life that depend on it.) "Conservation means the greatest good to the greatest number for the longest time" is how Pinchot summed up the concept, echoing the utilitarian philosophers of the 1800s [25].

With the growth of mechanized transportation (trains, planes, and automobiles) and the sciences of animal and plant breeding, the long trend of greater productivity and smaller employment began in the United States. In 1900, 37 percent of the population was employed through agriculture; in 1990, only 1 percent [26]. A great change took place during the 1930s. With the Depression gripping the nation, the Dust Bowl combination of drought and economic privation of the farmers of the Southwest and West led the federal government to organize the Soil Conservation Service. This agency as well as others sponsored by state universities have come to be known as "Extension Services," which many states provide to help farmers with technical assistance.

Forestry today remains one of the bitterest confrontations between industrial interests and environmental activists. The majestic old-growth forests of the Pacific Northwest are vastly shrunken, and yet logging companies seek to exploit the remaining ones. Over the past few years, a knock-down drag-out dispute over the spotted owl, an endangered species, resulted in a clear win for environmental interests. Notably, environmental activists were joined in the campaign by supporters of tourism, hunting, and fishing, which shows how economic and environmental interests have become much more complex in their intertwinings.

Over the past decade, foresters have compensated for the growing shortage of large, old-growth forests by developing a host of new technologies that utilize wood particles as a composite. Plywood is the best-known such composite; it employs a veneer of wood layered with adhesives and particle board. More recently, "oriented-strand" board, laminates, and other high-tech versions of the venerable plank of wood have been developed. "Lumbering in the Age of the Baby Tree" is the headline that the *New York Times* used to sum up the trend [27]. This article points out that, in the latest evolution of logging and forest regeneration, lumber companies are developing "fiber farms," where fast-growing woody plants are grown under conditions very much like those of a wheat or corn farm and are harvested in a few years (as opposed to 30 or more years for a tree planted for eventual harvesting). The picture that fiber farming conjures up is drastically different from our usual concept of a forest and of forest logging. But perhaps the success in fiber farming will reduce the pressure to exploit old-growth forest reserves, thus giving society the best of both worlds.

Small versus Big Agriculture. During and after the 1940s, the use of newly developed pesticides had become common in agriculture. In the 1950s, the use of breeding pens or "animal factories" became established for chickens and other animals, thus superseding small herds or groups of animals raised by farmers as a sideline to their crop production. *Agribusiness*, both as a concept and as an actual, dominating element of the food production and processing business, has now become firmly established. Critics of big agriculture argue, quite rightly, that federal agricultural policy has tended to favor the large farming businesses over the individual farmer. Agriculture professionals, in a competitive race for more efficient, more productive farming and food processing, have unwittingly helped big agriculture as well, through the development of machinery that has high capital cost and low human labor input (see also the discussion of agricultural engineering in Chapter 3). The small farmer, however, has a shortage of capital and a surplus (or, at least, ready supply) of labor. A number of environmental-activist organizations are philosophically allied with a variety of small-farming movements across the country. The latter are fighting for their very survival; the former are acting out of a belief that both agriculture and urbanization have grown too big in modern culture and that the better way to organize society is through the development of small towns that support themselves agriculturally.'

This small-versus-big confrontation over agricultural (and social) policy is one of the more fascinating elements of the green movement today. Its outcome is very much in doubt in a world of international economic competition and hopeless poverty and starvation in the underdeveloped nations. For the professional green-collar scientist, a decades-long tradition of rationalizing agriculture to higher efficiency and productivity is hard to overlook. The challenge for today's scientists is to develop technologies that both support small-scale agriculture and provide better economic and environmental performance to society at large.

Current Employment Trends. Four out of five forestry and conservation scientists work for government at the federal, state, or local level, according to the Bureau of Labor Statistics (BLS). Most of the remainder work for agribusiness and forestry and fishing businesses. BLS counted 27,000 such scientists in 1988 and predicts that the profession will rise by only 8.3 percent during the 1988–2000 period, a rate that is half the growth of all occupations.

BLS also estimates that there are 25,000 "agricultural and food" scientists. It predicts that their number will rise by 20.9 percent by the year 2000.

A final employment category worth noting is that of farm manager. These professionals may have a business or a science background; their 1988 enumeration was 131,000, and the occupation will grow by 29 percent through the year 2000. Most significantly, this above-average growth will occur while the number of farmers will shrink by 266,000 from 1988's count of 1.14 million.

Education

Tables 12a, 12b, and 12c provide a view of the full range of agricultural and other sciences in which a student can concentrate. Note that Table 12a covers the same data as Table 9; Table 12a is included here because of programs of study such as botany and microbiology, which are part of the life sciences.

Table 12a   *Life Sciences Degrees Awarded, 1987–1989*

Degree	1987	1988	1989
Bachelor	38,114	36,761	36,079
Master's	4,954	4,769	4,933
Ph.D.	3,423	3,598	3,533

Table 12b   *Agricultural Sciences Degrees Awarded, 1987–1989*

Degree	1987	1988	1989
Bachelor	6,834	6,392	5,920
Master's	1,841	1,762	1,684
Ph.D.	680	726	752

Table 12c   *Renewable Resources Science* Degrees Awarded, 1987–1989*

Degree	1987	1988	1989
Bachelor	2,819	3,030	2,832
Master's	950	1,007	907
Ph.D.	188	217	229

*Includes conservation, fishing and fisheries, forestry, and wildlife management, among others.

Programs in agricultural sciences, forestry, and other renewable resources begin from a perspective of making use of nature. This is not to say that the programs of study are scientifically or intellectually unsound; rather, it is an assertion that the education of future foresters, farm managers, and public servants is felt to revolve around a knowledge of current industrial and business practices, production techniques, marketing, and public policy. The catalog of the University of Maine's College of Forest Resources makes this stance clear: "Maine's forest resource is the foundation of the State's economy. One reason for the existence of the College [of Forest Resources] is to insure a continuous flow of well-educated professionals and technicians to manage this important resource" [28].

All of these professions require an increasingly diverse range of scientific and professional skills; the undergraduate curricula are packed with courses and concentration areas, all of which vary from school to school. A prospective undergraduate or graduate student is well advised to compare the program themes of a variety of schools before making a choice.

Forestry students, for example, can study programs that concentrate on logging and timber operations, forest biology, forest recreation, and forest business administration, among others. Agricultural science majors can concentrate on various types of agriculture, animal science, plant science, horticulture, and landscape architecture or in preveterinary programs and agribusiness management. In terms of the sciences that are studied, forestry undergraduates study introductory biology, plant physiology, silviculture (the science of tree cultivation), ecology, entomology (the better to know the parasites of trees). Agricultural majors study biology and agronomy (the science of plant–soil interactions), soil science, animal nutrition, farm equipment and technology, and plant or animal physiology. In addition, some schools offer courses highly specific to the agriculture, horticulture, animal husbandry, and forest products of the region where they are located.

Wildlife management, which falls under the educational category of renewable resources, represents a form of applied ecology. Systematics, the study of plant and animal populations, is central to the profession. Besides the usual biology and other general science courses, wildlife managers study a series of applied courses in the management of forest resources.

Most undergraduate programs offer field experience, often as a required part of the curriculum. Some of these programs amount to summer jobs or a type of cooperative education between the school and the major agribusiness or forestry organizations (both public and private) in the region. Agriculture and forestry are learned by doing.

Graduate-level programs vary considerably as well, with the general tendency of driving the student toward specializing in some technical or business aspect of these programs. Some schools combine an undergraduate agribusiness program with an M.B.A. program. The more technically minded can concentrate in subjects such as remote sensing (i.e., using satellite imaging to perform resource surveys), soil science, pesticide development and usage, water resources management, and the like.

As in the pharmaceutical industry, the impact of the new biotechnology is large and growing in both agriculture and forestry. Genetically manipulated plants and animals are being tested for their economic viability. Another example of this technology's application is the development of a bacterial technique to prevent freezing; by adding this microbe to a water spray, plants can be protected from the cold. There has been, and will continue to be, a steady trafficking of new technology between the inventors—research biologists—and the users on farms or in forest lands.

Environmental Impact

Agriculture and forestry are the front lines of the environmental conflict. The acreage devoted to these two activities far exceeds any other business or social activity, and, strictly speaking, forests (including parks) represent the primary reserve of wild species on the American continent.

Here is one simple fact to show that all is not well in agricultural technology. David Pimentel, an entomologist at Cornell University, has estimated that in 1945 about one-third of crop yields were lost to pests, disease, and weeds. In the late 1980s, some 225,000 tons of pesticides (a 3,000 percent increase over 1945) were applied to U.S. agricultural land, and the amount of crop yields lost to pests, disease, and weeds was—surprise!—about one-third [29].

Of course, production volumes have grown in the interim, but not by 3,000 percent. What has happened is that the many species that farmers know as "pests" are developing tolerances for the more traditional, more common pesticide chemicals. Farmers and the insect world are engaged in an agricultural arms race to see who can be first to develop either the better pesticide or the better resistance to pesticides—and nature is winning.

The chemicals that are applied to fields and crops are often long-lived ones that then dissolve into soil and run off the ground into rivers when rain falls. The pesticides also seep into groundwater, and now many parts of the country have drinking water that is contaminated with these chemicals. A considerable number of pesticides have been banned (DDT was not the first, when it was banned in the 1960s; in previous decades, farmers had applied arsenic and mercury compounds!). But, when new regulations were passed during the 1970s, many currently used compounds were "grandfathered," meaning that, while new chemical formulations had to run a rigorous course of tests and approvals before being sold commercially, formulations that were in use when the laws were passed continued to be used unabated.

Pesticides are only one of many issues affecting agriculture and forestry. A long list of environmental issues could be drawn up; most of them would revolve around the following central facts:

■ As more wild land across the world is devoted to serving human interests (farming, forestry, etc.), the habitats of numerous plant and animal species are lost.

■ With modern agricultural and forest-harvesting techniques, soil and water become polluted or stripped of nutrients.

■ The topsoil itself that supports plant life is being degraded.

■ The worldwide reservoir of plant life that counters the rising carbon dioxide concentration of the atmosphere (the cause of global warming) is being lost, especially in tropical regions.

■ The ability of small local populations, ranging from aboriginal tribes in jungles or tropical forests to the American small-farm operator, to sustain themselves in a stable economic system is being lost, resulting in greater urbanization with its attendant environmental ills.

■ Wild, uncivilized, and unpolluted natural ecosystems—even those valuable only for no more than their lack of human traces—are being lost, usually forever.

Many of these problems are not the result of any particular agricultural or forestry technology; rather, the stresses caused by growing populations around the world are at fault. Overpopulation is the ultimate environmental issue, but it is one that will be addressed by political and social policies rather than by changes in technology.

In a sense, all agricultural and renewable resources scientists have been green-collar workers for as long as their professions have existed. No agricultural scientist sets out to cause the destruction of topsoil or the pollution of groundwater. Nevertheless, these are among the critical problems that the cumulative efforts of scientists, farmers, foresters, and society at large are causing. What is to be done?

Some answers may be found in a pathbreaking, controversial report issued by the National Academy of Sciences (NAS) in 1989, *Alternative Agriculture* [30]. The academy defines alternative agriculture as follows:

■ More thorough incorporation of natural processes such as nutrient cycles, nitrogen fixation, and pest–predator relationships into the agricultural production process

■ Reduction in the use of off-farm inputs with the greatest potential to harm the environment or the health of farmers and consumers

■ Greater productive use of the biological and genetic potential of plant and animal species

■ Improvement of the match between cropping patterns and the productive potential and physical limitation of agricultural lands to ensure long-term sustainability of current production levels

■ Profitable and efficient production with emphasis on improved farm management and conservation of soil, water, energy, and biological resources [31]

Although many types of "natural" or "alternative" agriculture seem to demand that farmers go back to a plow pulled behind a horse, the concepts just described do not *necessarily* ban modern technology; rather, they seek to guide the technology's use in harmony with the soil, the weather, and the inclinations of farmers themselves. The challenge to agronomy, soil science, and the related agricultural sciences is to develop technologies that can enhance this effort without sacrificing farm productivity.

Alternative Agriculture goes on to provide case studies of successful farms that practice all or some of these techniques. In general, the farms tend to be smaller ones, owned by a family rather than an agribusiness corporation. However, when a trend takes hold, agribusinesses readily jump onto the bandwagon. Numerous efforts are afoot to establish standards of "naturalness" in organically grown foods to enlighten consumers who seek foods free of synthetic residues (and for which they pay a substantial premium). Environmental activists urge consumers to "vote with your pocketbook" when it comes to issues like organic foods. The agribusiness enterprises will adapt to this new market when the voice of the consumer is heard loud enough.

The NAS report goes on to specify the research needs if alternative agriculture is to be widely adapted: "U.S. agriculture has always taken pride in its ability to apply science and technology in overcoming the everyday problems of farmers. Many states, however, are losing by retirement and attrition the multidisciplinary agricultural research and education experts capable of bridging the gap between laboratory advances and practical progress on the farm. . . . Insufficient numbers of young scientists are pursuing careers in interdisciplinary or systems research. . . . An effective alternative agricultural research program will require the participation of and improved communication among problem-solving and systems-oriented researchers, innovative farmers, farm advisers, and a larger cadre of extension specialists" [32].

Another example of agricultural research, far removed from the farm, occurs in Woods End, Maine, where the Woods End Research Laboratory is headquartered. Led by William Brinton, the firm has become a renowned center for solving nearly intractable problems with composting organic matter. Composting is the method of reducing leaves, wood, or other organic matter back into the soil through the degradation action of microorganisms and fungi. In nature, it is what decomposes dead, fallen trees and leaves, creating the rich soil out of which new plants grow. At Woods End, however, the technology is being applied to waste matter from chicken and egg farms, food-processing residues, and, most recently, toxic wastes on military bases in conjunction with an environmental engineering firm.

"Over the years, Mr. Brinton has turned the humble art of composting into a high-tech affair. Computers calculate needed ratios of ingredients such as manure, which adds bacteria and fuel for desired reactions," said the *Wall Street Journal* in a glowing, page 1 article on Woods End [33]. "Mr. Brinton has some grand visions for his industry," the article goes on to say. "One is a farming revolution in which compost helps growers get off their water-polluting chemical fertilizer habit."

In the larger arena, composting is also becoming a useful technology for municipalities, who find, every fall, that their precious garbage-landfilling capacity is preempted by yard wastes—leaves, grass, and wood. Many cities now collect yard waste separately, compost it, and sell the resulting soil enhancement back to the residents of the community.

David Dindal, a forestry professor from Cornell University, regularly regales environmental conferences with a talk entitled "Learning to Love the Maggot." As a researcher on the biota of the forest floor, Mr. Dindal has a clear understanding of the organisms that make open-air composting processes work. A good way to sum up his presentation is simply to contemplate all of the "pests" that homeowners pay dearly to eradicate. These pests are what enables composting to work, and their absence indicates a failed compost pile. The bugs include maggots—of course—as well as mites, beetles, wasps, spiders, and even rats. In-grown cultural biases against these organisms compel many sanitation managers to question their presence, yet Mr. Dindal points out that each species higher up the food chain clears the way for the next compost pile.

In forestry, the fiber farm technology mentioned earlier puts a decided technical direction on wood resource management. No one contemplates clear-cutting an old-growth forest in order to plant row on row of fast-growing trees that can be harvested every five or so years rather than the 30 to 50 years it typically takes for trees to mature. But what if such fiber farms are established in regions where indigenous plant life is scarce due to previous human use? Such highly managed wood crops are certainly not a "natural" vista to observe. But what if, on the other hand, forestry companies could succeed in cultivating trees assembly-line style and thus spare virgin forests from exploitation? And what if the products of such efforts result in lumber products that are both stronger and cheaper than currently used materials?

Forestry and agriculture have exacted a terrible toll on the environment, especially on the most pristine and dramatic fields, woods, and lush valleys that used to cover the countryside. But the future benefits of a more environmentally sound nation have already been planted. Today's agriculture and renewable resources scientists have their work cut out for them.

Earth Sciences and Geology

Overview

Physics likes to think of itself as the king or pinnacle of sciences since it deals with fundamental issues of matter, energy, and the universe. If so, then geology and the related earth sciences (oceanology, meteorology, atmospheric science, hydrology, and several others) may be thought of as our queen mother. The stars may be where humanity is going, but the Earth is where we come from and where our roots are. This romanticized view of a body of scientific knowledge may seem irrelevant, yet geology still contains within it a history of our origins. Ancient cultures attributed nearly all actions of the Earth (volcanoes, earthquakes, storms) to divine causes partly because they were at a loss to provide any other explanation. To them, geology refused to undergo mental abstraction; unlike mathematics, which can be analyzed in one's mind only, geology must be observed.

Geology outgrew its religious underpinnings with the need for knowledge for mining and with the need for mapmaking as the New World became explored. In this century, it has come to be dominated by the search for petroleum and other energy sources—a mutual dependency that has uncovered new sources of energy (and, with them, terrible environmental consequences) and new knowledge of how the Earth works. Yet, in the midst of satellite surveys of rock strata and geochemical analyses of minerals, the ancient yearnings and wonderings remain. It is for this reason that the discovery of an astronomical origin to the famed "K–T" boundary—a stratum of rock that divides the Age of Dinosaurs from what followed—is still winning grudging acceptance from the earth sciences community and has vast implications for humanity's vision of the Earth and its place on it. For the first time, there is clear-cut evidence that something can happen—may have already happened—that could end our climate and our civilization almost in the blink of an eye. This realization of the fragility of the Earth's climate colors the debate over newer issues, such as global warming or the loss of biodiversity. The pessimistic believe that the Age of Humanity may already be going the way of the dinosaurs.

In the meantime, earth scientists study, do research, write papers, and teach. In the employment arena, they help guide the national debate on environmental issues, and they are employed to correct previous injuries to the environment and to see to it that new projects (highways, buildings, factories) are constructed in harmony with the Earth. The prospect of a long-sought goal—the prediction of earthquakes—now seems in view.

History and Current Assessment

The Origins of the Earth Sciences. Perhaps more so than any other science, the origins of the earth sciences are bound up in the religious and philosophical yearnings of ancient cultures. When the tools of science and inductive reasoning are absent, there are few other ways of confronting mysteries such as storms, floods, earthquakes, and volcanoes than through supernatural beliefs.

Thus, in most ancient cultures, these manifestations of the Earth's instability were attributed to gods and, to a certain extent, were believed to be the consequences of human evil or failings. The Greeks attributed the actions of oceans to Poseidon; the Jews in the time of Moses could call on their God to separate the seas; and practically every active volcano in the world had a god associated with it.

As nautical travel became more common, new knowledge in the form of geography and mapmaking became important, and these efforts indirectly led to an effort to systematize mountains, oceans, and the actions of winds. Another root of the earth sciences is mining. Ancient cultures first just took what they could find from the Earth's surface but then began digging deeper, following veins of ore and learning about the composition of rock strata. Weather and meteorology, however, were essentially a complete blank until the development of scientific instruments (to measure air pressure and temperature, for example) in the post-Renaissance era. Happenings in the sky were indistinguishable from astronomy as well—which itself was indistinguishable from astrology.

Beginning in the 1500s, and spurred by the great circumnavigations of Spanish, Portuguese, and English explorers, the earth sciences had a vast new field of study—the New World. Mapmaking took on greater significance as did the use of stellar navigation and compasses. The new mountain ranges and flora and fauna did much to inspire "natural philosophers" of the era (who would be surprised at the divisions among earth sciences and among all sciences that exist today). A very important writer of mining and mineralogy, Georgius Agricola, wrote essentially an encyclopedia of earth sciences during the 1500s. It is notable for not attributing magical or mystical properties to the minerals it describes.

Developments in the 1600s to Early 1900s. In the late 1600s, with scientific societies well established in the major European countries, geology became a favorite theme for speculating. Robert Hooke, an Englishman, presented papers in 1667 on one of the great puzzles of the time—the presence of fossils in rocks. In the eighteenth and nineteenth centuries, the emerging knowledge of chemistry helped provide structure to the study of rocks and minerals; like the biologists of the era, who were busy categorizing all the new plant and animal life found in the New World, geologists and chemists were busy establishing new mineral and even chemical classifications. Most of the elements of the periodic table were found during the 1800s, usually in new minerals.

The 1800s were also notable for the culmination of the great debates over the fossil and geological records. The discoveries of the New World included fossils that had never been seen before, weakening the belief that fossils were simply the old remains of animals seen in everyday life. The "giants" of geology of this era—Georges Cuvier in France, Charles Lyell in England, Louis Agassiz in Switzerland, and Alexander von Humboldt in Germany—established the concept of geological strata as a record back in time of the Earth, accounted for the formation of mountains and the occurrence of earthquakes and volcanoes, and mapped the currents of the oceans. Charles Darwin, a protégé of Lyell, began his scientific investigations in geology but switched exclusively to evolutionary biology after his journey on the *Beagle* in the 1830s. Investigations in hydrology, the science of groundwater, also proceeded apace.

Humboldt was also a central figure in the development of climatology and meteorology; he was the first to map isotherms (lines of identical temperature) in the oceans and sky. Meteorological research was important during the nineteenth century mostly for nautical purposes; in the United States, meteorological stations were instituted as part of the Department of War (the predecessor to today's Department of Defense). With the tremendous expansion westward during the late 1800s, the U.S. Geological Survey was established in 1879.

A new wave of scientific instruments and techniques, such as radiocarbon dating, X-ray crystallography, analytical chemistry, and magnetometry, helped continue the growth of earth science knowledge in the early 1900s. One of the great geological theories of modern times—the existence of plate tectonics—was proposed early in this century (by a German meteorologist, Alfred Wegener, in 1915) but was not accepted until the 1960s. During the late 1800s, investigations of the upper atmosphere became common through the use of balloons and, later, airplanes. The development of aviation itself created a tremendous demand for more accurate weather information.

Atmospheric science, which existed only in traces prior to 1900, took a significant jump when rocketry became established in the post-World War II period. The chemistry of the upper atmosphere and the existence of the Van Allen belt were studied during the 1950s. Balloons and high-flying aircraft had preceded the rocket-based surveys.

From about the 1920s onward, geology has become highly dependent on the petroleum industry (and vice versa). The incredible wealth generated when a new oil field is found has spurred tremendous advances in geophysics, structural geology, micropaleontology (the study of fossilized protozoa, which are markers for the presence of oil), and other earth sciences. Some of the best records of what exists under the Earth's surface are now contained in the laboratories of the leading petroleum companies around the world. Oil companies have become the leading employers of both practicing geologists and geological researchers.

The K–T Boundary and Its Implications.   With over 300 years of intensive study, one might believe that the basic outlines of the geological record and the forces that drive geological change have been well established. One would be wrong. Within the past 15 years, a new piece of knowledge has gone from being a wild-eyed theory to (almost) becoming established dogma. This is the interpretation of the K–T boundary, the small stratum of rock that separates the Cretaceous and Tertiary geological periods. There are many such boundaries in the geologic record, but this one is notable because it signifies the end of the Age of Dinosaurs, 65 million years ago. The boundary can be found around the world (as indeed nearly all such boundaries can be, which was one of the bits of evidence that established plate tectonic theory). A nuclear physicist, Luis Alvarez, postulated in the late 1970s that this boundary contained evidence of the collision of the Earth with a meteor or comet at precisely that time, followed by enormous changes in the Earth's climate that led to the dying off of the mighty dinosaurs. Alvarez found an unusually high concentration of the element iridium in the K–T boundary and linked this fact with the knowledge that many meteors are high in iridium content.

This concept, seemingly pulled from the worst of science fiction fantasizing, soon took on new force as geologists found not only iridium but also small bits of "shocked" rocks—droplets or flakes of stone that have been liquefied or compressed, as might happen when a meteor crashes into the Earth. The race is now on to determine just where this meteor fell; the latest research points to an area in the Caribbean and eastern Mexico. This concept has gone from theory to (almost) dogma in a blindingly quick period, and its implications do no less than color our view of the universe.

For instance, the astronomer Carl Sagan won worldwide attention with the theorizing about "nuclear winter," an abrupt change in the Earth's climate caused by even a "small" nuclear war. This theorizing has subsequently been applied to a climate change caused by global warming, which would be characterized by gradual changes that build up forces that then reach a climax very rapidly. In the aftermath of the Iraq–Kuwait war in early 1991, scientists were questioning a climatological change almost as the oil wells began burning.

Another example, much more direct in its implications and in the actions that nations and industry have taken, has occurred over the past 20 years regarding the ozone layer of the Earth. A theory postulated by two chemists at the University of California (Davis) in the early 1970s—that chlorofluorocarbon compounds were destroying the ozone layer above the Earth—was confirmed in the early 1980s. For the first time, an international accord, the Montreal Protocol of 1987, was agreed to by most of the industrialized nations; this accord bans the production of chlorofluorocarbon compounds.

Neither global warming nor ozone layer destruction would have the force in people's imaginations without the confirmation of the K–T cataclysm that geology provided. If it happened before, it can happen again; the real anger sets in when people realize that it may not occur through an extraterrestrial event like a meteor or comet but through the ignorant, foolish practices of humanity.

Current Employment Trends. Today, the earth sciences are characterized by the extremely multidisciplinary nature of the research. Recall that the K–T boundary theory came from a physicist and that plate tectonic theory was proposed by a meteorologist. Various earth science research organizations now regularly conduct multidisciplinary research projects and then pool the resulting data to arrive at new scientific results. Earth science education contains the same multidisciplinary drive.

Today, nearly half of all geologists, geophysicists, and oceanographers are employed by the petroleum and natural gas industries. About another quarter are employed by federal or state government. Of the remaining quarter, about half are employed in consulting (usually at environmental engineering or construction companies), and the remainder teach or work in other areas. There were approximately 42,000 such earth scientists in 1988, and the projected growth rate is 15.7 percent, which is about average for all occupations.

Slightly less than half of the 6,000 meteorologists at work today are employed by the federal government, primarily at the National Oceanic and Atmospheric Administration (NOAA). The remainder work in a variety of business consulting or research services, such as private meteorological companies, or teach. The projected growth rate is 29.6 percent; however, this represents an addition of only 2,000 scientists, and when both the total and the addition are so small, the projection is subject to error. Undoubtedly, employment opportunities for meteorologists will grow.

Education

The degree totals in Table 13 include six separate programs tracked by the National Center for Educational Statistics: geological engineering, geophysical engineering, atmospheric science and meteorology,

Table 13 *Earth Sciences Degrees Awarded, 1987–1989*

Degree	1987	1988	1989
Bachelor	5,003	3,775	3,325
Master's	2,160	2,005	1,880
Ph.D.	471	545	563

geological sciences (which includes geology), oceanography, and earth science. This is one of the more diverse assemblages of an academic concentration, and indicates the many different ways that university programs address the earth sciences.

As befits the multidisciplinary nature of earth sciences work, the bachelor degree serves only as an introduction to the profession. Many students go on to advanced study; the student who does not do so is advised to begin to specialize in one or another earth science as early as possible during the undergraduate years.

Academic programs vary significantly from school to school; a comparison of curricula is therefore a worthwhile effort in contemplating undergraduate or graduate schooling. Typically, geological studies begin with chemistry and math courses (through calculus), followed by a survey course of geology. Even in a specialized geological program, a wide range of courses follow: petrology (the study of rocks), paleontology (fossils), stratigraphy (the analysis of rock strata, mountains, and the like), structural geology, mineralogy, geochemistry, sedimentology, and others. At some schools, there are courses on the geology of the region in which the school is located.

Many programs also include a course or two on geological instrumentation, which can be a field of study all its own. Several laboratory courses are usually required, and some schools sponsor summertime field research. The computer is having a dramatic impact on geological research, especially for structural geology and stratigraphy. An emerging trend is the use of satellite data, which can be used to analyze both the surface and the underlying chemistry and physics of the Earth.

For students who know that they are headed for employment in construction or in oil exploration and production, many schools offer programs in geological engineering. The range of types of geological study are more limited, and in their place more basic science courses are taken, as well as specialized courses in industrial practices. An even larger engineering specialty is petroleum engineering, which is tailored exclusively to the needs of the petroleum industry. Mining engineering is taught at a few schools, especially in western regions and in the states that produce significant amounts of coal.

At the graduate level, all of these specialties and others can be studied in detail. There are decided influences to geological study based on the locale of the institution: Freshwater lakes are studied in the Midwest; coastal conditions, on the eastern and western seaboards; mining and petroleum, in the western mountain states and Texas. Many schools have private- or government-sponsored programs that are associated with the school and that offer work–study programs to graduate students.

Meteorology is primarily (but not exclusively) studied at the graduate level. Sometimes, it is located in the physics and astronomy department rather than in an earth sciences department.

Environmental Impact

Geology, like astrophysics, holds a special fascination for us because it addresses fundamental questions about where we come from and where we are going—riding, as it has been said, aboard Spaceship Earth. Out of pure intellectual curiosity, we would like to know where the hypothesized meteor that caused the end of the dinosaurs landed, and we are also intrigued about the primeval arrangement of the continents that now float like barges over the surface of the Earth. Along with the other earth sciences, however, geology matters very much in a practical, workaday sense.

These everyday concerns can be neatly summed up by mentioning two common fluids: oil and water. Multinational petroleum companies are the source of new knowledge about much of what the Earth's geology is, both on land and in the oceans. Oil exploration and production are two of the most severe stresses put on wilderness environments and remote areas of the Earth. Oil companies have peppered much of the populated or developed regions of the Earth already; now the voracious appetite for oil has driven engineers and scientists to the most remote regions on the planet: the North Slope of Alaska, the deep jungles of the Amazon, and the storm-tossed seas of Northern Europe.

Oil is the source of employment, too, for most privately employed earth scientists. And those not working to find or produce oil are usually working on the location and production of water, for drinking or irrigation purposes. Both in terms of water's source and in terms of how its use is regulated, water is divided between *surface water*—that which exists in lakes, rivers, and streams—and *groundwater*, which is pooled under the surface. Groundwater emerged as a crucial issue during the 1980s, as the realization dawned that nearly half of the U.S. population depends on it as a source of potable water, but more and more of it was either becoming contaminated by industrial wastes or was becoming overexploited and was, therefore, inaccessible.

The only earth science professions that do not touch directly on oil and water are meteorology and atmospheric science. The old saying that the weather is something everybody talks about but that nobody does anything about no longer holds true, for we have found, much to our dismay, that human activity is, in fact, affecting the weather by altering the chemistry of the Earth's atmosphere. The intertwined issues of ozone-layer depletion and global warming have set the stage for a tremendous boost of interest in atmospheric science and meteorology.

All these issues—oil exploration and production, water resource management, global atmospheric change—are ones that affect wide swaths of society, and ones about which environmental activists and the general public have expressed the deepest concerns. Thus, the earth sciences are enjoying a new wave of popularity, and this popularity has translated into higher levels of funding for research. "NOAA Revived for the Green Decade" was the headline of a recent article in *Science* describing how the National Oceanic and Atmospheric Administration, having survived eight years of Ronald Reagan's attempts to put it out of business, is now seeing its budget boosted by millions [34]. NOAA, under its administrator John Knauss, took the lead in organizing a Committee on Earth Sciences to pool funding resources among NOAA, the National Science Foundation, the National Aeronautics and Space Administration, and other federal agencies whose scope touches on global-change issues. This unity has helped all the agencies win sizable funding increases during a time when the entire federal budget is being hammered by cost concerns.

The federal government figures largely in most of the earth sciences. Following is a rundown of the leading agencies, administrations, and offices.

Department of the Interior

Bureau of Mines

Established in 1910, BOM's mission is to ensure the development of new technology for minerals exploitation and mining equipment technology, to assess mineral policy alternatives, and to evaluate and develop mine-reclamation technologies. Underground and strip mines for coal production were a big issue in the 1960s as a result of the destruction of wildernesses after mining was completed and the emissions of acidic wastes that spoiled streams. Both issues were addressed by legislation and regulatory changes, and have largely faded as popular protest themes. Mine operators now use alkaline treatments to neutralize mine drainage, and are required to commit funds to restoring land after a strip mine is closed. Evolving issues on mining and mineral technology are the development of chemical methods of mineral recovery (such as the use of cyanide-based chemicals to leach gold from weak ores), the generation of methane gas from coal mines, and the problems of disposing of mine tailings (the wastes left after an ore has been refined).

BOM is a research organization. The actual regulation and enforcement of mining pollution regulations is the responsibility of other Interior agencies, the Office of Surface Mining Reclamation and Enforcement, and the Minerals Management Service. BOM operates laboratories in Pennsylvania, Minnesota, and six western states.

Bureau of Reclamation

BuRec's name harks back to the days when landowners felt that arid wilderness was agricultural or ranching land that needed to be "reclaimed" from nature, which had somehow wasted the land by not giving it enough moisture. The agency's work is conducted almost exclusively in the western states, where during this century it has built some of the largest dams and hydroelectric plants in the world. BuRec's efforts have been central to some of the most epic battles fought between state and federal government, farmers and ranchers, and conservationists, who still count the dams built by the agency as monuments to the conservation movement's failures.

These days, most of the largest rivers have already been dammed up or declared inviolate. A handful of expansion projects are planned by the Bureau for existing dams, and there is always maintenance work to be done. Also today BuRec is trying to broker agreements among wilderness users and preservers as a means of providing future guidance for how natural resources are to be used. It also continues to experiment with a variety of techniques to minimize the environmental impact of its dams, such as building fish ladders to allow migratory fish to return upstream to spawning grounds.

U.S. Geological Survey

USGS is a more-than-century-old agency that acts as mapmaker and resource-assessor to the nation. In more recent years, it has taken on an important role in studying groundwater issues, in flood control and water-resource management, and in evaluating the conditions on the Continental Shelf (the regions just off the eastern and western coasts in relatively shallow seas).

One might think that all the maps of the United States that need to be made have already been drawn up for decades, but this is emphatically not the case. One of the more recent technological developments has been to use satellite imaging systems to develop maps. These maps may show cartographic features as well as mineral resources, vegetation, and urban development. The agency will be expanding its research efforts for monitoring global change in coming years.

USGS employs geologists, geophysicists, hydrologists, and oceanographers, in addition to a variety of other natural scientists and engineers. All are employed at bachelor's, master's, and doctorate levels. There are offices in roughly half the states of the nation, as well as Puerto Rico and the Virgin Islands.

Bureau of Land Management

BLM is responsible for overseeing the more than 270 million acres of land that are the property of the federal government. BLM, like the Bureau of Reclamation, is regularly entangled in controversial issues pertaining to land use and resource management. Among these issues currently are the sale of timber from old-growth forests in the Pacific Northwest, the commercial use of lands in Alaska, and the policies for managing ranching in the western states.

The skills that BLM seeks among job applicants include geology and hydrology, as well as forestry, biology, and animal science. BLM also employs archaeologists and anthropologists, who are responsible for evaluating the artifacts uncovered during excavations of federal land.

Department of Commerce

National Oceanic and Atmospheric Administration

NOAA, which is primarily a science agency, was created in 1970 to bring together several federal activities that had been going on for almost as long as the United States had existed. Among these are the Coast Survey (established by Thomas Jefferson), the National Weather Service, and the National Marine Fisheries Service. NOAA is also the funding administrator for a variety of programs that sponsor research at universities, under a program called Sea Grants.

NOAA's star is shining much brighter these days as a result of the growing concern over the Earth's atmosphere. NOAA operates a variety of satellite and high-altitude aircraft systems, which have played a major role in determining the extent of ozone depletion, the effects of acid rain, and the problems caused by the growth of greenhouse gases in the atmosphere.

Environmental Protection Agency

EPA, of course, is the central agency to all the activities described in this book. While EPA has a variety of laboratories that perform studies on the earth sciences, its charter is primarily for the regulation and enforcement of environmental laws. Thus, many of its employees are involved in reviewing the plans of private companies or landowners who seek to expand factories, build on undeveloped land, or make use of water resources. EPA's responsibility is to make sure these activities are conducted in a lawful manner.

EPA divides the United States into ten regions (see Appendix A), and hiring is conducted at each of these regional offices, as well as at headquarters in Washington. The agency, which is soon to become a Cabinet-level office of the executive branch, hires about 800 engineers, scientists, and other specialists annually.

One of the biggest efforts currently under way is the Superfund program, under which federal tax revenues are being committed to cleaning up abandoned dumpsites across the country. The program is very expensive, spending more than a billion dollars per year and employing thousands of earth scientists at engineering and consulting companies to which contracts are let to perform the cleanup work. Superfund is not without some controversy, mainly over the slow pace of cleanup work that is actually performed. Of more than 12,000 sites that have been identified across the country, only a few more than 100 have been cleaned up. In one form or another, Superfund will continue for years to come.

Federal service is not the only level of government at which earth scientists are employed; many state environmental or natural-resource agencies also hire scientists. Water resources are a major concern across the country; in the western states mineral resources are also important.

Besides oil and gas companies, the largest employers of earth scientists are engineering and technical consulting firms. These companies are hired whenever a construction project commences, to perform site surveys of the land, determine its underground conditions, and assist in designing environmentally sound structures. The work ranges from the simple—digging a waterwell—to the extraordinarily complex—developing a remedial plan for an abandoned hazardous waste dump that is causing groundwater pollution.

These companies have witnessed some of the most explosive growth of any type of business in recent years, with staffs growing by 40 to 50 percent annually, year after year. Hiring pressure is so intense that many firms resort to raiding each other's staffs. Such growth is not sustainable and, indeed, many of these companies have begun to slow down (but not shrink). The need for more comprehensive geotechnical services won't disappear any time soon.

Atmospheric scientists have a growing list of environmental activities to worry about, just as geologists do. With the passage of a renewed Clean Air Act in 1990, the analysis and control of air pollution problems has become much more elaborate, and will necessitate the expenditure of an estimated $20 billion per year by industry and the mass of consumers by the turn of the century. A critical subject of research in this area is the mapping of pollution plumes back to their source—to discover, for example, whether a high level of sulfur in the air is caused by coal combustion at utilities or by automobile exhausts. Such mapping requires the development of sophisticated computer models of air and weather patterns and, thus, the field is becoming increasingly oriented around computer technology.

The biggest weather models, of course, would survey the entire globe. There is a multinational effort under way now to develop "general climatological models" (GCMs) that can be helpful in determining the presence and consequences of global warming. These models require the very biggest supercomputers that exist; each time a new, more powerful generation of supercomputers is announced, the National Weather Service or other agency steps in line to buy one, in order to run their models more efficiently.

Environmental Health and Safety Science

This section has a companion in the next chapter, entitled "Environmental Health and Safety Engineering." The disciplines described here occupy a middle ground among three concentrations: science, engineering, and medicine. Theoretically, any disease or injury caused by the environment, ranging from cancerous tumors to workplace accidents, involves the services of medical doctors and therapists; therefore one could make the case that the entire range of health disciplines is part of the green-collar work force. In practice, however, there is very little trafficking between the many issues that environmental workers in general share, and those that the medical establishment shares. The exceptions are described here and in the corresponding engineering section.

The professions or academic specialties include environmental or public health, toxicology, and epidemiology. (The next chapter includes coverage of industrial hygiene and safety engineering.) As the details of the following section show, most of these professions have existed for decades independently of overt environmental concerns, at least as we understand them today. Current events, however, have overtaken them. Many burning environmental questions concerning risks caused by the presence of toxic chemicals in the air or water, or the hazards of common industrial practices, can be addressed only through the application of the expertise of these professionals. More recently, the same principles that were developed originally for workplace hazards are now being applied to wildlife or aquatic biota, to determine the dangers caused by industrial activity to these life systems.

The scientific modes of inquiry and analysis of industrial safety and environmental health are now thoroughly enmeshed with those of environmentalism generally. These health specialties will now grow in the same manner as that of the overall green-collar work force (if not faster, given the small size of these specialties in earlier years). The challenge these professions face is how to maintain their purpose—to improve human health—in the context of better health for all forms of life, and for the Earth itself.

History and Current Assessment

A large part of the medical and chemical research of ancient and medieval times dealt essentially with poisons—substances that caused some reaction when breathed, ingested, or absorbed through the skin. "The dose makes the poison" is an ancient principle that guided premodern doctors in treating patients with small amounts of arsenic, mercury, and many varieties of plant extracts that could kill, but were thought to cure disease.

Two trends began as medical doctors became more professional and better grounded in scientific knowledge during the eighteenth and nineteenth centuries. First, a distinction arose between the concern over the health of the individual and the health of populations (such as the residents of a city). This trend culminated in the development of "Health Committees" in major Eastern cities of the United States during the eighteenth century that enforced quarantines. Eventually these Health Committees became permanent features of civic government and, during the nineteenth century, the public health profession was created by civic-minded medical doctors [35].

The second trend, which gathered momentum during the late nineteenth century in the United States and Europe, was the development of pharmaceutical products that had some rational basis in chemical and medical theory. As the producers of nostrums and other "cures" for disease or ill health began to develop more efficacious medications, the need for rigorous analysis of the toxicological effects of medications became important. The work was spurred on by the passage of the Pure Foods and Drugs Act, signed by Theodore Roosevelt in 1906. (The extremely powerful U.S. Food and Drug Administration, however, did not come into being until 1938, with the passage of another law, the Food, Drug, and Cosmetic Act.)

These two trends helped create a need for professionals trained in the specific science and technology of public health and toxicology. Both of these specialties originated informally in the medical professions, but soon stood on their own as independent disciplines, with distinct methods of training. Public health, in particular, had to wrestle with the American Medical Association, the professional group of medical doctors, during much of the latter half of the nineteenth century not only for a separate identity, but even for a legitimate say in health issues. Then, as now, medical doctors were extremely protective of their doctor–patient privileges, and accepted any outside authority only very grudgingly. The first local boards of health already existed in the early 1800s, spurred into being by epidemics in most large urban centers; but it wasn't until 1879 that a national law on public health was established. Finally, the first university-level public health training and research center for public health was established at Johns Hopkins University in 1918 (just in time to witness the great influenza pandemic that killed millions around the world after World War I ended).

A third thread that winds through the history of environmental health and safety science is occupational safety. As the Industrial Revolution—and its lineal offspring, mass production—took shape in the United States toward the end of the nineteenth century, appalling accident rates were the norm. According to a Department of Labor study in 1913, the average death rate from industrial accidents was 73 per 100,000 workers; a survey published in 1916 conducted in the heavily industrialized county of Pittsburgh revealed that an average of ten workers were being killed weekly in the 1905–1906 period [36]. These accident rates were to no small degree worsened by the inhuman legal structure of the era, which put responsibility for workplace safety squarely on the workers themselves (see next chapter for details).

The early 1900s continued a generation-long battle over labor laws and union rights; it is no coincidence that concern over workplace safety arose in this time as a means of addressing at least some of the grievances of laborers. The Department of Labor itself was founded in 1913, the same year as the forerunner of today's National Safety Council. A year later, the American Public Health Association organized an Industrial Hygiene section and, in 1916, the medical establishment weighed in with the American Association of Industrial Physicians and Surgeons.

Fast-forward to the 1980s: The fatality rate from industrial accidents has sunk to an all-time low of 9 *per 100,000*, an 88% reduction from the 1913 survey [37]. The fact that the number of workers has nearly quadrupled over this time makes the decline all the more significant.

Two professional specialties dominate the industrial safety field: industrial hygiene and occupational safety engineering; these two tend to be oriented toward the immediate health problems caused by the workplace. A third, environmental medicine, focuses more on long-term illness, such as that caused by exposure to toxic chemicals, and also on the treatment and rehabilitation of injured workers. Environmental medicine is also concerned with the epidemiology of disease or injury as a result of exposure. Environmental medicine (sometimes referred to as "occupational" or "industrial" medicine) developed gradually over this century, as the needs of the industrial hygiene and safety engineering fields called for a response from the perspective of medical doctors.

Both the industrial safety professionals and the public health field received a boost during the Depression years, as social security and workman's compensation laws were established. Professionals' organizations for industrial hygienists were established in 1938 and 1939. World War II was something of a backward step for industrial safety, as many corners were cut to maximize production of war materiel, and as relatively inexperienced workers were brought in to replace those who had joined the military service. The intensified production patterns that the war effort brought on, together with the recognition that a safer workplace was a more productive one, helped bring a strong technical base to industrial safety. In the 1950s, research began on what would ultimately become a landmark campaign over the occupational and environmental risks of asbestos exposure. Meanwhile, the dramatic growth of the petrochemical industry created a host of issues over safety and health that would become hot controversies in the next decade. Similarly, the commercialization of peaceful uses of atomic energy created a new specialty—health physics—along with the development of safety and exposure rules for working with radioactive materials.

In the 1960s, all these fields grew significantly as new types of social-service legislation were passed, as a War on Poverty took hold, and as the environmental movement gathered momentum. In this decade, debate began on what would result in a flood of new legislation affecting all these fields: the Federal Hazardous Substances Law (1966); the National Environmental Policy Act (1970), which set up the Environmental Protection Administration (later, "Agency"); the Occupational Safety and Health Act (1970), which set up the Occupational Safety and Health Administration; a Coal Mine Safety Act (1969); and the Clean Air Act (1970), the first of the modern environmental laws.

Apart from industry or community health concerns, the new emphasis on the environment created a research opportunity for scientists and health professionals who could use the tools of industry or community health on wildlife and ecosystems. Thus, "environmental toxicology" came into being as a specialty in that field for studying the effects of industrial pollutants on natural systems. The veterinary field also took on an environmental slant.

With the passage of each new law, a three-sided relationship becomes organized among environmental health and safety scientists: federal or state regulators; industrial safety specialists; and academic or consulting specialists, who perform surveys or conduct research at the behest of government, and who help to expand the expertise of occupational safety staffers employed in industry. With the tidal wave of new legislation written into law during the late 1960s and early 1970s, there arose large, specialized communities of professionals devoted to each set of regulations the new agencies were establishing. During the 1980s, these professional communities began pooling their expertise, with one field borrowing from another.

The pattern set by the Comprehensive Environmental Response, Compensation and Liability Act (CERCLA, first passed in 1980 as the Superfund law, then expanded and reauthorized in 1986) demonstrates this coming-together trend. CERCLA began as a law aimed at the cleanup of abandoned hazardous waste dumps that were affecting the environment by contaminating groundwater. To identify such a site, the first indicator is usually the presence of contaminated water in wells used by homes or towns for drinking water. This is often identified by local public health officials. Once a problem has been identified, a remedial investigation/field study is conducted, which can include chemical analyses of the soil and then an evaluation by a toxicologist of the risks that contaminants at the site pose. Finally, when a determination has been made that the site needs to be cleaned up, industrial safety professionals are required to review the cleanup procedures to ensure that workers are not exposed unnecessarily to hazardous conditions.

When CERCLA was reauthorized in 1986, the requirement for community relations between industry and local residences was mandated. Town safety and public health officials now sit down with industrial safety specialists to work out an emergency response should a disaster occur. When a new factory is to be built (or a Superfund site is to be cleaned up), construction and operational plans by the industrial company or cleanup contractor are now open for review by the community, and changes are made to suit local concerns.

Over this century, environmental safety and public health has swung up and down as governments at the state and federal levels have waxed and waned over their progressive philosophies. When an administration responsive to rising social concerns is in power, new laws are passed and the safety and health professions get a boost, as they did during the 1900–1910 period, the 1930s, and the 1960s. They are poised to do so again in the 1990s.

Education

The degree totals in Table 14 cover only part of the environmental health and safety science field: degrees in public health and in toxicology. Many other degree programs are hidden in the "miscellaneous" educational categories, in which the National Center for Education Statistics lumps together small or specially designed programs.

Suffice it to say that there are not only many ways to study environmental health at universities; there are also many types of backgrounds that, with experience, can be a good preparation for an environmental health science position. A good example of this is social work, which lends itself readily to public health. Many of the environmental science programs that are rather undifferentiated as

Table 14 *Environmental Health and Safety Science Degrees Awarded, 1987–1989*

Degree	1987	1988	1989
Bachelor	373	391	384
Master's	1,721	1,845	1,845
Ph.D.	231	268	264

to what types of occupations they prepare students for can, with the right combination of coursework and professional interest, be a good preparation for the field.

The typical public health program is usually at a school of allied health sciences at a large university. Students learn a relatively small amount of biology and medicine, and then concentrate in the traditions and practices of the public health profession. Communicable diseases are of special concern, as is basic sanitation and water quality measurement. Upperclass-level topics include sociology, government practices, healthcare administration, and the special problems of the young, the indigent, the aged, and the handicapped. A major purpose of public health is disease prevention, which is accomplished through educational programs that public health officials develop and conduct at schools or community organizations.

Most public health degrees are earned at the master's level, which is generally regarded as the entry-level certification for professionals. Public health officials employed by the U.S. Public Health Service have the option of becoming commissioned officers, which provides certain legal and regulatory status, as well as an obligation to fulfill the mission of the Service.

Toxicology is usually part of the school of biology. Students take a certain number of biology courses to gain a basic understanding of how living organisms function. Then a series of statistics courses is usually required because of the importance of statistical analysis of data. The basic "principle" of toxicology is summed up in the relationship *dose–response*. That is, for a certain dosage of some compound, what short-term or long-term response develops? At upperclass (or graduate-school) levels, the student has the opportunity to specialize in a variety of areas: wildlife toxicology, medical toxicology, or occupational toxicology (sometimes called industrial toxicology).

Health physics is the term developed in the post-World War II period to define occupational health workers who dealt with radioactive materials. Originally of concern only to the military and to the developers of commercial nuclear power, the safety of radioactive materials now touches the lives of most of us. Essentially, health physics extends the usual training provided in industrial health and hygiene programs with courses geared directly to the health issues of radioactivity. Most health physics training is provided at graduate schools, especially those with some affiliation to the network of federal national laboratories.

There are a great variety of other paths into environmental health: industrial hygiene, nursing, health care administration, home economics, industrial relations, industrial or safety engineering, physical therapy, and others. In dealing with environmental health issues pertaining to the natural world (rather than to the workplace or to man-made environments such as cities), there are programs in veterinary medicine, environmental science, renewable-resource or wildlife management, and ecology (see the section on Biology). With these backgrounds and the appropriate work experience, the concerned individual can obtain additional training, either at graduate school or through a variety of continuing-education programs that professional societies offer.

Obviously, this field is characterized by a diverse array of professionals with varied types and levels of expertise. It is very new; some of the job titles and employers have just been started.

Environmental Impact

Over a century ago, the leading environmentalists were public health officials, who maintained that drinking and using contaminated water or living in proximity to sewage and municipal wastes were health threats. Indeed, this was common knowledge at the time, but few realized why; the transmission of disease via germ-carrying insects was only a theory, and most people thought that waste caused disease by spontaneously generating disease-carrying miasmas.

Public health officials helped win the day, making widespread epidemics a thing of the past. As technology pushed ahead during this century, public health officials could be said to have become a liability to the environment at large, because they led in efforts to drain swamplands or to blanket them with pesticides, as a means of eradicating pests. (Whether or not this practice is maintained—as it is in many parts of the world outside the United States–a moral dilemma is presented: How many human lives is one willing to lose through the greater threat of malaria or yellow fever, versus the number of wildlife species rescued, or wetland ecosystems preserved?)

Aside from the wetlands issue, public health in the early half of this century became more concerned with the delivery of healthcare systems (such as vaccination programs or visiting nurses for rural areas), and with food distribution and general social services. These concerns continue today, and are certainly as important as they were in earlier decades. The problems of poverty and deprivation have by no means vanished. Added to these issues, however, are the newer ones of urban air pollution and its effects on the aged or those with respiratory problems, of drinking water contaminated with industrial wastes, and of community-response programs to prepare for disasters.

In addition, through offices like the Centers for Disease Control, the U.S. Public Health Service is at the vanguard of research into the effects of long-term exposure to small amounts of hazardous chemicals. In 1985, the Service created a new office, the Agency for Toxic Disease Registry, which is a broad-based program to gather data from people who have been so exposed.

Such work is also dependent on the expertise provided by toxicologists and epidemiologists. Aside from the specific questions about determining the amount of exposure to toxic chemicals that people experience, the toxicology profession is involved in a lengthy program of reassessing health risk measurements in general. *Risk assessment* is the term used to identify a heavily statistically based, quantitative study of exposure and risk (for injury or disease). Federal rules for the cleanup of hazardous waste sites now require a risk assessment to be performed to determine whether the least dangerous cleanup techniques are being used. Risk assessments are now also becoming a standard part of business planning, as corporate managers evaluate the use of new technologies (or the replacement of one with another) on the basis of the risks that have been avoided.

The pharmaceutical and food-processing industries are major employers of toxicologists, primarily for "operational" toxicology, by which routine testing of the quality and contents of their products is conducted. Toxicological research goes on at pharmaceutical companies as well, since these firms are constantly developing new biochemicals that must be tested extensively. Research also goes on at medical schools and at research hospitals.

Traditionally, health physics professionals have been employed by the nuclear power industry and by the military facilities that produce or perform research on nuclear weapons or power. The commercial nuclear power industry is trying, yet again, to build a consensus for allowing the construction of new power plants. Since the Three Mile Island accident near Harrisburg, Pennsylvania, in 1979, not a single new plant has been ordered. Nevertheless, nuclear power now represents nearly 20 percent of today's electrical supply in the United States. Should new plants be built, the call will go out for more health physicists.

Whether or not these plants are built, there will be plenty of work at hand in the decommissioning of old plants, some of which are now approaching an age of 30 years, which was thought to be the limit to their useful lives. (Now that the end is near for some of these plants, though, their owners are having second thoughts.) An elaborate program of taking the plant apart and disposing of its radioactively hot components properly will require at least as much work as when the plants were first built. Health physicists will be involved in overseeing the dismantling procedures and in monitoring the health of the workers involved.

In a similar vein, the U.S. military establishment has now found that it has a monumental cleanup task ahead of it, at the many facilities operated by the U.S. Department of Energy, to clean up a decades-old backlog of accidental and purposeful releases of radioactivity. The Congressional Office of Technology Assessment cited statistics [38] that it will take some 20 to 30 years, and cost more than $150 billion, to perform this cleanup. It is the only line item in the Pentagon's budget that is rising, rather than shrinking. Again, health physicists and other safety professionals will be involved in supervising this cleanup.

Health physics may soon have another big-ticket item on its agenda: the concerns over low-level radiation from high-voltage electrical sources. This health risk has been studied for some time, but has become a legitimate environmental concern only quite recently. A series of epidemiological studies performed during the 1970s and 1980s identified certain concentrations of childhood cancer and other diseases in close proximity to high-voltage electrical sources, such as power lines or transformers. Now there is concern that all types of high-voltage equipment may need to be reevaluated. The potential changes this might require in industrial production and in consumer power use are enormous.

In terms of environmental health generally—that is, the health of ecosystems and large environments—environmental health scientists must compete with other professionals for attention and funds. Wildlife biologists, ecologists, foresters, and others are all sharing in this concern. There is much science that needs to be done before some definitive answers over the preservation of tropical forests, or the stemming of the loss of wildlife species, are answered. Environmental health professionals will have an influence on the policies that will develop in coming years.

CHAPTER THREE

Engineers and the Environment

Most engineering societies have a statement of purpose that runs something like this:

> [. . .] engineering is the profession in which a knowledge of mathematics, physics, and [any other appropriate science] gained by study and experience is applied with judgment to develop economic ways of using [various natural resources] for the benefit of mankind.

This lofty-sounding statement has three vital components: "science," "judgment," and "economic ways." (One might argue that the phrase "benefit of mankind" is equally important, but it is difficult to conceive of a profession that would freely admit that it is *not* for the benefit of mankind.)

"Science" is important to engineering because it is both the very language and the toolkit with which engineers work. Engineers create and guide technological artifacts—anything from a jet airplane to a bridge to a supercomputer. The technological artifact is usually suited to some human purpose, either for manufacturing or conveying something or to control some aspect of nature that society would like to domesticate (one thinks readily of how a dam silences a wild river). This artifact works as intended because it was designed and built according to rules adapted from scientific laws.

"Judgment" is equally important as science because any self-respecting engineer would quickly admit to the artistry or creativity with which scientific principles are applied. The engineer is no servant of scientists, no lowly technician who blindly and repeatedly applies some scientific principle to the matter at hand. Rather, engineers pick and choose among the fruits of scientists' endeavors, applying what they find might be useful to creating new or improved devices. In many cases, engineers create new science.

"Economic ways" is the phrase that is the great slayer of interesting engineering ideas. Unless an artifact can be made at a sufficiently low price or can be shown to be worth its expense when the savings earned by using it are calculated, it will never leave the developmental laboratory or will never be built. Engineers use economics as rigorously as any Wall Street financier would to evaluate the pros and cons of one product versus another or one way of doing things versus another.

Another way of summing up the point to engineering was expressed by someone lost to history: "Engineering is doing for a dollar what any damn fool could do for two." This saying seems rather disrespectful of the engineering professions, but it gets at the essential power and challenge of engineering. Engineering is the art of the possible rather than a dream of perfection. Engineering is also wrapped up almost completely in the warp and woof of human society, especially as expressed in production of items of economic value, such as manufacturing, agriculture, and natural resources.

Engineering study today is patterned after the great sciences, such as physics, chemistry, and biology. Students can now obtain a baccalaureate degree and then pursue a master's and a doctoral degree. It was not always so; the earliest modern engineers (i.e., those who first called themselves "engineers" during the early days of the Industrial Revolution) were primarily craftspeople and artisans. Common engineering activities such as building construction, boat building, or metal fabrication reach back to the dawn of civilization. Centuries later, as a body of scientific knowledge built up during the Renaissance and after, there was a time when scientists were theorizing about the very things that artisans were building and fabricating. In medieval civilization, much of the spur for technological development, by both scientists and artisans, was for warfare. Eventually, by the late eighteenth and early nineteenth centuries, the two merged; the Industrial Revolution began to take hold; and, more thoroughly in France and Germany than in England, engineering began to be taught at universities and polytechnic schools.

The United States borrowed the Continental model of engineering training in the early 1800s; the first engineering school was the United States Military Academy at West Point. Engineering study received a tremendous boost with the passage of the Morrill Act in 1862, which set up the land-grant colleges of the West and Midwest specifically to teach "useful" arts and agriculture. As the U.S. economy gathered momentum in the late nineteenth century, engineering became the preferred route to the management of the giant manufacturing enterprises of the era.

The 1900–1950 period is generally regarded as the heroic age of engineering. One after another, ancient natural calamities such as floods, outbreaks of communicable diseases, and droughts were brought under control by engineering. The "miracles" of heavier-than-air flight, automotive power, electricity, and electric illumination became established. Enormous dams stilled rivers and converted their fury to electrical production. Giant bridges spanned mountains and coastal bays, and skyscrapers altered the urban vista. Nature existed as an inhuman force to be harnessed to humanity's ends.

To be sure, this feeling was not unanimous. Pioneering naturalists like John Muir fought to preserve, as untouched by human industry, Yosemite and Yellowstone Parks. The denudation of midwestern forests, the extinction of the passenger pigeon, and the near-extinction of the buffalo were not ignored. A battle over the Hetch Hetchy dam near California raged for six years before a federal law permitted its construction in 1913 [1].

Herbert Hoover, the first engineer–president, was a towering force in the engineering professions before he entered politics. (The other engineer–president was Jimmy Carter. Between the two gentlemen, it may be another century before a politician with an engineering background ascends to the White House.) Around Hoover's time, substantial efforts were made to formalize engineering with licensing and certification requirements and to unite the disparate disciplines into a force for applying the principles of engineering to society at large. Given theoretical force by the economist Thorstein Veblen, the "technocracy" movement of the late 1920s and early 1930s "attempted to end the Depression by a dictatorship of the engineers," according to an excellent history of the topic by Edwin Layton, Jr. [2]. The movement never really got off the ground primarily because the engineers themselves were unable to unify either with one another or around a coherent political philosophy.

By the 1950s, the ills of rampant industrialism had become clear, and the desire on the part of nature-lovers to preserve wilderness areas was expressed in a number of federal laws. Engineering expertise began to be applied to some of these problems, and the training of engineers reflected the growing importance of workplace safety and the risks of industrial pollution, especially air pollution.

Corporations today are the focused force of their employees and stockholders, and the American-style market economy is the model to which the world is looking. Of late, they have tended not to be very united themselves, as witnessed by the orgy of hostile takeovers that occurred during the 1980s.

Three points are worth making on the question of the professionalism of engineers and its implications for addressing environmental issues. First, there are plenty of engineers who do not work for corporations. They are independent consultants, academics, and government officials. Among those who do collect a paycheck from corporations, many work for small companies whose goals are quite distinct from the Fortune 500. Second, many corporations have put themselves in the vanguard of the environmental movement. Edgar Woolard, chairman of Du Pont Co., styles himself as the firm's chief *environmental* officer rather than as chief *executive* officer. McDonald's Corp. consults with the Environmental Defense Fund on ways to reduce waste generation. Third, as demonstrated in the previous chapter, the work of pollution abatement and control has itself become a big, profitable business, worth over $115 billion and growing more rapidly than the economy as a whole. Many environmental companies have grown huge, with staffs of hundreds of engineers, while spending this money on behalf of corporate and government clients.

Debating the ethical and environmental orientation of engineering is valuable, and there is a refreshing sense of reevaluation and reassessment going on in engineering circles. In the meantime, there are pressing environmental problems to be addressed. Thousands of engineers are working on them now, and thousands more will be doing so in the near future. Studying engineering, either as an undergraduate or as a graduate student who is combining engineering with another undergraduate degree, is the most direct route to hands-on work on pollution abatement and control.

Looking Ahead. In the sections that follow, engineering disciplines having the most central involvement in environmental issues will be described in detail. Current estimates of the size of the profession and projections of future growth are derived from data published by the U.S. Bureau of Labor Statistics [3]. Numerical trends in graduating class sizes at all academic levels are also presented; these data are obtained from the Engineering Manpower Commission [4], an office of a Washington, D.C., organization called the American Association of Engineering Societies. For the latter data, the results of the years 1988–1990 are presented. The thought here is that, by looking at the trend in class sizes and the projected growth, a rough assessment of supply and demand of jobseekers can be made. Historically, engineering has been a boom-and-bust field, with class sizes swinging up and down, sometimes in sync with the job demand and sometimes out of sync.

In general, however, the demand for engineers is higher than for any other academic degree and has been so for many years. Unemployment rates for engineers have been extremely low also for many years. Engineers earn an average of $50,000 to $70,000 annually, based on various surveys made by the Engineering Manpower Commission and others. Newly graduated engineers get salary offers of $29,000 to $36,000, according to surveys made by the College Placement Council, a Bethlehem, Pennsylvania, group for college recruitment officials. At the doctoral level, engineers earn $50,000 or more if they join an industrial employer. In academia, these salaries are in the $25,000 to $35,000 range.

Chemical Engineering

Overview

Chemical engineering occupies a central position in the environmental world. The profession is closely tied to its major employer, the chemical industry, which takes roughly half of its graduates each year. In turn, this industry is generally regarded as a producer of pollution well out of proportion to its size in the industrial economy. The industry is estimated to produce roughly three-quarters of the hazardous waste in the country.

At its heart, chemical engineering is the study of *processes*—manufacturing steps in which chemical compounds are undergoing continual change in physical form or composition. Chemical engineers seek to improve the efficiency of these processes or, in cases where a new type of material is being commercialized, to devise the most efficient production steps.

In the environmental arena, chemical engineers are employed by manufacturers to reduce the production of wastes or pollution. Many pollution-control processes are themselves chemical processes. An air pollutant, for example, is extracted from a smokestack by a water spray, then mixed with a neutralizing compound that destroys or otherwise alters the pollutant. Chemical engineers are also highly sought individuals at engineering consulting firms, where they can be called on to assist manufacturers in meeting environmental regulations or to develop treatment processes for contaminated soil or water.

Notwithstanding the widespread applicability of chemical engineering to environmental issues, the profession is under something of a cloud at the dawn of the 1990s, at least as far as college students are concerned. Enrollments have slipped by nearly half since the mid-1980s, when record-setting classes were graduating. The recession of the early 1980s hit the profession severely, and the steady drumbeat of bad news about environmental ills caused by chemical manufacturing has combined with it to steer students away from the profession. A turnaround may be in the offing: Chemical engineers continue to win one of the highest starting salaries coming out of college at all academic levels. Historically, this has caused a surge in popularity for engineering students considering which major to enter.

According to the U.S. Bureau of Labor Statistics, there are about 49,000 working chemical engineers; the projected growth rate to the year 2000 is 16.4 percent, which is about the average for all occupations. The ratio between master's and bachelor degrees in 1990 was 31.5 percent. Among working chemical engineers, 6.3 percent are women, and 6.2 percent belong to African-American or Hispanic ethnic groups.

History and Current Assessment

Chemical engineering arose, primarily in the United States, at the turn of the century. In Europe, the tradition of industrial chemistry had been much more strongly established; indeed, not until the mid-twentieth century was a program of study comparable to chemical engineering established in Germany. Most of the earliest chemical engineers combined the study of mechanical engineering with courses in academic chemistry. "Chemical engineering" was taught at the Massachusetts Institute of Technology in the late 1880s and at a number of other schools before the turn of the century, but, without the standardization and accreditation that a professional society could supply, the programs were disunited [5].

The field received a considerable boost in the 1910s, when embargoes against Germany due to World War I created a dramatic new need for domestic chemical production. (Historically, much of the modern chemical industry was born in Germany, with the outcome of the research into dyestuffs derived from coal chemicals.) The growing need of the petroleum industry to refine crude oil into usable fuels for automobiles and other vehicles was another spur to its growth.

The period of the 1930s through the end of World War II saw the emergence of a wondrous array of synthetic chemicals and substances. The industrial laboratories of Du Pont Co. were responsible for the development of nylon in the 1930s; those of General Motors developed critical fuel additives and lubricants. Over this period, too, the Manhattan Project got under way, resulting not only in the production of refined, fissionable uranium but also in a host of new production processes for minerals and chemicals. Nuclear engineering is more or less an offspring of chemical and mechanical engineering.

By now, the basic body of knowledge of chemical engineering had coalesced around the concept of *unit operations*. This term refers to the combination of a process that changes the physical or chemical nature of a substance and the equipment that causes the changes. The quintessential unit operation is distillation, the process of heating or depressurizing a mixed fluid stream inside a pot or column, thus effectuating the separation of the components of this mixture. Others are straightforward processes that might be found in a typical kitchen as well as a chemical factory—mixing, cooking, straining (sieving), chilling.

Typically, chemical engineering work evolves into a partnership between chemists and engineers. Chemists, working in a laboratory with cup-sized quantities of compounds, develop a new material or production method. This basic knowledge gets turned over to the chemical engineering project team, which seeks to "scale up" the production process so that commercially viable quantities of the new material can be produced. A key element in this scale-up process is the "pilot plant," a miniature chemical factory (*miniature* is a relative term here; some of these pilot plants can be the size of a large house). Once the process is proved out, an engineering construction firm is hired to build the plant, again involving chemical engineering expertise. Finally, the chemical engineers may become involved in the day-to-day operations of the plant, especially when the production process varies continuously.

After World War II, the chemical industry, as well as the chemical engineering profession, took off. Production of synthetic fibers, plastics, agricultural chemicals, petrochemicals and refined minerals, and forestry products expanded rapidly. A considerable number of these new materials have no natural equivalent; this fact is the source both of the tremendous success of many of the new chemicals as well as of the environmental ills they cause. Without a natural source, there is no conventional way of degrading these materials either as they leak from chemical storage facilities or once the material is used up and discarded.

Chemical engineering continued a steady growth throughout the 1960s and slumped as the recessions of the early 1970s took hold. By the end of that decade, the two tremendous oil shocks that had raised the price of oil over $40 per barrel practically set off a stampede into chemical engineering. The federal government had announced elaborate synthetic-fuels research and demonstration programs, and there were forecasts that thousands more engineers would be needed. When the world price of oil fell and the U.S. economy slid into recession in 1982, chemical engineering was hit with a double whammy: Jobs seemed to evaporate, and the discipline received a bad reputation that it is still recovering from today.

According to a 1990 survey of the profession [6], roughly two-thirds of today's chemical engineers work in manufacturing. The other sources of employment are:

Engineering and construction services, 15.3 percent

Government, 5.2 percent

Academic, 1.1 percent

Self, 1.0 percent

Other, 11 percent

The primary job functions are project and design engineering, R&D, production, consulting, and administration. About 30 percent have a master's degree; about 7 percent, a Ph.D. The graduating class trends are shown in Table 15.

Education

Like most undergraduate engineering students, the chemical engineer takes a core curriculum of mathematics, physics, and chemistry courses. In later years, additional upper-level chemistry courses are required, including organic and physical chemistry. Depending on the school's program, courses in thermodynamics, fluid mechanics, mass and heat transfer, and process design are offered. Over the past decade or so, the subject of process control (using computer algorithms to model or operate chemical processes) has become popular. Laboratories are common, both in the general course requirements and in the departmental engineering courses.

At the master's level, it is possible to concentrate in a variety of specialties, including biochemical processes, chemical reactions, advanced process control, or polymer chemistry, among others. Environmental topics are growing in popularity. Depending on the region of the country where the school is located, local concentrations in manufacturing may be represented in the undergraduate or graduate curriculum. These include pulp and paper, pharmaceuticals, fuels and petroleum processing, and microelectronics fabrication, among others.

At the doctoral level, the basic science of how compounds are manipulated is intensively reviewed. These topics include kinetics, reactions and catalysis, biotechnology, fluid dynamics, process control, and computational chemistry.

Working chemical engineers can avail themselves of a variety of continuing-education options. The American Institute of Chemical Engineers offers an extensive array of courses, which are usually held

Table 15   *Chemical Engineering Degrees Awarded, 1988–1990*

Degree	1988	1989	1990
Bachelor	4,082	3,711	3,622
Master's	1,274	1,220	1,140
Ph.D.	657	680	667

as seminars while national meetings are going on. Many of these courses are designed as industry-specific training. Topics include environmental regulation, process safety, process control, engineering economics, and industry-specific courses.

Environmental Impact

Involved as it is with the production of some of the worst chemicals the environment has suffered to absorb, chemical engineering is a centrally located profession in environmental problems. "Chemical engineers face important research challenges associated with the imperative to protect and improve the environment," reads a study from the U.S. National Research Council, *Frontiers in Chemical Engineering* [7]. "The future of the profession and the industries that it serves will depend on the vigor with which chemical engineers approach these challenges."

EPA, along with most other long-range thinkers concerning industrial pollution, has developed a hierarchy of control options for solving environmental problems. The hierarchy is as follows: (1) prevention, (2) reduction, (3) recycling, (4) disposal. Chemical engineers have the tools to address each level of control.

For prevention or reduction, one of the most common methods is to redesign a process so that a waste-causing ingredient or processing technique is avoided. Many chemical reactions, for example, produce a variety of byproducts when only one primary product is desired. By introducing a catalyst or other agent that directs the reaction, production of these byproducts can be minimized. The cheapest pollutant-disposal method, as industry engineers are coming to believe, is not to produce the pollutant in the first place.

Recycling often pays off, too. Electronics manufacturers, to take an extreme example, use copious quantities of water to wash circuit components while they are being fabricated. This wash water can be recycled when a cleaning process is incorporated into the production line. In many instances, the recycling process can be analyzed just as a production technique would be.

Disposal is the ultimate control technique. Years ago, when regulations were absent, industry grew accustomed to dumping wastes in the ground. The belief was that, over the course of many years, the wastes would simply degrade into harmless constituents or become so diluted that their presence was unnoticeable. In the aftermath of Love Canal and other landfilling disasters, regulations have been written to control what can be disposed. Flammable, toxic, or reactive liquids can no longer be disposed without prior treatment, which requires the expertise of a chemical engineer. Landfilling and a closely related technique, deep-well injection, are still the most common disposal methods; even with the additional treatment requirements, they remain the lowest-cost option.

Treatment methods in use include the use of chemical agents that solidify the waste, neutralize it, or break it down. One attractive option is to use one waste (a contaminated acid, for example) to react with another, thereby destroying both. Incineration, in gigantic kilns that burn the wastes at high temperatures, is a desirable option for materials that are highly poisonous but that do not degrade easily in the environment. When the waste is incinerated properly, the producer is assured that any liability associated with its existence is also consumed. Usually, however, incineration is chosen only as a last resort because it tends to be the most expensive disposal method.

Chemical engineers use their training in chemistry, process equipment, and economics in each of these treatment methods just as they would when a new chemical is invented and its production is researched and commercialized. Large corporations employ many chemical engineers in this task, and the same skills can be turned to environmental problems. Corporations without these staffs and government agencies turn to engineering consulting firms that employ chemical engineers to accomplish the same goal. Once the process has been developed and the treatment machinery installed, the involvement of chemical engineers is reduced, although it is always possible for the chemical engineer to become involved in the process's operation as well.

Government agencies concerned with regulating the environmental activities of corporations call on chemical engineers as well. In many of these cases, chemical engineers are desirable job candidates simply because of their familiarity with chemistry and with basic manufacturing methods. There are numerous cases, however, where a detailed knowledge of chemical manufacturing is essential, and, in these cases, the chemical engineer is the most desirable job candidate.

Chemical engineering research into environmental technologies is growing rapidly. From the late 1980s to the early 1990s, Wall Street took notice whenever a new, entrepreneurial company was formed to commercialize some piece of engineering research, such as a new waste-treatment method. These start-up companies follow very much the same pattern as the microelectronics or biotechnology firms of earlier years; if the technology is proven to be commercially viable, it gets sold or licensed to larger firms, and the financial backers of the original firm strike it rich. Large corporations and research institutions also employ chemical engineers in the development of new technologies. Other areas of research to which chemical engineers are contributing are the design of inherently recyclable materials, air-pollution control, alternative energy schemes, and improved process safety and control.

Mechanical Engineering

Overview

Mechanical engineering is the second-largest (behind electrical) and, arguably, the second-oldest (behind civil) engineering discipline. The development of the machine—the hallmark of the Industrial Revolution—is the realm of mechanical engineering, and there were "mechanicians" (an archaic word referring to those skilled in mechanical arts [8]) long before there were schools devoted to the topic. The development of steam power, which then became applied to ships, trains, and industrial production equipment, solidified the concept of mechanical engineering around material objects in motion.

During this century, mechanical engineering has become deeply embedded in nearly every type of industrial production or manufactured structure and in agriculture as well. As houses and buildings take on more machinery to make them function properly (such as ventilating systems or elevators), they acquire more input from the mechanical engineering profession. The adding machine, one of the earliest forms of computers, was a mechanical device, and the mechanical component of modern computers is still very high.

In a conceptual sense, it is rare that the actual product of mechanical engineering talent—a machine—is itself a pollutant. It is equally rare, however, that the effect of such machines is pollution-free. Automobile and aircraft exhausts, smoke from power stations, and wastes from factory production lines are all the result of the creations of mechanical engineers. Avoiding or minimizing the production of these pollutants is now a prime directive of good mechanical engineering design. Correspondingly, the education of mechanical engineers pays more attention to the effects of machines. There are also, now, a wide variety of machines that are specifically designed for minimizing pollution.

There are some 225,000 mechanical engineers at work in the United States, according to the Bureau of Labor Statistics; the profession's growth rate to the year 2000 is projected at 19.8 percent, which is slightly above the average of all occupations. The ratio between master's and bachelor degrees in 1990 was 27 percent. Among working mechanical engineers, 3.7 percent are women and 5.5 percent are members of African-American or Hispanic ethnic groups.

History and Current Assessment

Two main objectives were addressed by early mechanical engineers—power and transportation. With the development of the steam engine in 1802, the ancient forms of power (wind, water, and the horse) had an artificial equivalent. Mechanical engineering was taught in a number of schools by the mid-nineteenth century, but not until 1888 did a group of businessmen gather to form the American Society of Mechanical Engineers (ASME). A critical problem at the time, which also exists to this day, was the continual explosion of steam engines aboard trains or ships. By the end of the century, the guidelines for constructing and operating these steam generators were codified into the ASME Boiler and Pressure Vessel Code. The latest (the 75th) version of this document runs over 11,000 pages.

Because devices such as steam engines and, later, automobiles and aircraft had such vital considerations for public health, ASME developed a tradition of providing standards that, in some locales, have the force of law. Metals are graded according to ASME codes, and the ASME stamp appears on everything from pump housings to jet turbine components.

The success of Cyrus McCormick's agricultural reaper in the mid-nineteenth century and Henry Ford's automobile by its end heralded a new mode of mass manufacturing that fueled the tremendous growth of the U.S. economy in the early 1900s. During this era, too, the commercialization and rapid growth of electricity created a new demand for mechanical engineering talents. The success of mass manufacturing in these decades in the United States and Europe was so profound that many intellectuals looked to it as a model for social organization. This so-called technocratic movement, in which many U.S. mechanical engineers participated, peaked during the 1920s and then faded away during the Depression.

The World War II era did not change mechanical engineering markedly, except for the mass production of aircraft and other military equipment. Since that time, the development of electronics has led to much more rigorous control of automated production techniques. Automation builds on the earlier mass-production techniques and has had a profound impact on manufacturing and commercial services.

In the past two decades, the diminished stature of the U.S. economy in international competition has put a special burden on mechanical engineering. Manufactured products both lower in price and higher in quality have cut into the profitability and market share of U.S. corporations. In many markets now, the environmental quality of manufactured products is a key selling point. "Mechanical engineers in the automobile industry can no longer design a car without regard for its operating and disposability requirements," says Terrence Dear, an industry engineer and vice president of the ASME Environment and Transportation Group. "Packaging and manufacturing professionals must consider using materials that are recyclable, or that can be turned into biodegradable and soil-enhancing compost. And safety and maintenance engineers [are] responsible for reducing risk, and for upgrading, repairing, and replacing equipment that might be leaking harmful pollutants into the air or water" [9].

Dear touches on the key functions that working mechanical engineers fulfill. A sizable number are responsible for creating new designs for manufactured products and subsystems. Because so much manufacturing is itself carried out by machines, there are mechanical engineers who both develop this machinery and operate and maintain it. The workplace environment is also an important factor for the safety of workers and the nearby community. Finally, the disposition of manufactured products—how they are packaged, shipped, used, and discarded—is of concern to mechanical engineers.

Mechanical engineers have taken to the latest generations of computers extremely well. Many design engineers spend their day at a computer workstation, where high-powered computers allow them to make speedy changes in a design and then run calculations on how the changes will affect overall performance. The development of such *computer-aided design* (CAD) software is also a major function of mechanical engineers.

Education

As Table 16 shows, mechanical engineering graduation rates have been on a slow decline for several years. Nevertheless, the profession remains the second largest one (behind electrical engineering), and its graduates find employment in a wide variety of industries and organizations.

Beyond the standard introductory math and science courses that all engineering students take, the options expand dramatically for mechanical engineering students. The multidisciplinary nature of the profession, with large numbers working in very diverse industries, requires a long course catalog.

Typically, students start their training with courses in mechanics, a branch of physics that deals with objects in motion. This is followed by basic courses in engineering materials, power and electronics, and thermodynamics. Next are courses in mechanical dynamics, automation and control, and machine design. Depending on the size of the program, course are then available in various industrial specializations, such as textiles, aerospace, power generation, microelectronics, automobiles, and others.

Master's-level programs continue these industry specializations. They also add courses in advanced control, CAD, engineering materials, and noise and vibration theory.

Doctoral-level programs involve many topics in applied physics, such as fluid dynamics, heat transfer, materials science, tribology (the study of lubrication), propulsion, and heat- or mass-transfer

Table 16   *Mechanical Engineering Degrees Awarded, 1988–1990*

Degree	1988	1989	1990
Bachelor	15,610	15,369	14,969
Master's	3,767	3,855	3,994
Ph.D.	738	795	900

systems. Bioengineering is a recent addition to master's and doctoral programs: Mechanical engineering can be applied to the development of prosthetic devices such as artificial hearts.

Licensure is available for mechanical engineers, especially those who work as consultants. ASME and other organizations provide extensive continuing-education programs.

Environmental Impact

Perhaps the dominant environmental problem that mechanical engineers face is air pollution from engines and power machinery, such as automotive exhaust and smoke from power plants, industrial furnaces, and incinerators. Improved designs in these engines and combustors are succeeding in reducing air pollution.

In automobiles, the use of "stratified charges" in which air and fuel are mixed in proportions closer to the ideal can reduce emissions as well as provide more power. Automotive companies have also added catalytic afterburners that complete the combustion of fuel after it leaves the engine as exhaust. Large-scale furnaces, such as those at power plants, produce ash, smoke, and toxic combustion by-products such as dioxin, sulfates, and nitrates. A common countermeasure is to route the exhaust gas through a second device or even third device, such as an electrostatic precipitator, for example, which takes out dusts, or a scrubbing system that neutralizes sulfur compounds by washing them with alkaline chemicals.

Most engines, whether in an auto or an airplane, are examples of "rotating" machinery; energy in the form of fuel is transformed into rotational motion, and gears and shafts convert this to propulsion. This concept of transforming energy into useful work is central to mechanical engineering, and thus these engineers are among the leading experts on other or, to use the preferred term, "alternative" energy. Alternative energy comprises a wide range of power production schemes, ranging from solar or wind power to heat pumps, fuel cells, batteries, magnetohydrodynamics—the list goes on and on. When (and if) the day comes that the new "warm" superconducting materials that were discovered in the mid-1980s by materials scientists become commercially available, it will undoubtedly be mechanical engineers who adapt them to power production and delivery grids.

Heat is energy, and another transformation of it is to extract it from a container, exhausting the heat and leaving coldness behind. This, in layperson's terms, is how a refrigerator works. During the

1990s and beyond, refrigeration is going to take on a new look as a result of the banning of chlorofluorocarbons (CFCs) that damage the upper atmosphere. CFCs were developed in the late 1920s as ideal refrigeration fluids that could be compressed, chilled, and warmed in a cyclical fashion for years without degrading. Under normal use, they are essentially indestructible (they can, however, be burned or chemically broken up under extreme conditions). A refrigerator (or an air conditioner) uses them in a mechanical compressor powered by electricity or by an engine.

With the banning of conventional CFCs by an international conference (the 1987 Montreal Protocol), the race is now on to develop alternative refrigerants or refrigeration systems. A group of similar, but relatively benign compounds has been proposed, as have various older refrigerants that fell out of popularity when CFCs were commercialized. The chemical companies that produce refrigerants employ mechanical engineers, along with chemical engineers and chemical scientists, to help devise production schemes. The manufacturers of appliances, air-conditioning machinery, and compressors must redesign their machines to use the alternative refrigerants. In some cases, new materials of construction, lubricants, and heat-transfer devices must be developed. The choices that design engineers will be making over the next few years will either maintain (or even increase) market share for their employers or cause the failure of the business as the market moves to the clear winners.

As mentioned previously, mechanical engineers have traditionally been more worried about the environmental problems caused by machinery rather than the machinery itself. There is a new school of thought on this issue, especially where high-volume, large-sized products like automobiles or appliances are concerned. The materials that make up these products are either too valuable simply to discard or too toxic (think of the reactive chemicals, for example, in auto batteries). Thus, some manufacturers are applying a "design for disassembly" philosophy to their products. These products not only should work as intended but also should be capable of being easily taken apart so that each component (glass, metal, plastic, etc.) can be recycled. This changed philosophy is little short of a revolution in product design theory.

Because mechanical engineers are concerned with the vibration caused by machinery in motion, they are the technological professionals to address noise pollution, a critical issue for aircraft manufacturers. The solutions include "antisound" devices, which electronically record and play back a noise out of phase with the original sound so that it is canceled out. (The effect is similar to two ripples on a pond canceling each other when they collide.)

Just as mechanical engineers design and operate the machines that extract minerals from the ground and purify them, so they can apply similar skills to processing wastes. Municipal garbage processing has had a stormy record over the past few decades. During the high-priced-energy 1970s, a substantial effort was made to develop a production line that could extract combustible materials from garbage while also recovering metals and glass. These "resource recovery" plants generally did not work, and they have been replaced by incineration plants that simply burn the garbage *en masse*. Now, in the 1990s, resource recovery is making something of a comeback partly due to the problems that the incineration plants have had with air-pollution generation.

ASME has an Environment and Transportation Group as one of the standing divisions that society members join. The subdivisions of this group are:

Aerospace
Environmental control
Noise control and acoustics
Rail transportation
Solid waste processing

In addition, other divisions with an environmental orientation include safety, plant engineering and maintenance, solar energy, and fuels and combustion.

Civil and Environmental Engineering

Overview

The most direct confrontation between the environment and engineering occurs in civil engineering. Civil engineers are the people who direct bulldozers that knock down mountains, who build dams that wreck white-water rivers and fishing streams, and who pave the countryside.

Civil engineers are also the people who cleanse cities and their surroundings of waste and sewage, preventing disease and public-health hazards. They are the professionals who design wildlife sanctuaries, provide fresh drinking water, and turn deserts into farmland. Civil engineering contains all the ambivalence we feel toward the environment as our home and, at the same time, as a hazard to be minimized. "We used to be praised for ridding the countryside of swamps," Samuel Florman, a noted engineering commentator (and civil engineer), said. "Now we're condemned for destroying wetlands" [10].

The heart of civil engineering, since its inception, has been building structures. In order to do this properly, civil engineering technology has extended to the properties of building materials, soil and rock science, and the effects of water in rain, in rivers and lakes, and in the ground. More than one-third of these professionals work as independent consultants (usually for building owners and developers and occasionally for industry). Publicly funded construction (i.e., public works) is a major part of the building that goes on in the United States, and nearly half of all civil engineers are government employees.

Of all engineering disciplines, civil engineering is the one that is most oriented around independent consulting engineering firms, which provide advice on public works for government officials and on buildings for land developers and owners. The bulk of this work consists of developing construction management plans and performing the actual construction. Other work includes building maintenance and the restoration of highways and water and sewage systems that we all look to government to attend to. A smaller portion of civil engineering services are directed toward factory owners and those who exploit natural resources, like oil, mining, and forestry companies.

Drinking water and public health have been concerns of civil engineers almost from the founding of the country. Many of the civil engineers who specialize in water and wastewater treatment go by the title of "sanitary engineers." In the mid-1950s, civil engineers and public health professionals formed a joint organization called the Joint Committee of the Advancement of Sanitary Engineering; in 1967, this now greatly enlarged organization changed its name to the American Academy of Environmental Engineers. From the 1950s forward, sanitary engineering programs at colleges' schools of civil engineering took up the term "environmental" engineering, attesting to the wider issues of water resource planning in which sanitary engineering was engaged. At some schools, environmental engineering has become a freestanding department; at most others, it remains a concentration within the civil engineering department.

According to federal data, about 37 percent of working civil engineers are employed in engineering and architectural services. These range from one- or two-engineer consulting practices to international design and construction firms that employ tens of thousands. About 43 percent are employed by city, state, and federal government, with the largest portion among the three at the state level. Most of the remainder work in manufacturing or natural resources. There are an estimated 186,000 civil engineers; their projected growth rate to the year 2000 is 17.4 percent, which is just above the average for all occupations. The ratio between master's and bachelor degrees in 1990 was a relatively high 39 percent. Among working civil engineers, 6 percent are women and 9.6 percent are members of African-American or Hispanic ethnic groups.

History and Current Assessment

Civil engineering is the oldest engineering discipline in the sense that humans were building homes and other shelters before even recorded history. From the Renaissance forward, European kings sponsored experts who were "military" engineers, charged with developing forts, armaments, and the like. Leonardo da Vinci best exemplifies this tradition. Civil engineers adapted these skills to peaceful purposes from the mid-eighteenth century.

The oldest formal schools of civil engineering were founded in France in the late 1700s, and, by Napoleon's time, the public works of that country were the wonder of the civilized world. In the early 1800s, the United States was dependent on the importation of civil engineers from France and England (where civil engineering was formalized into a profession around 1770, with apprenticeships to experienced artisans). The United States Military Academy (West Point), founded in 1802, provided formal academic training to military engineers; many of these worked in the Army Corps of Engineers and then entered private service upon military retirement. By the mid-1800s, there were about 500 "civil" engineers, and the American Society of Civil Engineers was founded in 1852. (The Army Corps of

Engineers performs many environmentally related activities to this day and is charged with certain regulatory responsibilities by both nineteenth- and twentieth-century environmental legislation. It employs 40,000 today, including substantial numbers of civil and mechanical engineers [11].)

Civil engineering underwent a boost in education and numbers when the Morrill Act was passed in 1862, setting up the network of state land-grant universities that dominate the college scene to this day. A special emphasis was placed on "useful" arts in agriculture and science, and civil engineering was one of the central disciplines to this emphasis. By the late nineteenth century, the principles of professional licensure were also established. Federal and state legislation eventually mandated that a professionally licensed civil engineer be involved in public works projects. To this day, civil engineering is the discipline in which the greatest proportion of its practitioners obtain a professional license.

Civil engineering in the nineteenth century was dominated by the successive new transportation technologies. In the early part of the century, and in the East especially, this technology was for canals. By the mid- to late 1800s, canals were supplanted by railroads, and bridge building became a critical skill. The Brooklyn Bridge, for many years the largest suspension bridge in the world, was completed in 1883.

It is all but forgotten today, but sanitation and outbreaks of epidemics were dominant themes of nineteenth-century American life, especially in the rapidly growing cities. Periodically, thousands were killed during summer outbreaks of cholera and yellow fever. People knew that raw sewage was a health hazard, but it was believed to be hazardous because of the fumes generated by decay. The germ theory of disease was a major debate in scientific and medical circles during that century, and not until the early 1900s did public health officials clearly understand that sanitation involved the prevention of bacteriological contamination of drinking water. "The organization of the American Public Health Association in 1872 clearly indicated the emergence of a new medical specialty," writes the historian John Duffy [12]. "By this date dozens of new professions were beginning to appear . . . the public health field contributed to their growth by creating a demand for professionals such as sanitary engineers. . . ."

Water and sewage systems were among the major public works projects that cities undertook in the late 1800s; spending for them remains a major portion of city budgets today. Civil engineers developed new tunneling and water-transportation techniques; today, the rehabilitation of the "infrastructure" projects dating back to this era is a critical concern in cities throughout the East and Midwest.

Somewhat later, but soon with equal intensity, the problems of solid-waste disposal grew in importance for city managers and public health officials. Garbage was too precious a commodity simply to dump in a landfill in the 1800s [13]. Most cities had scrap-heap districts where wastes were separated by garbage pickers or turned into manufacturing commodities by rendering plants. Only the residue was burned. The many health and public nuisance problems that these activities caused, coupled with the growing efficiency of commodity producers (such as textiles, building materials, and chemicals from coal or oil), led to the abandonment of most of these activities by the 1920s. Giant incinerators were built in many cities, and the ash from these plants was landfilled. By the 1950s, however, air-pollution woes caused many cities to shut the plants down. Landfilling of raw garbage proceeded apace, and, now, with landfill space at a premium in many regions, incineration (with modern air-pollution-control devices attached) is making a comeback.

The historian Martin Melosi points out [14] that dealing with garbage was a major spur to the establishment of engineering departments in many city governments in the early 1900s. As the issue of garbage was understood to be less of a medical problem and more of a bulk transportation problem (i.e., simply, how to get the stuff away from population centers), "faith in technology fostered the belief that since the water-carriage problem had been solved by technical means refuse could likewise be mastered through the skills of the engineer."

In the early decades of this century, the railroad began to be superseded by the automobile. Highway construction proceeded quickly through the 1950s, when the federal Highway Act established a public trust fund to build high-speed interstate highways across the nation. By the 1970s, these highways had become a dominant element of the countryside and of inner cities. Hundreds of thousands of civil engineers have been involved in highway construction throughout this century.

Highway construction has both borrowed from and contributed to the civil engineering work that manufacturers perform. Coal and mineral companies are major tunnelers and earth movers (for strip mines). Oil companies sponsor the bulk of geological studies that go on around the world, and the movement of water through underground strata has become better understood through oil and gas exploration. By tradition and common concern, agriculture and federal land-management agencies (the Bureau of Land Management, the Bureau of Reclamation, and the Soil Conservation Service) share concern over water resources, irrigation, and land use, especially in the American West.

In sum, the major foci of civil engineering today are building construction; water, sewage, and solid-waste transportation and disposal; and highways and other transportation systems. A common theme to each of these areas of technology is construction, and thus many civil engineers are engaged in the development and production of building materials, especially steel, concrete, earth, and wood. By tradition and by practice, both civil and environmental engineering are the central area of technical expertise for environmental problems.

Literature of the American Society of Civil Engineers notes that there are 23 subsections to which members belong. They are:

Air transport
Aerospace
Codes and standards
Cold regions
Computer practices
Construction
Energy
Engineering management
Research
Engineering mechanics
Environmental engineering
Geotechnical engineering
Highways

Hydraulics
Irrigation and drainage
Lifelines earthquake engineering
Pipelines
Structures
Surveying and mapping
Urban planning and development
Urban transportation
Water resources planning and
   management
Waterways, ports, coasts, and
   oceans

Education

Civil and environmental engineering enrollments have dropped somewhat in recent years, as Table 17 shows, but the decline appears to have stabilized.

Following the usual set of science and math courses that all engineering undergraduates take, civil engineers take courses in surveying and mapping, structural mechanics, basic building de-

Table 17a *Civil Engineering Degrees Awarded, 1988–1990*

Degree	1988	1989	1990
Bachelor	7,714	7,688	7,587
Master's	3,041	3,050	2,940
Ph.D.	518	554	539

Table 17b *Environmental Engineering Degrees Awarded, 1988–1990*

Degree	1988	1989	1990
Bachelor	192	138	137
Master's	329	427	471
Ph.D.	63	49	51

sign, metal structures, and fundamentals of materials science. Upper-level courses include soil and fluid mechanics, hydraulics, and CAD. In light of the strong business orientation of civil engineering work, many students opt for courses in engineering and construction management, economics, law, and accounting. Concentrations in environmental or sanitary engineering, geotechnical topics, transportation planning, hydrology, and others are often available.

At the master's level, more advanced courses on many of these same topics are offered. Many civil engineering students combine their master's-degree studies with preparatory courses for the initial professional-licensure test. Many also take on more business courses. Another lively area of civil engineering education is the use of computers, which have been programmed to run many of the intricate structural calculations that civil engineers make when designing a structure. One technique in particular, finite-element analysis, has evolved into a key method for determining the stresses that occur throughout a structure like a bridge in very fine detail.

Doctoral-level civil engineering can take a great variety of directions. Studies may relate to environmental topics, such as hazardous-waste management, limnology (the study of lakes and streams), aquatic chemistry, biology and coastal engineering, and microbiology. At all levels of education, a remarkable number of courses are devoted to the study of soil. The course catalog of the Georgia Institute of Technology, for example, lists the following courses: soil and rock engineering, flow through porous media, sediment transport, soil mechanics, physical and physiochemical properties of soils, soil testing, terrain evaluation, soil construction, soil stabilization, and advanced theoretical and applied soil mechanics.

Relative to most other engineering disciplines, a considerable number of business courses are offered to civil engineers, which is a natural outcome of the profession's strong orientation toward construction management. Early in their careers civil engineers are expected to be able to oversee a construction crew and to complete such projects on time and within budget.

There are plenty of civil engineering professors, and most of them conduct research just as any other engineering professors would do. However, in the world of business and commerce, relatively little civil engineering research is conducted. Other disciplines that are closely tied to an engineering discipline, such as the combination of electrical engineers and the electronics industry or aerospace engineers and the aerospace industry, benefit from the strong R&D programs that private companies sponsor. Civil engineering firms, however, tend not to sponsor such research. As a result, opportunities for the doctoral civil engineer are somewhat limited outside of academia.

A major factor in the educational process for civil engineers is obtaining professional licensure. Of today's working civil engineers, a relatively high percentage have their P.E. license, and, as noted, some schools make the preliminary steps to obtaining this license part of the educational process. Licensure starts with passing an "engineer-in-training" (EIT) examination, a rigorous, eight-hour test of fundamentals of science and engineering. Then, depending on the state that grants the license, three or four years of work experience are required, which must be under the guidance of an already-licensed professional engineer. Finally, a second examination, also eight hours in duration, must be taken and passed.

Those who seek certification as a professionally licensed environmental engineer undergo a second series of tests and work experience. These requirements are set by the American Academy of Environmental Engineers and include eight years of engineering experience, four of which are in a supervisory role. A written examination is supplemented by an oral one. Those who meet all of these requirements are certified as "diplomate" environmental engineers and can append "D.E.E." after their names on business correspondence. There are 2,500 such diplomates.

The American Academy of Environmental Engineers is jointly sponsored by 11 professional organizations. These represent a noteworthy cross-section of the professional interests of environmental engineering in the United States today. They are:

Air and Waste Management Association

American Institute of Chemical Engineers

American Public Health Association

American Public Works Association

American Society for Engineering Education

American Society of Civil Engineers

American Society of Mechanical Engineers

American Water Works Association

Association of Environmental Engineering Professors

National Society of Professional Engineers

Water Pollution Control Federation

Environmental Impact

As the preceding listing makes clear, civil engineering is intimately involved with environmental assessments and pollution prevention. While civil engineers are often perceived as the environment's enemy (since they tame wild rivers with dams, pave the countryside, and build in pristine forests and wetlands), their work has a large potential for doing good for the environment as well. It is not uncommon now for state highway departments to "build" a wetlands area or wildlife preserve by removing manufactured structures and establishing the proper water flow.

Civil engineers are also responsible, by and large, for garbage disposal projects, irrigation and sewage construction, and a variety of projects associated with electrical power generation. The latter includes coal transportation and storage, electrical-transmission systems, power plant construction, and facilities for the disposal of ash from coal-burning plants. In cases where a dam is built for hydroelectric power, civil engineers oversee the dam's construction and the planning that goes into the design and operation of the reservoir behind the dam. Many of these projects are among the most bitterly contested environmental projects in the country. There are obviously many such disputes where the environmental impact is clearcut: If a certain dam is built, then a wild river or stream ceases to exist. Others are less so: Some coal-burning plants, for example, have a complex system of pumping the ash byproduct into an artificial lake; when the plant no longer operates, the lake is drained, topsoil is added, and an open field is all that remains of a waste-disposal problem that could have caused serious air or water pollution.

Waste disposal, especially of toxic industrial wastes, is another dramatic environmental confrontation. In previous years, such dumps were simply pits dug in the ground; soil was thrown over heaped-up waste until it became uneconomical to raise the height of the dumps any farther. Today, both industrial and municipal landfills are highly "designed" structures. Hydrological surveys are conducted first to make sure that there are no underground streams or reservoirs that would be contaminated by the waste. The site is then excavated and lined with alternating layers of clay, gravel, and a thick plastic sheet. The goal is to minimize leaching of hazardous materials from the landfill once it begins accepting waste. In many cases, it is now mandatory to build an underground piping system that pulls any leachate from under the landfill that occurs; this leachate is then treated much as sewage would be.

There is more than a little irony in the "discovery" by William Rathje, a professor at the University of Arizona who organized an ongoing program called the "Garbage Project," that there is very little decomposition at municipal landfills [15]. Rathje's group digs shafts down into old landfills, much as an archaeologist would excavate an ancient city, and records the types and conditions of wastes encountered. "The notion that much biodegradation occurs inside lined landfills is largely a myth," he says. What gets overlooked in this realization is that the minimization of degradation (in turn, causing the generation of malodorous gases and leachates) was the goal of the engineers who designed the facility! Many liquid wastes are now banned from landfills, and steps are being taken to minimize the incursion of rainfall into landfills.

Turning this question on its head, scientists at the Georgia Institute of Technology are experimenting with the addition of the appropriate microbes so that leachates that are collected from a landfill are returned to that landfill and degraded as they percolate through it, just as sewage is treated at a municipal sewage plant. Other engineers (and several businesses) have successfully recovered the methane gas generated by a landfill (the product of decomposition), purified it, and sold it to municipal gas utilities. Thus, the gas in your stove used for cooking your morning's breakfast may be the by-product of the garbage you threw out a decade ago!

The pros and cons of these disposal techniques are open to debate and will not be settled here. What is clear, however, is that technologists including civil engineers are formulating solutions to pressing social problems, such as the disposal of municipal waste.

Civil engineering companies, over the past decade, have literally feasted on a new federal program that looks as though it will continue for decades to come. This "Superfund" program has now been copied at the state level in many states. EPA, which manages Superfund, collects a tax from manufacturers and spends it on the cleanup of old or abandoned industrial waste dumps. Love Canal is now a Superfund site, as are thousands of other old dumps around the country. The U.S. government itself, at its national laboratories and military bases, has hundreds more such dump sites. When Superfund was reauthorized in the mid-1980s, its budget was increased to nearly $2 billion per year. The thought was that a few years of Superfund activity would clean up most of the worst dumps, and the program would shut down. Now, with over 12,000 sites on a "National Priority List" and with cleanups at some sites taking as long as ten years, the existence of Superfund appears to be nearly perpetual.

At Superfund sites, a survey of the underground conditions (in cases where wastes have been buried) must be conducted by a hydro-geological firm. Often, this will necessitate digging a series of wells around the site and taking samples of the contaminated groundwater. Once the below-ground conditions are known, a complicated *remedial investigation/feasibility study* (RI/FS) is conducted to determine what type of treatment technology is appropriate to the environmental problems at the site. The range of technologies that are under consideration for hazardous-waste sites is large and growing. It includes incineration of contaminated soil, chemical treatment, solidification via high-energy techniques like microwaves, stripping volatile chemicals from groundwater by airing it, and the use of biological agents (microbes) that can degrade the wastes *in situ*. It may not be environmentally elegant, but one of the more common treatment techniques is to remove the contaminated soil from the site and ship it to another, better-designed landfill.

The Superfund program is not without some controversy. Billions of dollars have been spent, but relatively few sites have been successfully ameliorated. "About 60 percent of EPA's Superfund spending thus far has been for site studies, administration, and management," noted the Congressional Office of Technology Assessment (OTA) in a 1989 report [16]. The report estimated that as much as $500 billion may be spent over a period of decades to complete the cleanup of some 10,000 sites. "It is essential," OTA said, "to view Superfund as an experimental program tackling a new problem with an inexperienced work force and limited technologies."

If nothing else, this assessment demonstrates that the problem of cleaning old dumps will consume the efforts of many civil engineers for years to come. And, as these engineers gain experience, the cleanups will proceed more expeditiously. In the meantime, the production of industrial wastes has by no means slowed down; if anything (and partly due to environmental regulations that extend the definition of *hazardous*), waste generation has gone up. New landfills and treatment facilities are being built. The role of the civil engineer in this process, according to a position paper issued by the American Society of Civil Engineers, is to:

1. Apply technical knowledge to determine which site selection methods and environmental data are appropriate.
2. Carefully collect environmental data, as necessary.
3. Assemble and use these data accurately regardless of which technical site selection method is used.
4. Most importantly, recognize the need to present results of this process in a manner which enables fair-minded (technical and nontechnical) individuals to assess the risks of proposed facilities within the context of normally accepted risks otherwise encountered in our technological society.

Site selection of hazardous-waste disposal facilities is without question the most controversial environmental issue that industry and communities face. The costs of disposal have risen dramatically, and more manufacturers are seeking ways to cut waste generation drastically. Waste will continue to be generated, however, and, if it is not incinerated or otherwise chemically destroyed, it and its residues will ultimately have to be landfilled. Civil engineers will be called on regularly to provide their expertise in controlling risks and costs to society.

A final area of environmental impact by civil engineers concerns building materials. The production of concrete, lumber, steel, glass, and, increasingly, plastics that goes into building construction is, to put it mildly, earthshaking; annual capacities for these materials are measured in the billions of tons (or billions of board feet). While the forestry, chemical, and mineral industries are the main suppliers, engineering-construction businesses, including architectural and civil-engineering firms, are the specifiers and purchasers of these materials. A substantial fraction of civil engineers work for the finished-goods producers, such as cement or gypsum manufacturers, dimensional lumber manufacturers, and the like.

There are two central environmental aspects to this specifying and purchasing function: (1) the recycling of old building materials and (2) the use of recycled materials from other waste streams (commonly, materials from municipal solid waste) in new construction. To take one example, the manufacturers of polystyrene foam are attempting to establish businesses in which used food packaging is recycled into building insulation or acoustic tile. General Electric Company, a major plastics producer, is attempting to establish a plastics-use hierarchy in which relatively high-valued plastics (i.e., those that sell for over a dollar a pound) are first used in highly technically specific applications like food packaging, then reused in automotive or computer components, and then recycled into building materials. (In each case, the period of time from when the product is first fabricated to when it is disposed lengthens at each of these steps. When, finally, the plastic is used in a home or building, it will reside there for decades.)

Recycling, on the whole, is a very entrepreneurial business these days, with small, undercapitalized firms attempting to grow and establish dependable sources of supply and steady customers of the recycled goods [17]. Construction materials are definitely a part of this entrepreneurial effort and, in terms of the tonnage of materials involved, could become the dominant market for recycled goods. Civil engineers, working with these recycling entrepreneurs (or joining in the cause themselves) can make a major contribution to this effort.

Nuclear Engineering

Overview

"Battening the hatches" is a nautical phrase referring to a sea captain's preparation of the ship for a storm. With all the doors, windows, and hatches closed and with proper steering, the ship will survive a severe storm unharmed. In the nuclear industry and the nuclear engineering professions, the hatches have been battened since 1979, when the Three Mile Island power plant disaster occurred near Harrisburg, Pennsylvania. No new nuclear power plants have been ordered in the United States since then, and, as of the first half of 1991, only three plants were left whose construction was not yet complete. After that, the order book is empty. During the intervening years, hundreds of other plant proposals were canceled.

Nuclear power generates about 20 percent of U.S. electricity, and may, due to concern over the pollution caused by fossil fuel combustion, be headed for a renaissance. At the same time, a 50-year legacy of sloppy nuclear weapons production has left the U.S. Department of Energy (DOE), the agency that is responsible to the Defense Department for nuclear weapons and fuel production, with a cleanup project whose cost has been estimated at $155 billion. Even today, before the cleanup program has hit full stride, DOE expects to be working on the program through the year 2019. (A 22-year-old college graduate would be 50 years old by then, which easily demonstrates that one could devote the bulk of one's career to this program.) The Office of Technology Assessment has concluded that there is no dependable way of predicting either the ultimate length of time or the cost of the cleanup.

Nuclear power and nuclear waste cleanup are the two issues that will keep nuclear engineering going well into the future. Even so, college students have slipped away from nuclear engineering programs in droves. Only 264 students graduated with B.S.E. degrees in the subject in 1990, which is less than half the number in 1980. Industry adjusts to the paucity of job candidates by training other engineers or technologists in the necessary skills and by paying higher salaries—the normal adjustments that the job market makes when a shortage of appropriately trained professionals exists.

Traditionally, nuclear power has not been perceived to be part of the matrix of environmental issues facing the nation; it has always been held separate, under its own regulatory control and, not unintentionally, away from the public eye. Many antinuclear activists are not necessarily pro-environment activists. All this is changing, however, as the Environmental Protection Agency, under congressional prodding, has exerted greater authority over the industry and DOE. And the intermingling of energy and environmental issues—the production of air pollutants, the desire to reduce oil imports, and the need for more electricity production—will tighten this nexus in the future.

Nuclear engineers work as power plant designers and operators. Billions of dollars are spent annually to refurbish existing power plants, and this maintenance work requires engineering design skills. Designers thus have work even when a new plant is not being planned. Nuclear engineers are also trained in a topic called *health physics*, which is the general term for monitoring the effects of radioactivity on humans and the environment. For cleanup or disposal work, nuclear engineers are employed by engineering and consulting companies that are contractors to DOE for cleanup work.

There are about 15,000 nuclear engineers, according to federal data, and their projected growth rate to the year 2000 is zero; there will be the same number then as now. However, job openings will be steady due to the normal pace of retirements, job changes, and other departures from the working ranks. Almost as many master's degrees were awarded in 1990 as bachelor degrees (see Table 18), indicative of a high level of technical expertise among working nuclear engineers.

Education

Nuclear engineers are basically chemical or mechanical engineers who are familiar with the handling and use of radioactive materials. The profession could hardly be said to exist prior to the 1940s, when

Table 18 *Nuclear Engineering Degrees Awarded, 1988–1990*

Degree	1988	1989	1990
Bachelor	306	303	264
Master's	221	245	236
Ph.D.	102	90	115

the United States began the Manhattan Project to build an atomic bomb. However, there have been—and continue to be—diverse applications of radioactivity and nuclear technology aside from bomb making and power generation. Radiation therapy is one obvious example; another is the production of instrumentation, sensors, X-ray machinery, and the like. Scientists were working on such devices prior to World War II, and new applications, such as synchrotron radiation (for materials research) and X-ray lithography (for microelectronics production), continue to evolve.

At the undergraduate level, however, the curriculum is dominated by nuclear power. Courses include basic reactor design, reactor operations, design theory, fundamentals of health physics, radiation shielding, and transport of nuclear materials through different media. A central technology that is either embedded in a variety of these courses or that is given its own title is thermal hydraulics, the study of heat transfer and fluid flow within a reactor, which are critical to the safe operation of a reactor. Some schools will also offer an elective course in nuclear fusion. (This technology seeks to generate power by combining small atoms into larger ones rather than, as is the case in nuclear fission, by large atoms breaking down into smaller ones. Nuclear fusion is what the sun does to generate heat and light.)

Options really open up in master's and doctoral programs. Undergraduates with an engineering degree can pursue a master's in nuclear engineering, which is usually tailored toward advanced study of nuclear power. The graduate-level programs are combined with a variety of other programs, including health physics, engineering physics, radiology or radiation biology, and energy engineering. The fact is that nuclear technology is a key portal to the study of the fundamental aspects of matter, to medical research, and to certain aspects of physics. Nuclear engineering programs share in these themes.

In response to the lessened prospects of nuclear power, some academic programs have altered their focus somewhat. "In the past, nuclear power and nuclear science have shared equal emphasis in Cornell programs," reads the course announcement of Cornell University's nuclear engineering program in a graduate-school catalog [18]. "Nonpower applications of nuclear phenomena, atomic physics, and plasma physics now form an increasingly larger part of the University's teaching and research programs."

Another factor in choosing among graduate schools is the horsepower of their laboratories. The larger universities have an impressive array of ion beam generators, neutron and electron beam sources, gamma irradiation cells, tokamak fusion reactors, cyclotrons, and other devices. Georgia Institute of Technology has a five-megawatt nuclear reactor, which is not far from having a commercial-scale nuclear power plant on campus! In all seriousness, many of these facilities represent substantial investments by the federal government in fundamental physics research and, in some cases, have large staffs of scientists devoted primarily to conducting research with these machines.

Over the years, a considerable number of training regulations have been imposed on utility companies. Many engineers take advantage of programs such as the Institute of Nuclear Power Operations to become more familiar with power production.

Environmental Impact

There are 112 operating nuclear power plants in the United States, supplying about 20 percent of the electricity the nation uses. While the absolute number is highest in the world, as a proportion of power generation, U.S. figures are actually rather low. France, for example, generates 75 percent of its power from nuclear plants; Germany (before unification) generates nearly 40 percent.

Nuclear power is easily as controversial as hazardous-waste disposal as a community issue; the NIMBY syndrome is in full force. However, in the 1990s, nuclear power has begun to be perceived in a new light due to the growing concern over the emission of carbon dioxide and other "greenhouse" gases. The complete absence of such emissions from nuclear power generation changes its environmental worthiness. The nuclear industry—utility companies and the contractors that serve them—has already jumped into the breach with a set of white papers seeking to reinvigorate nuclear power. In conjunction with the production of the National Energy Strategy, a U.S. Department of Energy action plan for future energy policies, the Nuclear Power Oversight Committee said, "The National Energy Strategy must recognize that expanded reliance on nuclear energy is essential to this nation's, and the world's, energy supply" [19].

In anticipation of this hoped-for nuclear renaissance, equipment contractors are developing plans for new types of reactors, the "evolutionary" and "passive" advanced light-water reactors. The Nuclear Regulatory Commission will soon rule on the safety and certification of these designs. Utility companies will then seek to build new plants on the basis of a standardized design, thus greatly expediting the final certification of each plant. (Previously, each new plant design had to be reviewed from the very start to completion of construction.)

There remains a gigantic hole in this argument—the inability of the government and industry to come up with an acceptable method of disposing nuclear waste. The Department of Energy, which has responsibility for this element of the nuclear complex, has staked its claim on a desert region in Nevada, Yucca Mountain, and has started preliminary construction of a repository there. Serious questions exist, however, concerning the geological stability of the site, which must be capable of retaining the waste for thousands of years (until the radioactivity level in the waste decays), and the feasibility of carrying out the disposal. Although the site is on federally owned land, the state of Nevada has also expressed its reservations.

Whether or not more new nuclear plants are built, they will be a part of the nation's energy mix for at least the next 30 years. The utility companies that have installed these plants depend on nuclear engineers to run and maintain them. Federal regulations, established and administered by the Nuclear Regulatory Commission (NRC), require the presence of a licensed plant engineer at all times while the facility is in operation. Extensive performance checks and tests are also required on a regular basis. NRC itself is a major employer of nuclear engineers as well; it totals 3,400 employees and recruits actively on college campuses [20].

The vast cleanup program that the U.S. Department of Energy is engaged in will take nuclear engineering, health physics, and other nuclear-related professions into a new dimension. Environmental engineering and consulting firms, having gained experience as government contractors under the Superfund program, are now angling for business in cleaning up the so-called nuclear weapons complex. This complex encompasses 14 facilities in 13 states, covering 3,350 square miles and employing over 100,000 people. DOE is in the process of reevaluating the need for all of these facilities since, presumably, there will be fewer nuclear warheads needed in this era of warmer relations with the former Soviet Union. As facilities are shut down, the decommissioning process will entail removing radioactively "hot" equipment and materials and disposing them in waste dumps. (Yucca Mountain is intended for "high-level" radioactive wastes, mainly spent fuel rods from nuclear plants. "Low-level" wastes, which are mostly materials that have been irradiated by the high-level wastes, do not require as restrictive a storage method and are being disposed at a variety of sites around the country.)

Both for nuclear power and for the cleanup of nuclear wastes, extensive research programs are being funded by the utility industry and DOE. Much new science will have to be developed to address these issues, and these research programs will keep nuclear scientists busy for years to come. Special mention should also be made of the nuclear fusion research program, which is a decades-long effort to demonstrate the feasibility of this form of power generation. Fusion research, according to some wags, is *the* energy source of the future and *always* will be. Already, about 30-years' worth of research has been conducted on it, and final, successful demonstration is believed to be another 25 to 40 years in the future. DOE has funded the current research program at $200 million to $300 million annually since the early 1980s, but Congress has become disenchanted with the low level of progress in the program. Rather than seeking to increase funding, DOE is in a mode of trying to hold onto what it can get to keep the program alive. Fusion has the promise, as its proponents continually assert, of producing power without the generation of radioactive waste. It is likely that research will continue indefinitely on fusion, but it also seems likely in these fiscally constrained times that its funding will be reduced.

Electrical Engineering

Overview

In the early 1980s, the term *high technology* came to mean the ultimate in technical innovation, and high-technology companies were the darlings of investors on Wall Street. To most people, high technology is synonymous with computers and electronics. Thus, the high priests of high technology are electrical and electronics engineers.

Electrical engineering is by far the largest of any engineering discipline, with an estimated 439,000 practitioners in the United States. The growth rate for this profession is quite high—about 40 percent, according to the Bureau of Labor Statistics. Like mechanical engineering, the second-largest engineering discipline, electrical engineering is deeply embedded in all facets of manufacturing and in many business and government services as well.

Given its broad distribution throughout society, electrical engineering is bound to get involved in environmental activities. Most electrical engineers work in electronics applications—the production of microchips, printed circuits, and consumer electronic devices like radios and televisions. About 10 percent work in the utility industry, generating and transmitting the electricity that runs our houses, offices, and factories. The same environmental issues that affect mechanical engineering work also apply to electrical engineers who are involved in power generation.

History and Current Assessment

Electrical engineering in the United States started with the commercialization of scientific research into electricity in the late nineteenth century. Basic appliances such as the telephone (invented in 1876), the light bulb (1878), and the electric motor (1888) soon began to change many aspects of life in that era. Learning how to produce and then provide power for the massive amounts of these products occupied the attention of the early electrical engineers. The Institute of Electrical and Electronics Engineers, Inc. (IEEE), the leading professional organization of these engineers, was founded in 1884.

By the turn of the century, radio had been theoretically demonstrated, and, by the 1920s, radio broadcasting became common. This communications medium, together with the telephone and telegraph, created a second strain of electrical engineer, then called the "radio engineer." Where power generation involves thousands of volts and amperes of electricity, radio gets by with a few millivolts gathered out of the air as a radio signal. The same distinction occurred in Germany, where the former was called "heavy current" and the latter, "light current." By the end of World War II, the momentum was very much with these radio engineers, who were aided immeasurably by the invention of the vacuum tube (in the early 1900s) and the transistor (in 1948).

The Institute of Electrical Engineers merged with the Institute of Radio Engineers in 1963. Today, about 90 percent of working engineers are involved with low-voltage electronics rather than high-voltage power.

In the World War II era, electrical and electronics engineering enjoyed a tremendous boost as a result of research into new weaponry. The development of radar and sonar, radio communications, targeting devices, and, toward the end of the war, missiles, all depended on the skills of these engineers. Coincidentally during the war, television began to make an impact in the civilian population.

Military contractors, especially aerospace firms, have since become big employers of electrical engineers. The space program launched in the early 1960s, with the goal of putting a man on the moon before the decade was over, intensified this involvement. The integrated circuit—arguably *the* technological development of the twentieth century—was developed, with support from the Defense Department and NASA, as a weight-saving device for missiles and rockets. According to a December 1990 survey of electrical engineering readers, *IEEE Spectrum* magazine found that 60.4 percent of its respondents were employed at companies doing some degree of military work [21].

During the 1960s also, the computer came into its own as an industry. IBM developed its 360-series mainframe computer in the middle of the decade and soon had a multibillion-dollar business on its hands. A decade later, two college dropouts working in a garage developed the first successful personal computer. The two, Steve Jobs and Steve Wozniak, helped create another multibillion-dollar business in computers.

The success of the computer during the 1960s led to the creation of an entirely new profession—computer programming. This profession, combining logic, mathematics, and electronics, was practiced originally by mathematicians, physicists, electrical engineers, and just about any other scientist or engineer who understood the vast potential of the computer. Eventually, formal programs were set up in computer programming, and many of these programs were placed in the electrical engineering department. As they grew, however, and as the focus of electrical engineering remained on designing and building computers rather than on writing their instructions, computer programming became an independent department. Many electrical engineers continue to be involved in programming; yet another academic concentration, computer engineering, has also come into being (see the later section on computer and science engineering.)

Electrical engineering today is broadly distributed throughout industry and commerce. Products for both industrial and consumer applications are developed by electrical engineering designers and are manufactured by electrical engineers in factory management. It is not too much of an overstatement to say that wherever electricity is flowing—through the home, in the car, over the radio waves—electrical engineers have been involved. The Institute of Electrical and Electronics Engineers, the leading professional organization, subdivides its membership according to the following divisions (membership figures are for 1988):

- Circuits and Devices (34,404 members) includes integrated circuits and microchips, the electronic circuits that these are wired into, and related solid-state devices.

- Industrial Applications (18,089) includes the factory managers and the engineers concerned with designs of control equipment for factory lines and power plants.

- Communications Technology (38,841) incorporates radio, television, telecommunications, and all the other methods of communicating.

- Electromagnetics and Radiation (28,745) involves the many signaling techniques for military applications, such as radar and phased-array systems, as well as nuclear and plasma sciences.

- Computers (90,223) is the biggest division.

- Engineering and the Human Environment (20,562) comprises engineering management, education, professional communications, and the societal implications of technology.

- Power Engineering (23,311) includes the engineers who work at public utilities or other power sources.

- Signals and Applications (31,650) covers the various types of advanced electronic signals and includes aerospace systems (avionics), ultrasonics, and speech and signal processing.

- Systems and Control (32,219) is the engineering of large, distributed electrical and electronic systems, including factory automation, robotics, and the like.

A relatively high number of electrical engineers go on to get a master's degree; in 1990, the ratio of master's to bachelor degrees was 36 percent (see Table 19). About 8 percent of working electrical engineers are women and 6.2 percent are members of African-American or Hispanic ethnic groups.

Education

To look at a circuit board or electrical network is to see mathematics made into physical objects. Whereas civil or mechanical engineers have a certain degree of artistic latitude in how their designs are made, the electrical engineer has a rigorous set of equations to resolve in the execution of a design. This is not to say that electrical engineering is less creative—the cornucopia of appliances and electronics in our homes attests to that—but that the education of electrical engineers is strongly oriented around mathematics.

Following the basic science and math courses, undergraduate electrical engineers take courses in computer programming, basic circuit design, and the basics of electronic devices. These are followed with courses in electromagnetics, communications (one such course has the felicitous title of "Random Signals and Noise"), semiconductor theory, and electric power production. A plethora of options or engineering specialties—military avionics, telecommunications, advanced computer design, nuclear power, optoelectronics, and others—are offered.

Doctoral-level studies reach deeper into the fundamental principles of circuit design, computer programming, and materials research. In the latter area, the topic of solid-state physics is important. Today's electrical engineering researchers are developing semiconductor components that take advantage of the so-called quantum effects of subatomic particles—a technology that only a few decades

Table 19 *Electrical Engineering Degrees Awarded, 1988–1990*

Degree	1988	1989	1990
Bachelor	24,367	22,929	21,385
Master's	7,335	7,520	7,691
Ph.D.	1,003	1,139	1,262

ago was being developed by physicists working at the large atomic accelerators at the national laboratories.

Advanced materials research is also important to applications such as high-efficiency batteries, which will become important in future generations of electric automobiles. Another application of materials research is to solar energy, particularly the form called *photovoltaics*, which converts sunlight directly into electricity.

The size and breadth of electrical engineering technology makes it one of the most lively areas of research. As new types of materials are developed, the electronics applications multiply rapidly, creating yet more opportunities for inventing new technology. The most obvious example of this is the discovery of "warm" superconductors—materials that do not have to be chilled nearly to absolute zero ($-460°F$) in order to conduct electricity with no resistance. The new materials, combinations of copper, oxygen, and rare-earth metals, can act as superconductors at temperatures of around $-293°F$, which is still very cold but is in the range of relatively cheap liquid nitrogen. The great potential of these superconductors is that an electrical-transmission line made with them would lose no power while transmitting the electricity. Other applications are in microelectronics, magnetics, and transportation.

There are many continuing-education opportunities from colleges, large employers themselves, and rather innovative arrangements such as the National Technological University, which transmits course materials over data communications lines to students across the country. In addition, engineers in the nuclear power industry can receive additional training from the Institute of Nuclear Power Operations, an industry-sponsored group.

Environmental Impact

Electricity and the devices that use it are deeply embedded in all aspects of our lives. To the extent that our life styles affect the environment—a point no one would argue—electrical engineering also affects the environment.

The most glaring aspect of this is electrical production. Nearly all types of power production have serious environmental impacts: Coal-burning plants produce air pollution and ash that must be disposed; nuclear plants produce radioactive wastes; hydropower from dams drastically alters the flow of rivers and streams. These hazards are well known, and billions of dollars have been committed to controlling them and reducing their risks.

More recently (over the past five years), electricity itself has come under question as an environmental hazard. (Naturally, high-power electricity is itself a health hazard.) A variety of studies have indicated that the electromagnetic field that is generated whenever current is stepped up or down by transformers (so-called low-frequency radiation) can subtly alter the human body's chemistry. Some studies indicate heightened cancer rates in the vicinity of strong electrical fields and among electrical-transmission-line workers. The risk of this hazard, if confirmed, will surely not mean the end of electricity as a power source (we might as well stop breathing air), but it could require dramatic alterations in how high-power transmission is accomplished and in the designs of machinery that use heavy amounts of current.

The "Holy Grail" of many environmentalists is the commercialization of solar energy, which has the potential of pollution-free power production. The source of the energy—sunlight—is free. Millions of dollars have been spent on solar energy production, either through "active" solar systems that concentrate the sun's heat to produce steam (which can then be used to generate electricity) or through photovoltaics, which are essentially electronic devices that convert sunlight directly into current. Active solar energy is marginally cost-effective, especially in regions where sunlight is relatively undiminished by clouds (e.g., in desert regions) and pollution-control requirements are high. Photovoltaics remain uneconomic except for highly specialized applications, such as providing power for satellites or other remotely stationed equipment. Solar energy has definite potential for the future, but it remains frustratingly outside the range of cost-effectiveness today.

Another aspect of utility operation is to reduce its demand as a means of reducing the pollution its production causes. So-called negawatts (negative watts) are "generated" when high-efficiency fluorescent lamps replace incandescent ones or when better electrical efficiencies are built into appliances and factory equipment. The electric motor, a ubiquitous device at factories, can be constructed with better components that increase its efficiency. Paradoxically, by reducing demand for electricity, local utility companies may become more profitable because they avoid the costs of constructing new plants or installing new pollution-control equipment. This trend is a dramatic turnaround for electricity producers, and many electrical engineers are reexamining how power is used in homes, offices, and factories to seek out new conservation candidates.

These efforts are critical for economic as well as environmental reasons. DOE has found that, while nonelectric energy (i.e., fossil fuels used in autos or for heating and cooling) decreased by 4 percent between 1973 and 1989, electric energy grew by 51 percent, which is almost in lockstep with the growth in GNP. More efficient use of electricity reduces the amount of oil that has to be imported while allowing the economy to continue to grow. As a result of requirements for innovative technologies to be applied under the Clean Air Act, electrically powered automobiles will become more common in the future. This, too, will require new electrical engineering technology.

In the microelectronics realm, a critical issue is reducing the pollution caused by microelectronics manufacturing. It has been common, for example, to use CFCs to clean circuit boards and microchips as they are being fabricated. These CFCs will be banned in coming years, and the electronics manufacturers are scrambling to find replacements. One promising alternative, already in use by some manufacturers, is a class of chemicals called *terpenes*, which are derived from renewable resources such as tree sap or fruit rinds. Similar issues are at stake involving the metals and chemicals used to produce microchips— highly toxic silane compounds, acids, and metals like nickel or copper, which are pollutants when dissolved in rinse water.

There are many intriguing, open-ended questions about the effects of the computer on the environment. The computer—emphatically a product of the electrical engineering profession—was not long ago thought of as a means of creating the "paperless" office of the coming "information society." Rather than mailing letters and photocopying records, we would enter this information into computer-driven storage media, use long-distance telecommunications lines to distribute it, and, in general, be more efficient in storing and accessing it.

Instead, as an interesting essay by Robert Herman and others in *Technology and Environment* points out [22], the computer has created an explosion of paper. A kindred device to the computer in modern offices—the photocopying machine—only intensifies paper demand. "Consumption in the United States of writing and printing paper increased in 1959–1986 from about 7 to 22 million tons, and in the short period 1981–1984 the use of paper by U.S. businesses rose from 850 billion to 1.4 trillion pages," writes Herman. "So perhaps it is not surprising that in the information era, the trees of the world are at risk. Moreover, the equivalent of about 1,500 pounds of petroleum is required to make a ton of paper . . . One wonders which will last longer—energy or the trees."

Herman's essay is devoted to the concept of "(de)materialization," which, succinctly put, addresses the rise or fall of modern industrial society's dependence on materials to sustain itself. Per pound of silicon, copper, and steel, today's computer is vastly more powerful than those of five or ten years ago. Yet, since this growing power makes the computer a more valuable possession by more people, more tons of silicon and the other materials are consumed by society. Computer technology continues to evolve, and the powerful nexus of computers, telecommunications, and information storage—all of which are the products of electrical engineering technology—is exerting a growing influence on our lives. The paperless office may yet arrive; conceivably, the computer may make offices as we understand them today all but extinct. (Anyone who has seen a "high-tech" executive in a car with a laptop computer, a cellular telephone, and a portable fax machine can readily question the need to gather in a headquarters office building.)

In the meantime, computer hardware and software are the bread and butter of environmental work: Databases of pollutants are generated; analytical instruments run automated tests on air, water, and soil contamination; engineering workstations become a basic tool for performing designs of environmental equipment and remediation plans. The industrial use of computers, as controllers for automated manufacturing steps, has become an essential component in achieving higher efficiencies and reducing waste across the board. "Intelligent" controls for the heating and air-conditioning of buildings help make them more energy-efficient. To the extent that electrical engineers bend their efforts to building better computers and industrial controls and guide their usage, these engineers are helping improve the environment.

Other Engineering Disciplines

The Engineering Manpower Commission, an arm of a Washington, D.C., umbrella organization of engineering professions (the American Association of Engineering Societies), keeps tabs on 20 distinct engineering disciplines and lumps the remainder in a miscellaneous "other" category. Five of these 20—chemical, mechanical, civil and environmental, nuclear, and electrical—have been described in the preceding sections. The other 15 have varying degrees of involvement with environmental issues, just as any technical profession does these days. But environmental issues are of such lesser importance to them, or they are so small, that their impact on environmental protection is overshadowed by the five that have already been described. A capsule summary of some of the other engineering disciplines, with their respective environmental involvement, follows.

Aerospace Engineering

There are about 78,000 aerospace engineers, who are concerned primarily with the design and construction of aircraft, spacecraft, and the equipment associated with flight. The profession divides neatly among engineers concerned with propulsion systems (engines and rockets), structural design of wings and fuselages, and aircraft electronics (avionics). A few specialize in the high-tech materials needed for modern aircraft construction, such as new metallic alloys, composite plastics, and the like.

Current environmental issues among aerospace engineers include those that are common to all engineers who work on transportation systems—increasing the energy efficiency of the craft and reducing the pollution caused by combustion of fossil fuels within the engine. When automobile manufacturers began getting serious about fuel efficiency in the 1970s, they looked to the body of knowledge developed by aerospace engineers in designing structures that slip through air with reduced resistance. Aerodynamic styling has changed the look of autos, trucks, trains—and even bicycles. Most automakers now have aerodynamic laboratories with wind tunnels patterned after the labs first developed in the aerospace industry.

On the pollution-control front, the debate, in the late 1960s, over the effects of nitrous oxide exhaust gases from supersonic jets spurred researchers to start looking at the chemical makeup of the stratosphere. Ultimately, this research has led to the banning of CFCs and the growing concern over the greenhouse effect. Attention continues to be focused on aircraft exhausts as well.

Many other transportation engineers pay attention to noise pollution, but the problem is of greatest concern to aircraft designers. Noise pollution is a dominant issue in siting new airports, and aircraft manufacturers are competing to produce quieter aircraft. The control of noise leads one inevitably into the study of vibration, and this research has applicability in a wide variety of applications in other types of noise control and in sound generation and reproduction.

Some aerospace engineers, at least, are going to be at the forefront of atmospheric and meteorological research in the 1990s as NASA develops its plans for a network of orbiting stations that will monitor atmospheric patterns. These satellites will carry instruments that can measure the chemical composition of the upper atmosphere so that a better understanding of global warming will be gained.

Such satellites are already being used in a variety of meteorological, geographic, and geological studies of the Earth, all of which have a dramatic impact on the understanding of global environmental issues. Such *remote-sensing technology,* as the field is called, is being used to survey the distribution of minerals and water and even to locate underground waste dumps.

At the moment, the aerospace industry is contracting severely due to the reduction in arms sales both domestically and internationally. But over the longer term, aerospace engineers are looking to the NASA satellite programs and even to the interplanetary trips to Mars or the Moon as future opportunities.

Agricultural Engineering

Given its tremendous influence on the environment, it is surprising that agricultural engineering is rarely thought of (except by its practitioners) as being in the vanguard of environmental research and innovation. One reason for this is undoubtedly the small size of the profession, which has roughly 10,000 practitioners. Most of these engineers work for the manufacturers of agricultural machinery (tractors, combines, harvesters, and the like), and this close industry–professional affiliation is probably another reason.

Agricultural engineering dates to the late 1800s, when the unquestioned success of farm machinery in increasing farm productivity led to the growth of large machine-manufacturing firms. The American Society of Agricultural Engineering (ASAE) was founded in 1907. Its growth was aided by the strength of the network of land-grant colleges in the Midwest and West, where most agricultural engineering departments were then and are today.

Besides tractor-powered machinery, agricultural engineers develop mechanical systems for irrigation and for distribution of seeds, fertilizer, and pesticides; farm structures; and conveying and processing equipment for agricultural produce. Most work on plant and grain production; some also work on technical issues involving animal husbandry.

The mechanization of agriculture has drastically cut farm employment, ultimately leading to the depopulation of farming regions and the decline of the very community from which most agricultural engineers come. This issue has not gone unnoticed by the profession, whose leaders have sought a reevaluation of the types of technological development for which they are responsible. "ASAE's view of agriculture's future was expressed in the 1976 'Horizons Extravaganza' which painted 21st-century farming as an empty landscape peopled by monstrous mechanisms almost as intelligent as their creators and requiring little human guidance to accomplish enormous tasks," notes an unusually forthright history of ASAE, sponsored by the society itself [23].

Agricultural engineering is hardly the only profession at fault for unintended changes in agriculture, and as the agricultural community looks to develop small-scale alternative agricultural technologies, agricultural engineering could be a vital resource. Other environmental issues in which agricultural engineering technology is involved include soil and water conservation, tropical deforestation, pesticide and fertilizer use, the adaptation of new biotechnology to food production, and energy conservation. Liquid fuels derived from agricultural biomass (specifically, ethanol from corn fermentation) are edging closer to being an economically viable alternative to oil. (Its cause has been aided by the fact that an ethanol/gasoline mixture, "gasohol," burns more cleanly in auto engines.)

The back-to-nature movement of the 1960s turned away from any application of modern technology to food production. The organic-farming movement of the 1990s, however, is using highly advanced technology to produce high yields without the heavy use of fertilizers or pesticides. Closer monitoring of soil conditions is helpful in this effort, as is the rotation of specific crops to maintain soil nutrition. Natural insect or animal predators help control pests.

Organically grown produce is generally more expensive than crops that use conventional agricultural techniques. But if consumer demand is high enough and durable enough and if agricultural engineers can help devise lower-cost production methods, organic farming may become the preferred technique of the future.

Computer and Science Engineering

Today's environmental professionals are creating the standards of proper practice as they go to work every day. Since the professions are so new, they are able to take full advantage of the latest technology; in essence, they have a blank slate to work with in devising methods of analysis and control of environmental hazards.

Thus, it is not surprising that the use of computers and computer programming is widespread at environmental science and engineering businesses and laboratories. In 1989, for example, when the first annual "Toxic Release Inventory" (TRI) was released by EPA, the output of 300 toxic chemicals by 17,500 manufacturers was made available on computer tapes by EPA [24]. Now, a community-activist group can obtain detailed data on the pollution caused by a local manufacturer; armed with this data, it can seek improvements in the manufacturer's operations.

The TRI is just one example of the power of computer databases in codifying vital environmental data. EPA also maintains databases of waste-prevention and waste-remediation technologies, of proper safety practices among environmental workers, and of the toxicological effects of industrial chemicals.

All of this creates a greater demand for computer hardware and software, which are the products of computer scientists and engineers. It would be next to impossible to determine how many of these computer professionals are employed specifically by environmental organizations; on the other hand, it is clear that nearly every medium-sized or larger environmental organization has a staff of computer specialists.

Computer science is a very large field; the number of graduates is approximately 36,000 annually, and the Bureau of Labor Statistics counts nearly a million computer programmers and systems analysts in the national economy. Computer engineering, an offshoot of electrical engineering, is much newer and much smaller; about 4,300 graduate from colleges annually, and the number of working computer engineers is probably in the range of several tens of thousands.

Computer science developed as a field of academic study in the 1960s as the computer itself became commercially important. Previously, those who programmed computers had mathematics, electrical engineering, physics, or other science-oriented backgrounds. The field has subdivided over the years between programmers, who write the code that makes up a computer program, and systems analysts, who are the architects of systems of programs that run computers or that help develop new types of computers. (Generally, programmers work for systems analysts.)

Computer engineering developed as more and more electrical engineers devoted themselves totally to computer design and production. Many computer engineering departments were hived off electrical engineering departments in the 1970s and 1980s. In a simplified description, electrical engineers help produce microelectronic components; computer engineers connect these components to make a functioning computer; and computer scientists write the software that runs the computer.

The computer is expected to create enormous growth in demand for trained professionals in coming years. The Bureau of Labor Statistics projects the growth rate through the year 2000 at around 50 percent, which is among the highest of any occupation it surveys. The growing environmental activity in the United States will help boost this along. Computer scientists work at environmental firms to keep computer networks functioning and to develop methods of archiving essential data. Environmental work in the field—at a waste dump, for example, or when a scientist does a survey of life forms in a tropical forest—often requires new types of instrumentation, which are themselves designed and produced by computer engineers.

A research-oriented application of computer science is the development of software models of natural processes, such as the diffusion of pollutants into the atmosphere or the spread of contaminated groundwater under a hazardous waste landfill. Currently, the grandest of these models is the *general climatological model* (GCM), which seeks to determine the long-term effects of global warming on the Earth. Designing the model to run one way or another drastically changes the results 50 or 75 years from now.

A rather famous model dramatically raised the level of debate over environmental issues in the early 1970s. This was the Club of Rome report on the "Project on the Predicament of Mankind," which was then widely published as "The Limits to Growth" report [25]. This model of economic production, population growth, and environmental stresses was developed by Jay Forrester, a pioneering computer scientist at the Massachusetts Institute of Technology. The model, which ran on mainframe computers at MIT, predicted disastrous exponential growth in pollution, along with exponential declines in the availability of resources, if then-current trends of environmental production continued. The embargo of oil from the Middle Eastern OPEC countries following the 1973 Arab–Israeli war fanned the flames of near-panic over these predictions. Later, other studies generally discredited the near-term predictions of the model; too little accounting was made of changes in manufacturing practices and other adjustments that human society can make in the face of changing conditions [26].

The limits-to-growth model was one of the earliest of many later models and helped spur the development of futurology as a field of study. Modeling is significantly more sophisticated today, and the outcomes of these models often show the serious consequences of global trends. There is much more work to be done in modeling and program development.

Industrial Hygiene and Safety Engineering

One of the relatively unheralded achievements of modern manufacturing is its workplace safety. At the turn of the century, the death rate from industrial accidents was estimated at 73 per 100,000 per year; the equivalent figure today is around 9 per 100,000. This performance is, of course, important to industrial workers themselves—whose lives are at stake—as it is for their employers—who are liable for worker injuries, and whose plants' very existence depends on safe manufacturing processes.

As with occupational health and medicine (described in the preceding chapter), however, the value of industrial hygiene and safety engineering go well beyond the plant gate. Many types of manufacturing operations—especially those in the chemical process industries—represent a significant risk to the environment at large. When a chemical plant blows up, or a railroad car filled with hazardous materials wrecks, whole towns need to be evacuated. The resulting cleanup can cost billions of dollars.

In an even larger sphere, the work that industrial hygienists and safety engineers perform sets the pattern for many types of environmental research. The concept of "threshold limit value" (TLV)—a common term in describing maximum exposures to toxic chemicals—originated in workplace safety. The very fundamental concept of risk assessment, which is the evaluation of the risks of some activity versus alternative methods, or versus the benefits obtained thereby, began in transportation safety. Engineers working there learned to prioritize highway-improvement expenditures by putting the money where it would do the most good—where there were the most frequent or the most severe accidents. Now this mode of analysis is being applied to the cleanup of hazardous waste sites (where, sometimes, risk assessment shows that it is safer to leave the contamination in place), to factory design, to situations involving the choice of chemical ingredients, and to many other applications.

Risk assessment has taken a much larger role in overall environmental policymaking. In a quest for "better science" at EPA, Administrator William Reilly put out a call for a rigorous evaluation via risk-assessment methods for ranking the hazards humanity faces. This, in turn, should lead to a more rational allocation of limited resources to counter these risks. Is it better, for example, to spend money on dumpsite cleanups, or to attempt to arrest the loss of biodiversity in wilderness areas? Risk assessment is not without controversy (the usual argument against it is that it can be used to justify no actions whatsoever on some environmental problems, since the cost is too high). But with better methodologies, the resources society commits to environmental improvements may be spent more wisely.

Safety engineering *qua* safety engineering is taught at a limited number of schools (see Appendix E), but it gains its identity more from professional societies and their members' activities than from academic study. Students take courses in industrial engineering, environmental science, environmental health, or other programs, and then obtain practical experience in industry or government. A variety of certification programs are available, such as the Certified Safety Professional, which is administered by the Board of Certified Safety Professionals (an arm of the Society of Safety Engineers).

These days, the importance of training as a safety function cannot be overemphasized. Manufacturers have come to realize that only through training will the majority of workers learn to use safe practices. Thus, a large part of the safety professional's work is organizing or conducting training seminars for workers. Another part is the analysis of accidents that do occur, to trace their origin back to flaws either in work practices or worker preformance. This function is sometimes called *forensic engineering.*

Most large manufacturing plants have an in-house safety staff, which works in conjunction with security, fire protection, and health specialists. Safety professionals are also employed at consulting firms, and by industrial insurance companies.

Community right-to-know laws have created another responsibility for safety professionals: conveying plans and information to local public officials and concerned citizens. In the aftermath of the Bhopal, India, accident of a Union Carbide Corporation subsidiary in 1984, in which thousands were killed by escaping toxic gas, these community-relations programs have taken on a much larger role. Good communication skills and a willingness to deal with sometimes caustic public opinion are necessary attributes for the safety professional employed in industry.

Mining and Petroleum Engineering

The two disciplines, mining and petroleum engineering, are usually taught by different departments at most colleges. They are combined here because the environmental impact of their technologies is very similar.

The common element of these professions is the extraction of commercially useful materials from the ground. (In many cases, too, they are employed by the same corporations—oil companies that own coal and mining subsidiaries.) The environmental impact of large strip mines and the exploitation of the oil reserves believed to be in the Arctic Nature and Wildlife Refuge on the northern slope of Alaska are two of the major issues of the day. Both mining and petroleum engineers study how to obtain natural resources from underground reserves. Mining engineering involves many of the same principles as civil engineering, especially when tunnels are built. Petroleum engineers, on the other hand, study hydrogeology, the movement of fluids through underground rock formations.

Few people worry about the environmental conditions deep underground in an oil reservoir (except, of course, the petroleum engineers who have to figure out how to retrieve the oil). Mining engineers, by comparison, must be very concerned with the workplace environment for miners deep in underground tunnels. In coal mining, the presence of methane gas in the vicinity of coal seams is a constant worry; it is the cause of mine explosions. Recently, the exhaust of this methane gas into the atmosphere has come under criticism as a contributor to global warming. In the United States, at least, many coal operators take advantage of regulations that permit the sale of recovered methane gas at premium prices; devising the techniques to recover and process this gas has been a major accomplishment of mining engineering. Another workplace hazard for miners is rock dust, which can cause silicosis in human lungs. As with methane generation, proper ventilation is the key.

During the mid-1980s, the price of oil dropped dramatically, and oil companies cut back staff severely as a result. Many petroleum engineers were able to convert their expertise directly to the environmental remediation field, which was then beginning to boom. The critical skills involved an understanding of underground rock and water formations—the bread and butter of good petroleum engineering. Since then, the domestic oil industry has recovered somewhat, and most graduating petroleum engineers are hired into this industry. But the swings that occurred during the 1980s demonstrate the applicability of petroleum engineering expertise to environmental issues.

Both mining and petroleum engineers are concerned with the wastes produced by their respective activities. In mining, the waste is the dross left after valued minerals are recovered. At many mines, since this concentration or purification of minerals occurs at the mine mouth, the waste is produced where the minerals are recovered. In oil-well drilling, contaminated water and "mud" (rubble-like rock) are the waste by-product. Both activities are under regulations that strive to return the mine site or oil-well location to its original condition.

It used to be the case that a typical mine had a rock heap accompanying it; in the case of coal mining, this rubble was very often acidic, which then destroyed the water quality of streams and lakes in the vicinity. Now, these acidic wastes are treated to neutralize them, and the waste heap itself is covered over with topsoil, seeded with plants, and returned to a more-or-less natural condition. Some of the technology that was developed in this field is now being applied to the restoration of hazardous or municipal waste dumps. Most recently, in the case of gold mining, a technology called *heap leaching* has been developed. Low-grade gold-bearing rock (which is basically all that is left of gold resources in the United States) is piled into mounds and then sprayed with a solution containing cyanide compounds. Gold leaches out in the solution and is recovered by chemical treatment. The use of cyanide has obvious environmental hazards; gold miners are required to keep close control over its distribution. (Cyanide, unlike many other hazardous chemicals, will degrade into harmless byproducts relatively quickly; thus, it is usually not a long-term hazard.) Some mining researchers are investigating the use of bacteria or biologically derived compounds to accomplish the same sort of metal recovery as heap leaching. This *bioleaching* process holds the promise of a much more environmentally benign method of mineral recovery.

For petroleum engineers, the disposal of drilling wastes is often accomplished by reinjecting liquid wastes back into the well. This has the advantage of maintaining the underground pressure that causes the oil to flow out the well. (Such reinjection is a rapidly developing technology for recovering oil; petroleum engineers are also injecting carbon dioxide gas or water containing detergents to accomplish the same thing.)

Recently, the oil industry has been rocked by the realization that much of its equipment, when used repeatedly, gradually becomes radioactive. This radioactivity occurs naturally inside the Earth; the steady flow of slightly radioactive rock and fluid through the drilling equipment makes it "hot." DOE, which manages U.S. energy policy, and EPA are examining the problem, but no immediate solution is in sight. In the meantime, equipment companies that build and maintain oil-drilling equipment are making efforts to improve the workplace safety of their machine shops.

Mining and oil drilling, like the harvesting of forests, inevitably affect the environment around the work site and are ugly to contemplate regardless of how careful the engineers who perform the work are in taking precautions. These activities are of special concern in less-developed nations, hungry for the revenues that natural resources production offers and less fastidious about environmental effects. But both activities are essential to modern society. The challenge to these professions is to develop the least harmful means of extracting natural resources and the most successful means of restoring work sites to their original conditions.

Engineering Technology

Engineering technology is something of a shadow discipline, sharing many of the same subjects as regular engineering disciplines but lacking the stature or accreditation of the latter. There are programs in civil, chemical, manufacturing, mechanical, electrical, computer, and other forms of engineering technology. Some of these programs offer master's degrees; hardly any offer doctoral degrees. Although it lacks broad recognition, some 20,000 students graduate annually with associate, bachelor, or master's degrees in the various types of engineering technology.

Engineering technology grew in the 1960s and later out of two disparate trends: (1) the community college movement that took hold across the nation and (2) the desire on the part of some manufac-turers and other businesspeople to hire technically trained graduates who could immediately become productive members of the organi-zation's work force. Very often, a typical B.S.E. graduate has received substantial theoretical training in the design and research aspects of engineering but little training in basic industries, such as chemicals, electronics, machinery, construction, and the like. Instead of the advanced math and science courses typically required in engineer-ing, engineering technologists take applied courses on the type of industry that is of interest to them. Thus, when they graduate, they are relatively well versed in the customs of a specific industry. This type of training limits the graduate to career opportunities with only the specific type of business in which they are interested; the more theoretical training of an engineer is supposed to make the graduate more flexible in ultimate career directions.

Basically, each of the six types of engineering described in detail in the preceding sections has an engineering technology program that imitates it. The opportunities for environmentally related work follow the patterns described in those disciplines, with the exception that engineering technologists tend not to be involved in research. Engineering technology represents a somewhat more accessible technical training than most engineering programs; its existence offers the college student a chance to get involved in engineering-related technical work without hurdling the coursework that engi-neers are required to have.

CHAPTER FOUR

Green-Collar Professions

The preceding chapters explained the origins and current state of the leading scientific and technological disciplines, primarily as they are defined by college curricula. Many of these disciplines lead directly into jobs, which may or may not have a green-collar orientation. Many of these disciplines also apply to several distinct types of jobs in the environmental field.

To help organize your thinking on academic training and jobs, the following section lists many of the more prominent job titles in the green-collar field. The emphasis is on those for which a scientific or technical background is essential. There are, of course, other jobs for which this background is useful but not required.

Thinking About the Job Market

For most scientists, and for many technologists, the important career question is what scientific issues to pursue; the less important question is what type of employer. This is certainly a justifiable attitude for research positions, which share a certain commonality regardless of whether one's paycheck is provided by government, a university, or private industry. However, for all other types of green-collar work, the type of employer is a very important consideration.

The general stereotypes about employers are that private industry pays best; that the financial benefits in private industry are offset by the lack of freedom; and that government work pays poorly, but offers rapid immersion in a field, and provides a good springboard to a more lucrative private-industry job. These stereotypes are true, for the most part. The current university scene is one of scarce job openings, because schools are contracting somewhat in the early 1990s, as the number of college-age students declines. A turnaround in enrollments is expected later in this decade—by which time an undergraduate in college today might be winning a doctorate.

Government jobs happen to be good *at this moment,* but the swings in hiring trends by the federal government are rapid and unpredictable. As budgetary problems grow in importance, the notable growth in funding for EPA and other federal agencies may reach a plateau. On the other hand, federal government is also characterized by somewhat rapid turnover, creating new entry-level positions. EPA in the late 1980s and early 1990s was hiring about 800 new personnel each year.

The reason for high turnover in government employment is that the salaries in private industry are so good. Researchers with strong credentials in technology development can sometimes double their salaries by going private. Others develop a technology that looks promising, and through the combination of government research grants and Wall Street money, can become the founders of new environmental companies that can make the founder rich overnight. At the start of the 1990s, some inventors were plying the same route that many biotechnology and microelectronics researchers followed a decade previously, when "high-tech" stock offerings were the darlings of Wall Street. This type of development is extraordinarily unstable, and some researchers who think they are about to make a fortune instead wind up losing nearly everything they own.

Such start-up companies are the exception, rather than the rule, in private industry employment. Most jobs are at large, well-established manufacturing concerns, where environmental issues are handled as part of product design, factory management, and regulatory compliance. The next largest employment sector is consulting and business services. These are the firms hired by a manufacturer to inspect its pollution-control systems or waste-disposal practices in order to improve performance or comply with regulation. This has been the fastest-growing section of the green-collar job market, with some companies blooming at a rate of 30 to 50 percent per year for five or more years in a row.

Regardless of the type of employer, do not overlook the possibilities of teaching. "Interpretation" (explaining natural phenomena) is an important part of the work that government-employed park managers do; and even in private industry, the need for training to keep up with evolving regulations cannot be minimized. In universities, of course, teaching is an important job function for the young researcher.

Agronomist

Agronomy is in a ferment of new technology and new methods these days. While the traditional duties of agronomy continue—developing methods of planting, raising, and harvesting foodstuffs more economically—a host of new concerns are being raised, both within and outside of the agricultural sector of the U.S. economy.

For example, environmentally conscientious farmers and farm scientists are looking more closely at *low-input* agriculture. This term refers to the abandonment, or at least drastic reduction, of fertilizers, pesticides, and intensive plowing. As the channels for marketing environmentally "pure" foodstuffs develop and strengthen, more farmers are looking at low-input agriculture as a viable alternative to conventional farming practices. (Anyone with a smattering of a technical training is taken aback by the usual term that is given to these pure products—"100 percent organic"—as if crops grown with fertilizers and other chemicals are "nonorganic.")

Agronomy also is important in various types of nonfood growing, such as lawn care, landscaping, and land remediation. On the latter point, literature from the American Society of Agronomy states that "agronomists . . . are conducting research on the potential problems associated with recycling solid wastes into soil [and] are exploring techniques for reclaiming and revegetating drastically disturbed lands such as toxic waste dumps" (*Exploring Careers in Agronomy*, 1989, p. 10).

For the profession as a whole, the outlook is clouded by the severe downturn in employment caused by the slumping agriculture markets in the United States. Although food production has not shrunk, employment in the field has. Enrollments in colleges have shown a corresponding decline. However, many agronomy educators predict drastic shortages of suitably trained professionals in coming years.

Air Quality Engineer

Developing technologies both to analyze and control air pollution requires relatively sophisticated engineering skills. The new Clean Air Act, passed in late 1990, requires a complex set of counter-measures to air emissions. These include the reduction of so-called fugitive emissions (which are the small leaks that occur in factories, rather than what comes out of a smokestack), restrictions on automotive exhausts, reduction of sulfur dioxide and nitrous oxides from utilities and other power plants, and more study and control of indoor air quality. Simply to confirm the existence of some of these types of pollution is not a trivial task.

Most engineers involved with power production have a mechanical engineering degree, but studies such as chemistry, chemical engineering, or environmental engineering are also appropriate. Jobs occur at engineering consulting firms, in state government and at EPA, and among manufacturers and utilities.

Biologist

The study of biology is one of the core preparations for environmental work, and, since nearly 45,000 students graduate annually at all academic levels in this field, it is also one of the most popular college majors. The job title of "biologist" is rare because there are so many well-established specialties, such as aquatic biologist, biochemist, botanist, geneticist, zoologist, microbiologist, and others. (Ecology, generally a part of most biology programs, is treated separately here.)

Many biologists find work in environmental laboratories, working basically under the same conditions as chemists (see entry)—running tests and making evaluations. The key difference, of course, is that the biologist may be dealing with living creatures rather than test tubes and electronic analyzers. The *bioassay*, by which the health effects of a contaminant in water or air are measured by its effect on fish, microbes, plants, or other life forms, is a common feature of environmental studies.

Biology is the gateway to a great variety of other professions mentioned here, including ecologist, wildlife manager, toxicologist, industrial hygienist, and biostatistician. The entire realm of health care beckons, from physician, to epidemiologist, to health care researcher. Biologists tend to have advanced schooling; roughly one out of eight go on to obtain an advanced degree in biology, and many others go on to medical school or other forms of advanced education.

Microbiologists are finding fruitful opportunities in *bioremediation* work, by which naturally occurring microbes or genetically selected ones are used to detoxify underground aquifers. (The first genetically engineered microbe to win a patent, in fact, was one under development for bioremediation.) Many companies that service the wastewater treatment industry also employ biologists.

Average starting salaries are in the range of $18,000 to $24,000, depending on the type of employment (lower for straight lab work, higher for design or research). Projected growth is 15 percent.

Biostatistician

Biostatistics (and the more-or-less synonymous term *biometrics*) is the statistical analysis of health condition, usually of human health. Biostatistical work has become especially important in the risk assessments that are carried out in conjunction with pollution-control operations or with the determination of the cause of disease or injury. The split between a knowledge of biology and a knowledge of statistics is fairly even, but in most schools, the biostatistics are learned in the biology department. An advanced degree is often desirable. The heavy quantitative aspect of biostatistics makes it imperative that computer skills be well developed.

The statistical interpretation of health effects is one of the most controversial in medical circles. The connection between chemicals and cancer, for instance, has been in a state of turmoil for years over the validity of the Ames test as a measure of risk. Most biostatisticians work for the federal government, although there are many opportunities in the health care field in association with hospitals or contractors that provide this statistical service.

Chemical Engineer

A chemical engineering degree gives its holder broad entree into nearly all aspects of the environmental field except research (which would be open to the Ph.D. chemical engineer) and medical specialties. The irony is that chemical engineering enrollments have declined steadily since 1984, and half as many students are graduating now with a B.S.E. degree as did then. Salaries, not surprisingly, have shot upward and now start at around $35,000. In some states, a professional engineer (P.E.) license can be obtained, which is helpful for any engineer involved in public works projects (where the possession of a P.E. license is often mandatory).

The chemical industry and engineering/consulting firms are the highest bidders for chemical engineers and, with the supply shortage, are taking most of them. The heart of chemical engineering education involves an understanding of *unit operations*, the basic steps by which a material is transformed from its raw to finished state. This knowledge applies readily to projects like Superfund remediation (where one or a few unit operations are used). The familiarity with chemistry enables the chemical engineer to be adept at workplace safety, waste-handling or recycling activities, or air- and water-pollution control.

According to federal data, there are about 49,000 chemical engineers. Projected growth over this decade is 16.4 percent.

Chemist

The laboratory is the traditional home of chemists, but the need to gather data from polluted dumps or sick buildings is bringing them out of the lab. A steadily growing revolution in laboratory instrumentation enables chemists to perform many varied analytical tasks, such as sensing underground deposits, measuring the air quality high in the sky over a factory, or analyzing the combustion byproducts of automobile exhausts.

Laboratory employment, however, does not pay very well—about $24,000 annually—so many chemists go on for advanced degrees or seek employment opportunities outside the laboratory. Academic training in environmental studies would make the chemist a good candidate for working in consulting or assuming a managerial role in a laboratory, with somewhat higher pay.

Some chemists' positions are more involved with day-to-day operations, such as at a water-treatment works, where the varying quality of incoming wastewater calls for variations in the chemical treatments provided. And in industry generally, many chemists do research on improving production processes, reducing wastes, or inventing new products. Some of these jobs go by the title of "environmental chemist."

BLS says that there are about 80,000 chemists working currently; the single largest employer is the pharmaceutical industry. Overall growth is projected at 13.7 percent, which is average for all professions.

Civil/Environmental Engineer

The civil/environmental engineer is probably the most common type of engineer at work in the environmental arena today. Overall job prospects are in a slump currently due to the overheated construction business of the 1980s. By some estimates, we will be well into the second decade of the twenty-first century before all the unfilled commercial space in downtown cities is rented. Environmental engineering is usually offered in conjunction with a civil engineering degree, as a concentration or option, especially at the graduate level.

So, it is a good thing for the profession that the environmental business is booming. Civil engineers are best known for moving earth, and the Superfund projects across the country provide a natural application for this skill. Depending on the program attended, there are possibilities for combining civil and environmental training; in this case, the engineer learns more about groundwater, solid-waste disposal, and similar subjects. A large proportion of civil engineers in private practice seek to obtain a professional engineer license, which is mandatory in certain circumstances for public works design and construction.

Average pay for starting B.S.E. civil engineers is around $28,000. In government employment, it starts at around $27,000.

Community Relations Manager

Community right-to-know laws now require engineering firms or manufacturers to reveal detailed information on the expected risks of a cleanup action or for preparing for emergencies near chemical plants, utilities, and other factories. The conduit through which this information is passed is the community relations manager.

Essentially a function of the public relations department at large corporations, community relations management calls for a rather complete set of communication, diplomatic, and technical skills. Many managers lack an engineering or science degree, but, in order to be successful, such managers must be able to cope with the flood of scientific data and analysis that are issuing from Washington and state capitals.

Community relations managers find employment at consulting firms, especially those involved with the cleanup work paid for by the federal Superfund, and at manufacturers, especially chemical companies and others with a heavy burden of pollution-control responsibility. The skills learned and applied in performing community relations work lend themselves readily to environmental activism, public relations, and other communications-dependent professions.

There has not been, as yet, a thoroughgoing survey of job titles, salaries, and related issues for the profession, but, if the patterns of public relations professionals set the trend, starting salaries should be in the vicinity of $22,000 to $24,000. At the top of the heap, corporate environmental affairs managers can command salaries of $60,000 or better. As the recently organized National Association of Professional Environmental Communicators (see Appendix A) gets under way, more such data should become available in the near future.

Computer Specialist/Database Manager

The computer revolution of the past 25 years has certainly influenced the environmental field. Besides being a general-purpose office tool that any executive should have a passing familiarity with, the computer is used in highly complex research simulations of environmental conditions, both as a monitor for the vast array of manufacturing processes that must be tightly controlled to prevent accidental emissions and as a record-keeping device for the flood of paperwork that environmental projects create.

The multidisciplinary nature of environmental work means that no one profession or field of study has all or even most of the answers for an environmental project. Thus, there is a need for various specialists to pool their knowledge in a database to which all interested parties have access. EPA runs a series of such databases on existing regulations, preferred remediation technologies, hazardous chemicals, and many others. Every year, EPA makes available the "Toxic Release Inventory," a summing-up of all the pollution generated by industry; a computer-readable version of this inventory is used by local and national environmental groups to pinpoint what factories in what cities are a target for legal action.

On the research side, the subject of "modeling" is a dynamic focus for studying environmental issues. To predict, 50 or 100 years from now, the effects of global warming, computer scientists and physicists have developed a variety of *general climatological models* (GCMs) that simulate the actions and reactions of sunlight, weather, rainfall, and pollution on the Earth's climate. Today's regulatory decisions are being made on the basis of the output of these GCMs.

Database management, the gathering and sorting of data and information, is a key computer specialty throughout industry, consulting firms, and government. Graduates of computer science, information science, or library management can find opportunities among consulting firms, government agencies, and large corporations. The research applications of computers usually call for technical training in addition to computer science, in fields such as mathematics or physics.

The number of computer professionals throughout the U.S. work force is huge—some 1 million at least—according to federal data. The projected growth rate is high as well, pegged at 50 percent or better over this decade. Computer specialists who want to work in the environmental field should plan to take some courses in science, public affairs, or health administration to complement their computer courses.

Contract Administrator

Overseeing the work of hired contractors is a critical skill for most public agencies, which are given a budget and the responsibility to accomplish a set of goals by hiring private companies to carry out the work. The pattern is set by the construction industry, which is hired by a firm to design and build some structure while meeting a time and financial budget. There is quite a bit of construction-related work performed at various government environmental agencies, but environmental work also entails many other types of contracts, such as scientific studies, policy studies, surveys of technical specialists or the general public, and more.

The contract administrator's duty is to clearly understand the guidelines under which a contract is being offered, convey these guidelines to the contractor, and then see to it that they are met. The skills involved include cost estimation, an understanding of regulatory codes, and a familiarity with how the work is usually performed.

For these reasons, contract administration is seldom an entry-level job. More often, one gains experience by working for a contractor or as an assistant administrator.

Even so, one of the truisms of the workplace shows up dramatically in contract administration. In the private sector, it could be years before a newly hired engineer or business manager gets to administer contracts; at public agencies, this could be one's responsibility in just a couple of years.

The job is often specified such that an engineering background is required, but frequently, other types of training, including general business administration, are appropriate. Expertise in cost estimating is also valuable.

Earth Scientist

The earth sciences comprise geology, oceanography, soil science, atmospheric science and meteorology, and certain specialties in physics and astronomy. The earth-based specialties (geological engineering, paleontology, geochemistry, geophysics) suffered a decline during the 1980s, as enrollments and job opportunities plummeted due to the collapse of the oil-exploration business. Nevertheless, in 1988, 40 percent of such scientists worked for the oil and gas industries; the second highest total was the federal government (17 percent).

Atmospheric science underwent a big jump in interest during the 1980s as a result of the chlorinated-fluorocarbon (CFC) debate; this new interest will probably continue, if not strengthen, as a result of the global warming debate. These concerns translate into Ph.D.-level jobs in government and academia. Teaching positions are expected to open up further as this decade wears on, with more college-level teachers reaching retirement age and a projected growth in college-age students.

Ph.D.-level geoscientists get a starting salary of around $50,000 in private industry. In federal government employ, the starting pay is around $35,000. At the B.S. level, starting salaries for the two categories are, respectively, $23,000 and $17,000.

Dramatic things are in store for earth scientists due to the increasing use of *remote-sensing technology* (data from satellites). This technology is already being used to locate buried hazardous wastes in Eastern Europe (the data is from U.S. satellites), and its use in mineral exploration, agriculture, and natural-resource management is growing.

Ecologist

People who call themselves "ecologists" are generally involved in research, usually in the academic arena. Workers who apply ecological principles to environmental needs are foresters, soil scientists, wildlife biologists, and others.

As a study of living things, ecology is a subset of biology (see "Biologist"). It differs in that it is the study of systems of living things—an *ecosystem*. This is one of the more critical technical needs in the environmental field these days, as nature groups, industrialists, and wildlife lovers seek to preserve wild habitats and slow the extinction of endangered species.

Mid-1980s estimates of entry-level salaries by the Ecological Society of America were around $20,000, with Ph.D. holders commanding $55,000 or more. The study also showed that nearly two out of three researchers held academic positions. In academic research, the trend is usually toward specializing in the ecology of one system (or even one organism in a system), whereas in the working world of wildlife preservation the need is usually for ecologists who can deal with varieties of systems.

Environmental Protection Specialist

This job title is favored by EPA to describe, primarily, an entry-level position whose occupant can oversee a Superfund contract or monitor a manufacturer's record-keeping routines. A knowledge of applicable federal laws and regulations is essential. A scientific background is desirable but not essential, while quantitative skills such as accounting or statistics are a boost.

For EPA itself, the work essentially entails reviewing contracts and reports, making site visits to monitor actual conditions, and making judgments based on the health and safety criteria that have been established for various toxic compounds. The work is primarily administrative in nature. EPA rates it at GS 9–11, or roughly $25,000 to $30,000 per year.

In the private sector, this responsibility translates into an environmental compliance specialist, who is likely an assistant to an environmental manager. This specialist keeps tabs on new regulations and is responsible for writing mandated reports. In the consulting industry, an engineering or a technical degree is strongly advised; in private industry, generally, a technical degree should suffice. Starting pay is around $28,000.

Forester

Here is a situation pulled from recent newspaper headlines: Medical researchers discover that an extract, called *taxol*, from the bark of a species of yew tree is a potentially powerful cancer drug. The older the bark, the better the yield of the drug. The yew trees are not extremely rare; on the other hand, they do not cover whole mountainsides.

What does the forester bring to an issue like this? First, how many such yew trees are there, and where? A survey can be made. Second, if the choice is to harvest them (recognizing that each tree harvested diminishes the stock), how should it be done? Third, if there is a reasonable chance of domesticating the tree and growing whole fields of it, how is this to be done? The forester has many of the technical tools to answer these questions.

The yew tree is only the latest example of how humanity has found a useful purpose for the vast array of trees that cover the Earth's surface. The ultimate use, however, is one that calls that extensive coverage itself into question. The subject of deforestation—the elimination of old, stable forests, to be replaced by cattle ranching lands in Brazil or to be developed for housing and industry in the United States—is driving much research these days. Forests are one of nature's balancing wheels against the rise of carbon dioxide in the atmosphere and the resulting global warming. Yet, at the very time that carbon dioxide levels are increasing fastest, so is deforestation.

There are some 40,000 forestry and related conservation workers (nonscientists) in the United States, and another 27,000 foresters and conservation scientists, according to federal statistics. The growth rate for the near future is rather low—8 to 10.7 percent over the decade. But increasingly, the issues of land use, soil preservation, parks administration, and tree-dependent industries such as paper and lumber, will call on the forestry professions to provide guidance to industry and government.

About two-thirds of forestry professionals work for the federal, state, and local governments; the remainder are in private industry, usually at paper and lumber companies. Foresters also figure in recreation, land planning and preservation, agriculture, and environmental research.

Some 50 schools provide a bachelor degree accredited by the American Society of Foresters. An increasing trend in recent years is to require forestry professionals to become more familiar with other parts of the forest ecosystems—the wildlife, plant life other than trees, even the microbiology. In addition, with the increasing regulatory requirements, a knowledge of forestry and land-use rules is vital.

Geological Engineer/Hydrogeologist/ Hydrologist

This more technological (rather than scientific) look at the Earth is benefiting from the new emphasis on groundwater and Superfund cleanups. The concentration on underground physical conditions makes the profession something of a specialty, but then, what part of America does not need or use water from the ground? Hydrology, specifically, tends to focus on water-resources management (thus including above-ground and below-ground water) in support of agriculture and other natural-resource applications.

The growing problems in various parts of the country in obtaining adequate water supplies should make some states (in the West, in particular) more active in hiring these types of specialists. A decline in enrollments over the past decade should make finding a job easier now. Starting salaries are around $28,000 per year; oil companies pay considerably more.

Hazardous Materials Specialist

The transport, use, and disposal of hazardous materials is one of the front lines of environmental work. This job title, which has come into more common use due to federal environmental and workplace-safety laws, originally showed up only at chemical or oil companies. Now, it is common at pharmaceutical firms, hospitals, sanitation departments, fire departments, government environmental agencies, and shipping companies. There are plenty of these jobs at consulting firms as well.

The hazardous materials specialist (colloquially, the "hazmat" or "hazops"—for hazardous operations—specialist) works closely with industrial hygienists and safety engineers (see entries); the latter two professionals set the policies that assure a safe workplace environment, and the hazmat specialist carries them out. These duties include monitoring worker operations, inspecting storage areas or transport facilities, and seeing to it that the appropriate paperwork has been filed upon shipment or delivery of hazardous materials.

In hospitals, pharmaceutical firms, laboratories, and health care facilities, the job title is sometimes "biohazards specialist." The functions are the same, except that a knowledge of biological hazards (infectious materials, radioactive compounds, and so forth) is required instead of chemical knowledge.

A related specialty, which usually goes by the title of "emergency response specialist," involves professionals who handle fires, chemical spills, oil spills, and other disasters. When a fire department, for example, races to a warehouse fire, the safety specialists need to find out rapidly what chemicals or materials are present and how they may be best contained while the fire is smothered.

As these varied examples show, many different educational or experiential backgrounds are called on for hazmat specialists. One can study for a bachelor degree in safety engineering, industrial hygiene, or health technology. Alternatively, a general background in industrial work can be combined with certificate courses in hazmat operations (see Appendix E). Salaries will vary widely, depending on the level of responsibility, the type of employer, and the specialized knowledge or experience one has.

Health Physicist

Health physics is the term used to describe the effects of radioactivity and other forms of concentrated atomic energy on the human body. The profession originated (as did atomic energy itself) in the hush-hush military research of the 1940s that led to the development of the atomic bomb. During the 1950s and 1960s, peaceful uses of nuclear energy became more common: uranium mining, commercial power plants, medical therapies of various sorts, and diagnostics.

By design, the environmental problems of nuclear materials were kept quite distinct from those of other hazardous materials, as was the realization that the United States' programs for nuclear materials processing were as pollution-ridden as much private industry manufacturing. Now a bill of more than $150 billion for cleaning up military sites is coming due.

Health physicists get involved in ongoing uses of nuclear energy, or cleanup projects, in much the same way a safety engineer or industrial hygienist would. Because of the distinct effects of radiation on the human metabolism, however, specialized training is necessary. Much of this training takes place at the graduate-school level, although some practicing health physicists can maintain their professional status through continuing-education programs.

The basic work is overseeing the methods by which workers protect themselves from radiation hazards. New emission-control technology is continually being developed, and health physicists can review these developments to see what is appropriate to the production methods at a particular facility. In hospitals and clinics, health physicists also monitor the practices of health care workers. There are numerous research objectives, such as developing new monitoring techniques, new methods of analyzing exposure data, and the like. Like most other safety professionals, health physicists also expend much effort on training new workers.

The outlook for health physics is good at the moment, due to the expanding Pentagon program for cleaning up nuclear wastes. Prospects for uranium mining and commercial nuclear power depend on the decisions that utility regulators will be making in coming years regarding whether or not to build new power plants. In the meantime, though, a number of old nuclear plants that were built 30 or more years ago will start being decommissioned. The methods used to dismantle these facilities will require at least as much attention as was paid to their initial construction.

Industrial Hygienist

The Stealth bomber that figured in the recent Iraq–Kuwait war was produced by an aerospace contractor using the latest technology in polymeric composite materials. The wings and other body parts are not made from aluminum or other metal but rather are molded from liquid plastic resins, fiberglass, and other materials. Workers who constructed the planes complained of a host of mysterious maladies during the construction job. Are these illnesses job related? Are they related to the use of the new composites? Is there a way to protect against them if they are?

These are the sorts of issues that industrial hygienists address. In a time when new manufacturing techniques are being tried throughout industry, new safety standards must be instituted as well. Industrial hygienists are versed in human physiology and learn techniques to analyze worker operations to find where problems can occur. In turn, these workplace standards set the stage for all the usage instructions that consumers receive when they purchase paints, household cleaners, tools, and other products.

Most recently, a set of standards has evolved for carrying out environmental work, such as removing asbestos from buildings or cleaning up toxic dumps and spills. When thousands of workers were hired by Exxon Co. to clean up the Exxon Valdez spill, industrial hygienists went along to attempt to minimize health risks to those workers.

Undergraduate programs in industrial hygiene are rare. Most practitioners study a subject such as chemistry, biology, or engineering and then add on graduate courses in industrial hygiene. Starting salaries are above $24,000 and can rise quickly based on experience and employer. There are jobs among federal or state agencies (in particular, the Occupational Safety and Health Administration—see Appendix C), at large manufacturing companies, and among consulting firms.

Interpreter

Interpretation is the technical term for guiding or teaching visitors in the biosystems and natural history of the park or wildlife refuge they are visiting. The job involves the skills of a teacher and an awareness of what safety and park-use rules should be followed when, for example, a walking tour is being conducted. Interpretive jobs are very often seasonal, and the pay is minimal. In favor of the job, however, are the valuable skills it teaches those who plan to go on to develop more professional careers.

Being an interpreter is a good job for college students because the hiring season often corresponds with summer vacation. When looking for employers, be aware of opportunities available locally or at state or private parks—not just at the grand federal parks in the West.

Lawyer

Liability, penalty, criminal felony—these are some of the worries that keep corporate managers alert these days where the environment is concerned. Many federal and state laws passed during the 1980s included stiff penalties—including jail time—for business managers responsible for intentional pollution. In late 1990, according to a boastful U.S. Justice Department, indictments jumped 33 percent over the preceding year, conviction rates were running at 96 percent, and fines totaling $56 million had been assessed.

These legal concerns represent the ultimate outcome of pollution regulations. Most industry management tries to comply, and one of the main resources for developing a compliance record is the advice of an environmental lawyer. The latest laws are especially complex, and the interpretation of their regulations is an onerous task for industry managers. It is no surprise, then, that environmental law is the fastest-growing practice at law firms.

In the legal profession, the choices are generally among solo practice, joining a law firm, or working as a corporate lawyer. Not to be overlooked are government positions, through which many lawyers obtain highly valued experience in environmental regulation. While the big-time, large law firms, with 250 or more lawyers, can offer salaries of $75,000 and up to their new hires, the average income of all lawyers is actually considerably lower—around $35,000 for those starting out and rising to around $100,000 for the experienced.

An interesting facet of environmental work is the evolution of new types of regulations and enforcement procedures. Can one legislate recycling of postconsumer wastes? Can pollution "rights" be traded, much as stocks are bought and sold, in a market-driven effort to determine the industries where pollution can be controlled most efficiently? How can a debt-for-nature swap be organized to help an indebted Third World country preserve its forests? Many lawyers find themselves involved in recommending how best to bring all this about.

"To be a good environmental lawyer, first you have to be a good lawyer," comments Clyde Szuch, managing partner at Pitney,

Hardin, Kipp, & Szuch, a Florham Park, New Jersey, law firm. "An undergraduate technical degree would certainly be useful for the budding environmental lawyer, but it is not necessary."

Meteorologist

The weather forecaster plays an important role in agriculture, transportation, the military, and other activities where knowing day-to-day environmental conditions is important. In recent years, this concern has risen by several orders of magnitude as researchers realized that weather patterns were falling more and more under the influence of human activity. Ozone layer depletion, global warming, tropical forest destruction, and desertification are among the issues now brought together under the umbrella term "global change." Global change is certain to be *the* environmental issue at the beginning of the twenty-first century. This emphasis will greatly expand the research horizons—and the job opportunities—for meteorologically-trained scientists.

The weather forecaster to whom commuters listen while getting ready to drive to work is an *operational* or *synoptic* meteorologist. Many of these meteorologists work for the National Weather Service, a part of the National Oceanic and Atmospheric Administration. Scientists with a longer-term perspective on weather are called *physical meteorologists* or *climatologists*, and are concerned with the fundamental physical properties of the air and atmospheric strata that surround the Earth. Because of similarities in scientific properties between the atmosphere and the oceans, and the links whereby the patterns of one environment affect the other, oceanographers often have common interests with physical meteorologists.

It is possible to obtain employment as a meteorologist with a bachelor degree in some science (or in meteorology itself) but, increasingly, positions in the field are held by those with advanced degrees. A large portion of meteorological research involves instrumentation—new devices that can measure upper atmospheric properties; laboratory simulators of atmospheric conditions; models of weather phenomena that run on the biggest, fastest supercomputers. Thus, there is ample opportunity to specialize in electronics and instrumentation within the field of meteorology.

Noise-Control Specialist

Among the many programs that Ronald Reagan (well-known hearing-aid wearer) shut down during the early 1980s was EPA's research in noise control and the regulation of noise pollution. The business has by no means disappeared; all airports, for example, need to keep tabs on the noise levels around their facilities, as do many heavy-industry manufacturers. Acoustical engineering is a thriving field due to the growth of recorded-music media and advancing electronics. Some of this work is rubbing off in the noise-control arena, where, for example, manufacturers are developing methods of neutralizing noise by countering it with precisely offset sound frequencies. Noise control is of most concern to developers of heavy industrial machinery, where Occupational Safety and Health Administration regulations are still fairly rigorous. Noise control is also becoming more important to building dwellers.

Most research is the province of the advanced-degree holder. Starting salaries for Ph.D.-level scientists are in the range of $40,000 to $50,000; at the lower-degree levels, most engineers or scientists have salaries in the range of $28,000 to $35,000.

Occupational/Environmental Medical Doctor

Occupational or environmental medicine (the term that will be used hereafter) is a natural outgrowth of the developments in workplace safety and the recognition that environment plays an important role in human health. There are a great number of occupations concerned with human health in the environment: industrial hygienist, occupational safety professional, safety engineer, and so forth. The job title environmental medical doctor, however, signifies that this is the only one where a professional medical degree is required.

Just as medical doctors are surrounded by nurses, diagnosticians, therapists, medical record analysts, and other specialists when treating a patient, so is an environmental health doctor surrounded by safety and environmental health professionals. The doctor is the one who can prescribe treatment for a medical condition, and who performs research to evaluate unknown risks in various industrial or other synthetic environments.

To be an environmental health doctor requires going to medical school and, as other medical specialists do, concentrating postgraduate study in a specialty—in this case environmental health. Jobs are available either at clinics (where the sick or injured are treated) or in research.

A good example drawn from current research on environmental health is the topic of chemical sensitivity. Certain people have developed allergies to an entire host of synthetic chemicals—plastics, solvents, paints, food ingredients, fibers, and more—because of exposure to some potent chemical that caused a reaction with their immune systems. How these allergies are created and how their symptoms might be alleviated are the research questions that environmental health doctors are addressing. The environmental health doctor depends on extensive toxicological data, biostatistics surveys, and a knowledge of human physiology to make a determination in these cases.

The entire American health care system has been on a rapid growth curve for more than a decade, and only a moderate slowdown is expected in coming years. Within these generally improving employment conditions, environmental health is one of the strongest fields. Research hospitals have organized special practices for those who are believed to have unique problems in dealing with modern environmental hazards. In addition, the broader issues of the effects of pollution on human health in general will continue to grow in the future.

Planner

Everyone makes plans, but only planners make them for a living. Planning is a critical part of local and state government, as these agencies seek to guide the development of their economies, public services, and resource development on a rational basis. This rationality continually butts up against politics, history, tradition, and the individual desires of residents, constituents, and, not incidentally, taxpayers and voters. Planning can be a frustrating line of work, but it continually holds the promise of providing a better life for a larger fraction of the population, when natural and manufactured resources are used efficiently.

Planners accumulate information on current uses of public and private resources in a region, compare them with the desired future goals or needs, and try to develop a logical way of reaching these goals. Zoning regulations, for example, are a powerful tool for controlling the commercial, residential, and preservationist needs of a community. A city planner may recommend changing or establishing a zoning regulation to, say, preserve a historical landmark district or to prevent the overdevelopment of a lakefront.

According to the American Planning Association, the leading professional organization of the field, about two out of three planners work for government, with a quarter of the entire profession employed at the city level. The remaining third work in private business, education, or nonprofit organizations. Most have a master's degree or are in the process of obtaining one. Median salaries are around $24,000 for the relatively inexperienced, while those with more than ten years' experience earn above $45,000.

Currently, the straitened circumstances of many city and state budgets, especially among the most populous states, make employment prospects rather dim. However, the need for more and better planning continues to grow. Time and again, the success of transforming economic backwaters into "in" places where people and employers can relocate, while preserving the natural advantages of a region, has been demonstrated by professional planning.

Risk Manager

Risk management brings together the technical concerns of safety engineers, toxicologists, and industrial hygienists with the business concerns of corporate financial officers and administrators. It is an evolving position at most corporations, and the responsibilities vary from firm to firm.

In general, though, most positions share an interest in the liability insurance needs of the corporation and compliance with governmental regulations. "Risk management" as an academic discipline is taught at graduate business schools as part of a specialization in insurance issues. Other sectors of society, such as government agencies, insurance companies themselves, and environmental consulting firms, also are looking for the input of risk managers to help them deal with accident prevention and, when accidents occur, an apportioning of costs.

Typically, a risk manager examines the policies offered by insurance firms and compares them with the costs of self-insurance (which is becoming more common among high-risk industries due to the expense of purchased insurance). This manager will also keep apprised of new trends in governmental regulation because, as various activities come under such regulation, the responsibility for compliance carries with it a certain immunity to liability (provided that the regulations were fully met).

Thus, risk management combines the skills typically learned in an M.B.A. program with the specialized knowledge of the insurance industry. For this reason, an initial job in the insurance industry is often very helpful in getting a career going. Salaries depend on the type of employer and one's level of experience. For the top corporate jobs, sometimes reporting to the environmental manager or even to the board of directors, earnings can be as high as $100,000.

There is also a considerable amount of research being conducted with the goal of finding better predictors of the ultimate consequences of what activities are condoned today. Specialists trained in actuary science, statistics, public administration, and other programs are leading these efforts. There is little question that the responsibilities of the risk manager of the future will be quite different from those that exist today.

Safety Engineer

Safety engineers work in conjunction with industrial hygienists, hazardous materials specialists (see entries), and other professionals to assure a safe workplace. Many of the techniques developed by safety engineers carry over into the design of products that are used by everyday consumers; products such as tools, chemical compounds, heavy machinery, automobiles, and the like show the influence of safety engineering.

A very pronounced trend during the 1980s has been the development of so-called human factors; the term refers to the measurement of how individuals interact with machinery or how they use everyday items like chairs or ladders. *Human factors* and a related term, *ergonomics*, are strongly influencing the design of office equipment, computer workstations, airplane cockpits, kitchen utensils, and many other products. Because discerning consumers now demand ergonomically designed products, manufacturers are looking closely at the designs of their merchandise and are employing safety and human factors consultants to aid in improving these designs.

Safety engineers work at all major manufacturers, at public agencies, and for consulting firms. Many students combine an undergraduate degree in one or another engineering specialty with graduate schooling in safety engineering or with the many courses offered for safety and industrial hygiene (see Appendix E). However, an engineering degree is not mandatory. Starting salaries for B.S.E. graduates are around $30,000.

Soil Scientist

Soil science is one of the agronomy (see "Agronomist") specialties that has traditionally been most closely tied to agriculture. The majority of job slots have been with government, mostly for the benefit of agriculture through the Soil Conservation Service and related agencies. In private industry, a number of soil scientists have been employed by agricultural-chemical manufacturers, especially fertilizer suppliers. In the future, while this agriculture–soil science relationship will continue to dominate in terms of job slots, other sectors of the U.S. economy are calling for the expertise of soil scientists.

In particular, environmental consulting companies that perform Superfund-related cleanup work or that are involved in correcting or preventing the pollution of underground water reservoirs are hiring soil scientists. Landfills, much bemoaned by environmental activists and by city administrators, will remain a dominant factor in solid-waste disposal for years to come; the planning and operation of these facilities require soil science expertise. And, as land-use issues rise in importance in both populated and wilderness areas of the country, soil scientists are called on to help analyze and plan for environmental impacts.

Only a few hundred students study soil science in college these days; along with a slump in enrollments for nearly all agriculturally related majors, soil science has fallen as well. In recent years, there have been almost as many graduates with doctoral degrees as with bachelor degrees—an indication of the research orientation of the profession. Federal salaries range from about $16,000 to $28,000, depending on the degree held. Private industry is usually 10 to 20 percent higher.

Taxonomist

Taxonomy is a much honored but much ignored biological specialty today. That status is changing, however, as the issue of biodiversity comes to the fore.

The original biologists—even back to the time of Aristotle—were great organizers of families of living things. By comparing the characteristics of structure, habits, and physiology, these scientists were able to draw correlations among various types of life forms. This became a critical issue, of course, in the great debates on evolution of the nineteenth century. After that, however, taxonomy (or, to use the more modern term, *systemetrics*) began to fade from view. In this century, the field has been totally swamped by the attention paid to genetics and molecular biology.

Systemetrics is due for a revival, however, because it helps researchers address knotty questions about ecosystems, the effects of hybridization of species, and preservation of species. Now, working in concert with geneticists, taxonomists can address many of the uncertain questions about biodiversity and ecosystem maintenance.

The work remains much the same as it was a century ago. Taxonomists spend considerable time in the field (or in the jungle or under the ocean) collecting samples and making notes of wildlife habits. Back in the laboratory, precise measurements of physical dimensions and physiology allow the taxonomist to make decisions about how a life form should be categorized. Molecular biology assists in this effort by allowing the taxonomist to trace the DNA inheritance of a life form.

Nearly all taxonomists are affiliated with or employed by a university biology department. Some work for pharmaceutical companies (which depend on finding new plants as sources of medications) or conservation organizations. Prospects for overall employment of academic biologists are fair, especially later in this decade when the number of college enrollments is expected, once again, to rise.

Technical Writer

This title is being used to lump together a variety of positions that require skill in converting records or oral reports to finished documents. These positions share many of the same responsibilities as those of the community relations manager (see entry), with the proviso that, usually, the communications are between one organization and another rather than between an organization and the public.

A frequently seen title is "proposal writer." This individual has the responsibility for gathering together the technical and financial information that a consulting company develops in preparation for making a bid on a government or industry contract. The chances of winning these contracts are aided by delivering a well-written, polished proposal, and thus writers are hired to provide these finishing touches.

Once a project is concluded, a final report must often be issued, both to record what has been done and to provide useful information that might help in later projects. A job title sometimes seen in this context is that of "documentation specialist." Scientists conducting research are usually required to submit such reports when their studies are concluded, and some organizations employ editorial specialists to complete the documentation.

Yet another example can be seen among consulting firms or educational institutions that provide training for environmental specialists. Very often, there is no standard textbook for what is being taught; the instructor develops his or her own course material, which represents the collective experience of the organization offering the training. A writer can help prepare these materials.

A final example is writing for technical publications or book publishers. These organizations often employ journalists, but, in some cases, the job requires some level of technical training in addition to writing skills. With the right foresight, a journalism major can specialize in such technical writing by taking additional science or policy courses while in school or as a graduate student. Salaries vary considerably, depending on the type of employer and level of experience, but, usually, the technical writer can count on earning slightly more than the typical newspaper journalist, or currently around $19,000 for the recent graduate.

Toxicologist

Toxicology is the study of the adverse effects of the environment on human health. (There is also a subspecialty in animal toxicology.) The emphasis is usually on harmful chemicals; diseases caused by bacteria or other life forms are usually studied by biologists or epidemiologists.

Toxicologists spend much time in a laboratory, functioning essentially as detectives. For example, a certain medical condition may have been encountered; the toxicologist asks, what chemical is the cause of it, and where did this chemical come from? Due to this close connection between chemicals and human health, many toxicologists work in the pharmaceutical industry, both to ensure the safety of pharmaceutical compounds and to preserve the health of workers. Toxicologists were among the first to discover the link between lung diseases and asbestos, the degenerative effects of lead, and the dangers of air pollutants such as ozone and nitrous oxides.

It is possible to study toxicology at the undergraduate level, but many practitioners go on for graduate degrees. Some also take the route of obtaining a medical doctor degree.

Besides the pharmaceutical industry, jobs are available at chemical companies, food and cosmetics manufacturers, public health agencies, consulting firms, and in academia. For doctoral-degree holders, current salaries are in the range of $36,000 to $45,000. Certification is available through a variety of professional organizations.

Water Quality Technologist

A decade or so ago, it was common in most parts of the country to take water totally for granted. Relative to many other countries in the world, the United States was blessed with plentiful supplies of clean water.

In reality, these water supplies were already the product of much technical expertise in developing water resources, transporting them to where they were needed, and arranging for their distribution. The system ran very well with little public attention.

Today, the situation is changing. New sources of contamination appear, causing water wells to be shut down or water treatment plants to go temporarily out of service. A drought—not the first, but the first with California as the most populous state in the country—in western U.S. regions is changing agricultural plans dramatically.

All of these problems make the prospects for careers in water quality management brighter. This specialty, taught (usually at graduate levels) at many of the land-grant colleges of the Midwest and

West, calls for familiarity with a diverse array of physical and social sciences—chemistry, geology, hydrogeology, public administration, and agronomy. The simple fact of the matter is that, as population increases, more demands are put on all natural resources—water included.

Many water quality managers work for local, state, and federal government. Water quality managers oversee the operation of water and wastewater treatment plants, irrigation systems, and urban water-delivery systems. Other employers include agriculture and industries that are heavy consumers of water—pulp and paper manufacturing, public utilities, and food processing. Managers in these industries must assure the quality of water going into the production machinery of the plants, as well as maintain control over the contamination of the water resulting from its industrial use. Manufacturers and the engineering consulting firms that serve them are also required to assist in cleaning up previous contamination of groundwater and preventing future contamination.

Salaries vary considerably based on the type of employer and level of education. For bachelor-degree holders, starting pay is around $18,000 in government employ and approximately 10 to 20 percent higher in private industry.

APPENDIX A

Nonprofit Environmental Organizations

Air and Waste Management
  Association
P.O. Box 2861
Pittsburgh, PA 15230
(412) 232 3444

Alliance for Engineering in
  Medicine and Biology
1101 Connecticut Ave., NW
Washington, D.C. 20036
(202) 857 1199

Alliance for Environmental
  Education, Inc.
10751 Ambassador Dr., Suite 201
Manassas, VA 22110
(703) 335 1025

American Academy of
  Environmental Engineers
132 Holiday Ct., Suite 206
Annapolis, MD 21401
(301) 266 3311

American Association for the
  Advancement of Science
1333 H St., NW
Washington, D.C. 20005
(202) 326 6400

American Chemical Society
1155 16th St., NW
Washington, D.C. 20036
(202) 872 4600

American Conference of
  Governmental Industrial
  Hygienists
6500 Glenway Ave., Bldg. D-7
Cincinnati, OH 45211
(513) 661 7881

American Council of Independent
  Laboratories
1725 K St., NW, Suite 412
Washington, D.C. 20006
(202) 887 5872

American Entomological Society
1900 Race St.
Philadelphia, PA 19103
(215) 561 3978

American Farmland Trust
1920 N St., NW, Suite 400
Washington, D.C. 20036
(202) 659 5170

American Fisheries Society
5410 Grosvenor Lane, Suite 110
Bethesda, MD 20814
(301) 897 8616

American Forestry Association
P.O. Box 2000
Washington, D.C. 20013
(202) 667 3300

American Industrial Hygiene
  Association
475 Wolf Ledges Parkway
Akron, OH 44311
(216) 762 7294

American Institute of Aeronautics
  and Astronautics
370 L'Enfant Promenade, SW
Washington, D.C. 20024
(202) 646 7400

American Institute of Architects
1735 New York Ave., NW
Washington, D.C. 20006
(202) 626 7300

American Institute of Chemical
  Engineers
345 East 47th St.
New York, NY 10017
(212) 705 7338

American Institute of Mining,
  Metallurgical and Petroleum
  Engineers (AIME)
345 East 47th St.
New York, NY 10017
(212) 705 7695

American Institute of Physics
335 East 45th St.
New York, NY 10017
(212) 661 9404

American Institute of Plant
  Engineers
3975 Erie Ave.
Cincinnati, OH 45208
(513) 561 6000

American Nuclear Society
555 North Kensington Ave.
La Grange Park, IL 60525
(708) 352 6611

American Planning Association
1776 Massachusetts Ave., NW
Washington, D.C. 20036
(202) 872 0611

American Public Health
  Association
1015 15th St., NW
Washington, D.C. 20005
(202) 789 5600

American Rivers
801 Pennsylvania Ave., SE
Washington, D.C. 20003
(202) 547 6900

American Society for Microbiology
1913 Eye St., NW
Washington, D.C. 20006
(202) 833 9680

American Society of Agricultural
Engineers
2950 Niles Rd.
St. Joseph, MI 49085
(616) 429 0300

American Society of Agronomy
677 South Segoe Rd.
Madison, WI 53711
(608) 273 8080

American Society of Civil
Engineers
Student Services Dept.
345 East 47th St.
New York, NY 10017
(212) 705 7496

American Society of Consulting
Planners
1015 15th St. N.W., Suite 600
Washington, D.C. 20005
(202) 789 0220

American Society of Heating,
Refrigerating and Air-
Conditioning Engineers,
Inc. (ASHRAE)
1791 Tulie Circle, NE
Atlanta, GA 30329
(404) 636 8400

American Society of Mechanical
Engineers
345 East 47th St.
New York, NY 10017
(212) 705 7722

American Society of Safety
Engineers
1800 E. Oakton St.
Des Plaines, IL 60018
(708) 692 4121

American Water Resources
Association
5410 Grosvenor Lane
Bethesda, MD 20814
(301) 493 8600

American Water Works Association
6666 W. Quincy Ave.
Denver, CO 80235
(303) 794 7711

American Wilderness Alliance
7600 E. Arapahoe Rd., Suite 114
Englewood, CO 80112
(303) 771 0380

Association of American
Geographers
1710 16th St., NW
Washington, D.C. 20009
(202) 234 1450

Association of Environmental and
Resource Economists
1616 P St., NW
Washington, D.C. 20036
(202) 328 5000

Association of Ground Water
Scientists and Engineers
6375 Riverside Dr.
Dublin, OH 43017
(614) 761 1711

Association of State and Interstate
Water Pollution Control
Administrators
444 N Capitol St., NW
Washington, D.C. 20001

Board of Certified Safety
Professionals
208 Burwash Ave.
Savoy, IL 61874
(217) 359 9263

Canadian Council of Professional
Engineers
116 Albert St., Suite 401
Ottawa, Ontario K1P 5G3
(613) 232 2474

Canadian Forestry Association
185 Somerset St. West
Ottawa, Ontario K2P OJ2
(613) 232 1815

Canadian Geotechnical Society
170 Attwell Drive, Suite 602
Rexdale, Ontario M9W 525
(416) 674 0366

Canadian Institute of Mining and
Metallurgy
400-1130 Sherbrooke St. West
Montreal, Quebec H3A 2M8
(514) 842 3461

Center for Hazardous Materials
Research
320 William Pitt Way
Pittsburgh, PA 15238
(412) 826 5320

Center for Marine Conservation
1725 DeSales St., NW
Washington, D.C. 20036
(202) 429 5609

Chemical Institute of Canada
1785 Alta Vista Drive
Ottawa, Ontario K1G 3YG
(613) 526 4652

Citizen's Clearinghouse for
Hazardous Waste, Inc.
P.O. Box 926
Arlington, VA 22216
(703) 276 7070

Citizens for a Better Environment
942 Market St., No. 505
San Francisco, CA 94102
(415) 788 0690

Clean Water Action Project
317 Pennsylvania Ave., SE
Washington, D.C. 20003
(202) 547 1196

The Conservation Foundation
1250 24th St., NW
Washington, D.C. 20037
(202) 293 4800

Conservation International
1015 18th St., NW, Suite 1000
Washington, D.C. 20036
(202) 429 5660

Cousteau Society, Inc.
930 W. 21st St.
Norfolk, VA 23517
(804) 627 1144

Defenders of Wildlife
1244 19th St., NW
Washington, D.C. 20036
(202) 659 9510

Earthwatch
P.O. Box 403N
Watertown, MA 02272
(617) 926 8200

Ecology Center
1403 Addison St.
Berkeley, CA 94702
(415) 548 2220

The Engineering Institute of
Canada
700 EIC Building
2050 Mansfield Street
Montreal, Quebec H3A 1Z2
(514) 842 5653
(This is also the address of the
Canadian Society for Civil
Engineering, the Canadian
Society for Electrical
Engineering, and the Canadian
Society for Mechanical
Engineering)

Entomological Society of America
9301 Annapolis Rd.
Lanham, MD 20706
(301) 731 4535

Environmental Action
1525 New Hampshire Ave., NW
Washington, D.C. 20036
(202) 745 4870

Environmental Defense Fund
257 Park Ave. South
New York, NY 10010
(212) 505 2100

Environmental Law Institute
1616 P St., NW, Suite 200
Washington, D.C. 20036
(202) 328 5150

Freshwater Foundation
2500 Shadywood Rd.
Navarre, MN 55392

Friends of the Earth
218 D St., SE
Washington, D.C. 20003
(202) 544 2600

Geological Society of America
3300 Penrose Place
Boulder, CO 80301
(303) 447 2020

Green Cross Certification Co.
1611 Telegraph Ave., Suite 1111
Oakland, CA 94612
(415) 832 1415

Greenpeace USA
1436 U St., NW
Washington, D.C. 20009
(202) 462 1177

Green Seal, Inc.
1733 Connecticut Ave., NW
Washington, D.C. 20009
(202) 328 8095

Hazardous Materials Control
Research Institute
7237 Hanover Parkway
Greenbelt, MD 20770
(301) 982 9500

Human Factors Society
PO Box 1369
Santa Monica, CA 90406
(213) 394 1811

Institute for Local Self-Reliance
2425 18th St., NW
Washington, D.C. 20009
(202) 232 4108

Institute of Electrical and
Electronics Engineers, Inc.
345 East 47th St.
New York, NY 10017
(212) 705 7900

Institute of Environmental
Sciences
940 E. Northwest Highway
Mt. Prospect, IL 60056
(312) 255 1561

Institute of Industrial Engineers
25 Technology Park
Norcross, GA 30092
(404) 449 0460

Institute of Scrap Recycling
Industries
1627 K St., NW
Washington, D.C. 20006
(202) 466 4050

International Association of
Environmental Managers
243 W. Main St.
P.O. Box 308
Kutztown, PA 19530
(215) 683 5098

The Izaak Walton League of
America
1401 Wilson Blvd., Level B
Arlington, VA 22209
(703) 528 1818

Junior Engineering Technical
Society (JETS)
1420 King St.
Alexandria, VA 22314
(703) 548 5387

League of Conservation Voters
1150 Connecticut Ave., NW,
Suite 201
Washington, D.C. 20036
(202) 785 8683

National Association for
Environmental Management
4400 Jenifer St., NW
Washington, D.C. 20015
(202) 966 0019

National Association of
Environmental Professionals
P.O. Box 15210
Alexandria, VA 22309
(703) 660 2364

National Association of
Professional Environmental
Communicators
P.O. Box 06 8352
Chicago, IL 60606
(312) 781 1505

National Audubon Society
950 Third Ave.
New York, NY 10022
(212) 832 3200

National Environmental
Development Association
1440 New York Ave., NW,
Suite 300
Washington, D.C. 20005
(202) 638 1230

National Environmental Health
Association
720 S. Colorado Blvd.
#970 South Tower
Denver, CO 80222
(303) 756 9090

National Recycling Coalition
1101 30th St., NW, Suite 305
Washington, D.C. 20007
(202) 625 6406

National Resources Council of
America
1015 31st St., NW
Washington, D.C. 20007

National Society of Professional
Engineers
1420 King St.
Alexandria, VA 22314
(703) 684 2800

National Solid Wastes
Management Association
1730 Rhode Island Ave., NW
Washington, D.C. 20036
(202) 659 4613

National Toxics Campaign
37 Temple Place, 4th Floor
Boston, MA 02111
(617) 482 1477

National Water Well Association
6375 Riverside Dr.
Dublin, OH 43017
(614) 761 1711

National Wildlife Federation
1400 16th St., NW
Washington, D.C. 20036
(202) 797 6800

Natural Resources Defense Council
40 West 20th St.
New York, NY 10011
(212) 727 2700

Nature Conservancy
1815 N. Lynn St.
Arlington, VA 22209
(703) 841 5300

New Alchemy Institute
237 Hatchville Rd.
East Falmouth, MA 02536
(508) 564 6301

North American Association for
Environmental Education
P.O. Box 400
Troy, OH 45373
(513) 698 6493

Operations Research Society of
America
Mt. Royal & Guilford Ave.
Baltimore, MD 21202
(301) 528 4146

Organic Crop Improvement
Association
3185 Township Rd. 179
Bellafontaine, OH 43311
(513) 592 4983

Organic Food Alliance
2111 Wilson Blvd., Suite 531
Arlington, VA 22201
(703) 276 9498

Resource Policy Institute
P.O. Box 39185
Washington, D.C. 20016
(202) 895 2601

Sierra Club
730 Polk St.
San Francisco, CA 94109
(415) 776 2211

Society for Ecological Restoration
c/o University of Wisconsin
Arboretum
1207 Seminole Highway
Madison, WI 53711
(608) 263 7889

Society of Automotive Engineers
400 Commonwealth Dr.
Warrendale, PA 15096
(412) 776 4841

Society of Environmental
Toxicology and Chemistry
1101 14th St., NW, Suite 1100
Washington, D.C. 20005
(202) 371 1275

Society of Fire Protection Engineers
60 Batterymarch St.
Boston, MA 02110
(617) 482 0686

Society of Manufacturing Engineers
One SME Dr.
Dearborn, MI 48121
(313) 271 1500

Society of Plastics Engineers
14 Fairfield Dr.
Brookfield, CT 06804
(203) 775 0471

Society of Toxicology
1101 14th St., NW, Suite 1100
Washington, D.C. 20005
(202) 293 5935

Soil and Water Conservation
Society
7515 N.E. Ankeny Rd.
Ankeny, IA 50021
(515) 289 2331

Soil Science Society of America
677 South Segoe Rd.
Madison, WI 52711
(608) 273 8080

State and Territorial Air Pollution
Program Administrators and the
Association of Local Air
Pollution Control Officials
444 N. Capitol St., NW
Washington, D.C. 20001
(202) 624 7864

Student Conservation
Association, Inc.
P.O. Box 550
Charlestown, NH 03603
(603) 826 4301

Union of Concerned Scientists
26 Church St.
Cambridge, MA 02238
(617) 547 5552

Waste Watch
P.O. Box 39185
Washington, D.C. 20016
(202) 895 2601

Water Pollution Control Federation
601 Wythe St.
Alexandria, VA 22314
(703) 684 2400

The Wilderness Society
900 17th St., NW
Washington, D.C. 20006
(202) 833 2300

World Resources Institute
1709 New York Ave., NW
Washington, D.C. 20006
(202) 638 6300

Worldwatch Institute
1776 Massachusetts Ave., NW
Washington, D.C. 20036
(202) 452 1999

World Wildlife Fund
1250 24th St., NW
Washington, D.C. 20037
(202) 293 4800

Zero Population Growth
1400 16th St., NW, Suite 230
Washington, D.C. 20036
(202) 332 2200

APPENDIX B

Environmental Publications

Following is a list of publications about social issues, industrial practices, and some scientific research on environmental topics. At the same time, there is an emphasis on business publications. The main reason for this focus is to provide the publications that would be most useful to the job hunter; academic journals, while extremely valuable for environmental science, are written mostly for other scientists. Most of the business journals are not available on newsstands, and some of them actually restrict their subscriptions to those working in an industry. (You can usually get around this restriction by calling yourself a "consultant" on the subscription form.) Most large university libraries will have many of these publications on hand, as will many corporate libraries.

Air Pollution Control
Bureau of National Affairs, Inc.
1231 25th St., NW
Washington, D.C. 20037
(202) 452 4200

American Environmental Laboratory
American Laboratory Postcard Deck
30 Controls Dr.
Shelton, CT 06484
(203) 926 9300

American Industrial Hygiene Journal
American Industrial Hygiene Association
Box 8390
345 White Pond Drive
Akron, OH 44320
(216) 762 7294

Amicus Journal
40 West 20th St.
New York, NY 10011
(212) 727 2700
(House journal of the Natural
Resources Defense Council)

Analytical Chemistry
American Chemical Society
1155 16th St., NW
Washington, D.C. 20036
(202) 872 4700

The American Chemical Society
also publishes the following
journals of interest:
Biotechnology Progress
Chemical and Engineering News
*Environmental Science and
Technology*
Inorganic Chemistry
*Journal of Agricultural and Food
Chemistry*
*Journal of the American Chemical
Society*
Journal of Chemical Education
*Journal of Chemical Information
and Computer Science*
Journal of Physical Chemistry

*Annual Review of Ecology and
Systematics*
Annual Reviews, Inc.
4139 El Camino Way
Box 10139
Palo Alto, CA 94303
(415) 493 4400

Atmospheric Environment
Pergamon Press, Inc.
Maxwell House, Fairview Park
Elmsford, NY 10523
(914) 592 3625

*Behavioral Ecology and
Sociobiology*
Springer-Verlag
175 5th Ave.
New York, NY 10010
(212) 460 1500

*BioCycle, the Journal of Waste
Recycling*
The JG Press, Inc.
P.O. Box 351
18 South Seventh St.
Emmaus, PA 18049
(215) 967 4135

*Buzzworm, The Environmental
Journal*
2305 Canyon Blvd., Suite 206
Boulder, CO 80302
(303) 442 1969

CA Selects:
(a broad array of abstracts,
available in print or online)
Chemical Abstracts Services
2540 Olentangy River Rd.
P.O. Box 3012
Columbus, OH 43210
(614) 447 3600

California Environmental News

Tri-State Environmental News

Texas Environmental News

Environmental News Network
760 Whalers Way, Suite 100-A
Fort Collins, CO 80525
(303) 229 0029

Chemical & Engineering News
1155 16th St., NW
Washington, D.C. 20036
(202) 872 4600
(House journal of the American
Chemical Society)

Chemical Engineering
1221 Ave. of the Americas
43rd Floor
New York, NY 10020
(212) 512 2000

Chemical Engineering Progress
American Institute of Chemical
    Engineers
345 East 47th St.
New York, NY 10017
(212) 705 7576
(House journal of the American
    Institute of Chemical Engineers)

Chemical Week
Chemical Week Associates
P.O. Box 1074
Southeastern, PA 19398
(215) 630 6380

Chemosphere
Pergamon Press, Inc.
Maxwell House, Fairview Park
Elmsford, NY 10523
(914) 592 3625

Civil Engineering
American Society of Civil
    Engineers
345 East 47th St.
New York, NY 10017
(212) 705 7496

Clean Water Report
Business Publishers, Inc.
951 Pershing Drive
Silver Spring, MD 20910
(301) 587 6300

Conservation Biology
Blackwell Scientific Publishers, Inc.
3 Cambridge Center, No. 208
Cambridge, MA 02142
(617) 225 0401

Diplomate
American Academy of
    Environmental Engineers
132 Holiday Court, No. 206
Annapolis, MD 21401
(301) 266 3311

E, The Environmental Magazine
Earth Action Network, Inc.
28 Knight St.
Norwalk, CT 06851
(203) 854 5559

*Earth First! The Radical
    Environmental Journal*
P.O. Box 5871
Tucson, AZ 85703

EHP
National Institute of
    Environmental Health Science
Box 12233
Research Triangle Park, NC 27709
(919) 541 3406

*Ecotoxicology and Environmental
    Safety*
Academic Press, Inc.
1250 6th Ave.
San Diego, CA 92101
(619) 699 6742

Engineering News-Record
1221 Ave. of the Americas
New York, NY 10020
(212) 512 2500

Environmental Business Journal
Environmental Business
  Publishing, Inc.
827 Washington
San Diego, CA 92103
(619) 295 7685

*Journal of Environmental
  Economics*
Academic Press, Inc.
1250 Sixth Ave.
San Diego, CA 92101
(619) 699 6742

Environmental Management
Springer-Verlag
175 5th Ave.
New York, NY 10010
(212) 460 1500

*Environmental Science and
  Technology*
American Chemical Society
1155 16th St., NW
Washington, D.C. 20036
(202) 872 4600

EPRI Journal
Electric Power Research Institute
P.O. Box 10412
Palo Alto, CA 94303
(415) 855 2000

Farm Chemicals
Meister Publishing Co.
37733 Euclid Ave.
Willoughby, OH 44094
(216) 942 2000

*Fundamental & Applied
  Toxicology*
Academic Press, Inc.
1250 6th Ave.
San Diego, CA 92101
(619) 699 6742

*Game Bird Breeders, Aviculturists,
  Zoologists & Conservationists
  Gazette*
Game Bird Breeders, Aviculturists,
  Zoologists & Conservationists
1155 E. 4780 So.
Salt Lake City, UT 84117
(801) 262 4852

Golub's Oil Pollution Bulletin
World Information Systems
P.O. Box 535 Harvard Square
  Station
Cambridge, MA 02238

Graduating Engineer
Peterson's/COG Publishing
  Group
16030 Ventura Blvd., Suite 560
Encino, CA 91436
(818) 789 5293

Hazardous Materials Control
Hazardous Materials Control
  Institute
7237 Hanover Parkway
Greenbelt, MD 20770
(301) 982 9500

*Hazardous Waste & Hazardous
  Materials*
Mary Ann Liebert, Inc.
1651 3rd Ave.
New York, NY 10128
(212) 289 4697

Hazardous Waste News
Business Publishers, Inc.
951 Pershing Dr.
Silver Spring, MD 20910
(301) 587 6300

Hazmat World
Tower-Borner Publishing, Inc.
800 Roosevelt Rd.
Glen Ellyn, IL 60137
(708) 858 1888

*In Business, the Magazine for
   Environmental Entrepreneuring*
The JG Press, Inc.
P.O. Box 323
18 South Seventh St.
Emmaus, PA 18049
(215) 967 4136

Inside EPA
1235 Jefferson Davis Highway,
   Suite 1206
Arlington, VA 22202
(703) 892 8500

*International Journal of
   Environmental & Analytical
   Chemistry*
Gordon & Breach Science
   Publishers, Inc.
P.O. Box 786, Cooper Station
New York, NY 10276
(212) 206 8900

*Journal of American Oil Chemists'
   Society*
American Oil Chemists' Society
1608 Broadmoor Drive
Champaign, IL 61821
(217) 359 2344

*Journal of the Association of
   Official Analytical Chemists*
Association of Official Analytical
   Chemists
2200 Wilson Blvd., #400
Arlington, VA 22201
(703) 522 3032

Journal of Carbohydrate Chemistry
Marcel Dekker, Inc.
270 Madison Ave.
New York, NY 10016
(212) 696 9000

Journal of Chemical Ecology
Plenum Publishing Corp.
233 Spring St.
New York, NY 10013
(212) 620 8000

*Journal of Clinical Chemistry and
   Clinical Biochemistry*
(Zertschrift fur Klinische Chemie)
Walter de Gruyter, Inc.
200 Saw Mill River Rd.
Hawthorne, NY 10532
(914) 747 0110

*The Journal of Conservation
   Biology*
Society for Conservation Biology
3 Cambridge Center
Cambridge, MA 02141
(617) 225 0401

Journal of Environmental Health
National Environmental Health
   Association
720 S. Colorado Blvd., No. 790
Denver, CO 80222
(303) 756 9090

*Journal of Environmental Science
   and Health, Part A:
   Environmental Science and
   Engineering; Part B: Pesticides,
   Food Contaminants and
   Agricultural Wastes*
Marcel Dekker, Inc.
270 Madison Ave.
New York, NY 10016
(212) 696 9000

*Journal of Soil and Water
   Conservation*
Soil and Water Conservation
   Society
7515 NE Ankeny Rd.
Ankeny, IA 50021
(515) 289 2331

Journal of Toxicology
Marcel Dekker, Inc.
270 Madison Ave.
New York, NY 10016
(212) 696 9000

*Journal of the Water Pollution
   Control Federation*
601 Wythe St.
Alexandria, VA 22314
(703) 684 2400

National Parks
National Parks and Conservation
   Association
1015 31st St., NW
Washington, D.C. 20007
(202) 944 8530

Journal of Wildlife Management
The Wildlife Society
5410 Grosvenor Lane
Bethesda, MD 20814
(301) 897 9770

Natural History
P.O. Box 5000
Harlan, IA 51537
(1-800) 234 5252

New Age Journal
342 Western Ave.
Brighton, MA 02135
(617) 787 2005

Organic Food Business News
Hotline Publishing
P.O. Box 208
Williston, ND 58802
(701) 774 8757

*Pesticide Biochemistry &
   Physiology*
Academic Press, Inc.
1250 6th Ave.
San Diego, CA 92101
(619) 699 6742

Pollution Engineering
1935 Shermer Road
Northbrook, IL 60062
(708) 498 9840

*Progress in Energy and
   Combustion Science*
Pergamon Press, Inc.
Maxwell House, Fairview Park
Elmsford, NY 10523
(914) 592 3625

Pulp & Paper
600 Harrison St.
San Francisco, CA 94107
(415) 397 1881

REAP Newsletter
Iowa Department of Natural
   Resources
Wallace State Office Bldg.
Des Moines, IA 50319

Resources
Resources for the Future
1616 P St., NW
Washington, D.C. 20036
(202) 328 5113

Resource Recovery Focus
National Solid Wastes
   Management Association
1730 Rhode Island Ave., NW
Washington, D.C. 20036
(202) 659 4613

Resource Recycling
Resource Recycling, Inc.
P.O. Box 10540
Portland, OR 97210
(503) 227 1319

Science
American Association for the
   Advancement of Science
1333 H St., NW
Washington, D.C. 20005
(202) 326 6400

Toxic Substances Journal
Hemisphere Publishing Corp.
79 Madison Ave., No. 1110
New York, NY 10016
(212) 213 8368

Toxicological & Environmental
   Chemistry
Gordon & Breach Science
   Publishers
P.O. Box 786, Cooper Station
New York, NY 10276
(212) 206 8900

Transactions of the American
   Entomological Society
American Entomological Society
1900 Race St.
Philadelphia, PA 19103
(215) 561 3978

Waste Management: Nuclear,
   Chemical, Biological, Municipal
Pergamon Press, Inc.
Maxwell House, Fairview Park
Elmsford, NY 10523
(914) 592 3625

Waste Tech News
131 Madison St.
Denver, CO 80206
(303) 394 2905

Water Resources Review
U.S. Geological Survey
MS 20
12201 Sunrise Valley Dr.
Reston, VA 22092
(703) 860 6127

Water Well Journal
Water Well Journal Publishing Co.
6375 Riverside Dr.
Dublin, OH 43017
(614) 716 3222

Whole Earth Ecolog
available through bookstores or
Whole Earth Access
2990 Seventh Ave.
Berkeley, CA 94710
(1-800) 845 2000
(415) 845 3000

APPENDIX C

Federal Environmental Addresses

Most of the larger federal agencies have regional hiring offices in addition to the headquarters office in Washington. Also, the very largest federal agencies have hiring centers for divisions within the agency as well as the agency as a whole. Some of these divisional offices are listed here, under the title of the parent agency. The U.S. Environmental Protection Agency is listed first, including its ten regional offices. The publication *Career America*, from which all of these addresses were drawn, lists most of the regional and divisional addresses and should be consulted for more details.

ENVIRONMENTAL PROTECTION AGENCY

Headquarters Office

Recruitment Center
(PM-224)
401 M St., NW
Washington, D.C. 20460
(1-800) 338 1350
(202) 382 3305

Regional Offices

Regional Personnel Office
Environmental Protection Agency
Room 2203
John F. Kennedy Bldg.
Boston, MA 02203
(617) 565 3719
(CT, ME, MA, NH, RI, VT)

Regional Personnel Office
Environmental Protection Agency
Room 937-C
26 Federal Plaza
New York, NY 10278
(212) 264 0016
(NJ, NY, PR, VI)

Regional Personnel Office
Environmental Protection Agency
841 Chestnut Bldg.
Philadelphia, PA 19107
(215) 597 9372
(DE, MD, DC, PA, VA, WV)

Regional Personnel Office
Environmental Protection Agency
345 Courtland St., NE
Atlanta, GA 30365
(404) 347 3486
(AL, FL, GA, KY, MS, TN,
   NC, SC)

Regional Personnel Office
Environmental Protection Agency
230 South Dearborn St.
Chicago, IL 60604
(312) 353 2026
(IL, IN, MN, MI, OH, WI)

Regional Personnel Office
Environmental Protection Agency
1445 Ross Ave.
Dallas, TX 75202
(214) 655 6560
(AR, LA, NM, TX, OK)

Regional Personnel Office
Environmental Protection Agency
726 Minnesota Ave.
Kansas City, KS 66101
(913) 236 2821
(IA, KS, MO, NE)

Regional Personnel Office
Environmental Protection Agency
One Denver Place
999 18th St., Suite 500
Denver, CO 80202
(303) 293 1487
(CO, MT, ND, SD, UT)

Regional Personnel Office
Environmental Protection Agency
215 Fremont St.
San Francisco, CA 94105
(415) 974 8016
(AZ, CA, NV, HW, Guam,
   American Samoa, Trust
   Territories, Wake Island)

Regional Personnel Office
Environmental Protection Agency
M/S 301
1200 Sixth Ave.
Seattle, WA 98101
(206) 442 2959
(ID, OR, WA, AK)

DEPARTMENT OF AGRICULTURE

Office of Personnel
Central Employment Unit
U.S. Department of Agriculture
Room 1080, South Building
Washington, D.C. 20250
(202) 447 5626

Agricultural Research Service

Personnel Division
Building 003, BARC-West
Beltsville, MD 20705
(301) 344 1124

Forest Service

Washington Office
P.O. Box 96090
Room 906, Rosslyn Plaza East
Washington, D.C. 20090-6090
(703) 235 2730

Soil Conservation Service

Personnel Division
P.O. Box 2890
Washington, D.C. 20013
(202) 447 2631

DEPARTMENT OF COMMERCE

This arm of government, with 34,000 employees, has four regional "administrative support centers":

Personnel Officer
Eastern Administrative Support
  Center
253 Monticello Ave.
Norfolk, VA 23510
(804) 441 6516

Personnel Officer
Central Administrative Support
  Center
601 East 12th St.
Kansas City, MO 64106
(816) 758 2056

Personnel Officer
Mountain Administrative Support
  Center
325 Broadway
Boulder, CO 80303
(303) 497 6306

Personnel Officer
Western Administrative Support
  Center
7600 Sand Point Way, NE
BIN C15700
Seattle, WA 98115
(206) 526 6054

Bureau of the Census

Personnel Division
Room 3254, Building Three
Washington, D.C. 20233
(301) 763 5780

National Institute of Standards and Technology

Personnel Officer
Room A-123, Admin. Building
Gaithersburg, MD 20899
(301) 975 3008

National Oceanic and Atmospheric Administration

Personnel Division
6010 Executive Blvd.
WSC #5, Room 706
Washington, D.C. 20852
(301) 443 8834

DEPARTMENT OF DEFENSE
DEPARTMENT OF THE ARMY

Army Corps of Engineers

Civilian Personnel Division
ATTN: CEPE-CS
20 Massachusetts Ave., NW
Room 5105
Washington, D.C. 20314-1000
(202) 272 0720

DEPARTMENT OF ENERGY

Headquarters Operations Division
Room 4E-090
1000 Independence Ave., SW
Washington, D.C. 20585
(202) 586 8536

DEPARTMENT OF HEALTH AND HUMAN SERVICES

Public Health Service

OASH Personnel Operations Office
5600 Fishers Lane
Room 17A-08
Rockville, MD 20857
(301) 443 6900

Agency for Toxic Substances and Disease Registry

Personnel Office
1600 Clifton Rd., NE
Atlanta, GA 30333
(404) 639 3615

Centers for Disease Control

Personnel Office
1600 Clifton Rd., NE
Atlanta, GA 30333
(404) 639 3615

Food and Drug Administration

Division of Personnel Management
5600 Fishers Lane
Room 4B-41
Rockville, MD 20857
(301) 443 1970

National Institutes of Health
National Institute of
Environmental Health

Division of Personnel Management
9000 Rockville Pike
Bldg. 31, Room B3C15
Bethesda, MD 20205
(301) 496 2403

DEPARTMENT OF THE INTERIOR

Personnel Office
Office of the Secretary
Washington, D.C. 20240
(202) 343 6618

Bureau of Land Management

Division of Personnel
18th and C Sts., NW (MIB)
Washington, D.C. 20240
(202) 343 3193

Bureau of Mines

Headquarters
2401 E St., NW
Washington, D.C. 20241
(202) 634 4710

Bureau of Reclamation

Headquarters
18th and C Sts., NW
Washington, D.C. 20240
(202) 343 4626

National Parks Service

Headquarters
Branch of Personnel Operations
18th and C Sts., NW
P.O. Box 37127
Washington, D.C. 20013
(202) 343 4648

U.S. Fish and Wildlife Service

Headquarters
18th and C Sts., NW
Washington, D.C. 20240
(202) 343 6104

U.S. Geological Survey

National Center, MS-215
12201 Sunrise Valley Dr.
Reston, VA 22092
(703) 860 6127

DEPARTMENT OF LABOR

Occupational Safety and Health Administration

Office of Personnel Management
Frances Perkins Bldg., Room
  N3308
200 Constitution Ave., NW
Washington, D.C. 20210
(202) 523 8013

NATIONAL AERONAUTICS AND SPACE ADMINISTRATION

Headquarters, DP
Washington, D.C. 20546
(202) 453 8480

NATIONAL SCIENCE FOUNDATION

Staffing Assistant
Division of Personnel and
  Management
1800 G St., NW, Room 208
Washington, D.C. 20550
(202) 357 9529

NUCLEAR REGULATORY COMMISSION

College Recruitment Coordinator
Office of Personnel
Washington, D.C. 20555
(301) 492 9027

CANADIAN GOVERNMENT

Canadian Forestry Service
Place Vincent Massey
Ottawa, Ontario K1A OC5
(613) 997 1454

Department of the Environment
  Canada
Ottawa, Ontario K1A OE7
(613)

Geological Survey of Canada
601 Booth Street
Ottawa, Ontario K1A OE8
(613)

National Research Council Canada
Montreal Road
Ottawa, Ontario K1A OR6
(613) 993 9101

APPENDIX D

State Environmental Addresses

ALABAMA

Conservation and Natural
  Resources Department
64 N. Union St.
Room 702
Montgomery, AL 36130
(205) 242 3486

ALASKA

Environmental Conservation
  Department
3220 Hospital Dr.
P.O. Box O
Juneau, AK 99811-1800
(907) 465 2606

ARIZONA

Environmental Quality
  Department
2005 N. Central Ave.
Phoenix, AZ 85004
(602) 257 2300

ARKANSAS

Health Department
4815 W. Markham
Little Rock, AR 72201
(501) 661 2111

Pollution Control and Ecology
  Department
8001 National Dr.
Little Rock, AR 72219
(501) 562 7444

CALIFORNIA

Environmental Affairs Agency
1102 Q St.
P.O. Box 2815
Sacramento, CA 95812

COLORADO

Natural Resources Department
1313 Sherman St.
Room 718
Denver, CO 80203
(303) 866 3311

CONNECTICUT

Environmental Protection
  Department
165 Capitol Ave.
Hartford, CT 06006
(203) 566 5599

DELAWARE

Natural Resources and
  Environmental Control
  Department
89 Kings Highway
P.O. Box 1401
Dover, DE 19903
(302) 736 4506

DISTRICT OF COLUMBIA

Public Works Department
2000 14th St., NW, 6th Floor
Washington, D.C. 20009
(202) 939 8000

FLORIDA

Environmental Regulation
  Department
2600 Blair Stone Rd.
Tallahassee, FL 32399-2400
(904) 488 9334

GEORGIA

Natural Resources Department
205 Butler St., SE, Suite 1252
Atlanta, GA 30328
(404) 656 3530

HAWAII

Hawaiian Home Lands
  Department
P.O. Box 18789
Honolulu, HI 96805
(808) 548 6450

Environmental Health
  Administration
1250 Punchbowl St.
Honolulu, HI 96813
(808) 548 6455

IDAHO

Fish and Game Department
600 S. Walnut
P.O. Box 25
Boise, ID 83707
(208) 334 3782

ILLINOIS

Environmental Protection Agency
P.O. Box 19276
Springfield, IL 62794
(217) 782 3397

INDIANA

Environmental Management
  Department
105 S. Meridian St.
P.O. Box 6015
Indianapolis, IN 46206-6015
(317) 232 8162

IOWA

Natural Resources Department
Wallace Building
Des Moines, IA 50319-0034
(515) 281 5385

KANSAS

Health and Environmental
Department
Forbes Field, Building 740
Topeka, KS 66620
(913) 296 1500

KENTUCKY

Natural Resources and
Environmental Protection
Cabinet
Capitol Plaza Tower, 5th Floor
Frankfort, KY 40601
(502) 564 2043

LOUISIANA

Environmental Quality
Department
P.O. Box 44066
Baton Rouge, LA 70804
(504) 342 1222

MAINE

Environmental Protection
Department State House
Station 17
Augusta, ME 04333
(207) 289 7688

MARYLAND

Natural Resources Department
Tawes State Office Building
Annapolis, MD 21401
(301) 974 3041

MASSACHUSETTS

Environmental Affairs Executive
Office
100 Cambridge St., Room 2000
Boston, MA 02202
(617) 727 9800

MICHIGAN

Natural Resources Department
P.O. Box 30028
Lansing, MI 48909
(517) 373 1220

Pollution Control Agency
520 Lafayette Rd.
St. Paul, MN 55155
(612) 296 6300

MISSISSIPPI

Environmental Quality
Department
P.O. Box 20305
Jackson, MS 39289-1305
(601) 961 5099

MISSOURI

Conservation Department
2901 W. Truman Blvd.
P.O. Box 180
Jefferson City, MO 65102-0180
(314) 751 4115

Natural Resources Department
P.O. Box 176
Jefferson City, MO 65102
(314) 751 3443

Public Safety Department
P.O. Box 749
Jefferson City, MO 65102
(314) 751 4905

MONTANA

Natural Resources and
Conservation Department
1520 E. 6th Ave.
Helena, MT 59620-2301
(406) 444 6873

NEBRASKA

Environmental Control
  Department
State Office Building
P.O. Box 98922
Lincoln, NE 68509-8922
(402) 471 2186

NEVADA

Conservation and Natural
  Resources Department
201 S. Fall St.
Carson City, NV 89710
(702) 687 4360

NEW HAMPSHIRE

Environmental Services
  Department
6 Hazen Dr.
Concord, NH 03301
(603) 271 3503

NEW JERSEY

Environmental Protection
  Department
401 E. State St.
CN 402
Trenton, NJ 08625-0402
(609) 292 3131

NEW MEXICO

Health and Environment
  Department
1190 St. Francis Dr.
Santa Fe, NM 87503
(505) 827 0020

NEW YORK

Environmental Conservation
  Department
50 Wolf Rd.
Albany, NY 12233
(518) 457 3446

NORTH CAROLINA

Environment, Health and Natural
  Resources Department
P.O. Box 72687
Raleigh, NC 27611
(919) 733 4984

NORTH DAKOTA

Game and Fish Department
100 N. Bismarck Expressway
Bismarck, ND 58501
(701) 221 6300

Health and Consolidated
  Laboratories Department
600 E. Boulevard Ave.
Bismarck, ND 58505
(701) 224 2370

Parks and Recreation Department
1424 W. Century Ave., Suite 202
Bismarck, ND 58501
(701) 224 4887

OHIO

Environmental Protection Agency
1800 Watermark
P.O. Box 1049
Columbus, OH 43266-0149
(614) 644 3020

OKLAHOMA

Health Department
1000 NE 10th St.
P.O. Box 53551
Oklahoma City, OK 73152
(405) 271 4200

Public Safety Department
3600 Martin Luther King Ave.
P.O. Box 11415
Oklahoma City, OK 73136-0415

Wildlife Conservation Department
P.O. Box 53465
Oklahoma City, OK 73152

OREGON

Fish and Wildlife Department
P.O. Box 59
Portland, OR 97207
(503) 976 6339

PENNSYLVANIA

Environmental Resources
  Department
P.O. Box 2063
Harrisburg, PA 17120
(717) 783 2300

RHODE ISLAND

Environmental Management
  Department
9 Hayes St.
Providence, RI 02908
(401) 277 6800

SOUTH CAROLINA

Health Environmental Control
  Department
2600 Bull St.
Columbia, SC 29201
(803) 734 4880

SOUTH DAKOTA

Water and Natural Resources
  Department
Joe Foss Building
523 E. Capitol
Pierre, SD 57501
(605) 773 3151

TENNESSEE

Health and Environment
  Department
344 Cordell Hull Building
Nashville, TN 37219-5402
(615) 741 3111

TEXAS

Air Control Board
6330 Highway 2901 E.
Austin, TX 78723
(512) 451 5711

Health Department
1100 W. 49th St.
Austin, TX 78756
(512) 458 7244

Parks and Wildlife Department
4200 Smith School Rd.
Austin, TX 78744
(512) 389 4800

Soil and Water Conservation
  Board
P.O. Box 658
Temple, TX 76503
(817) 773 2250

Water Commission
P.O. Box 13087
Capitol Station
Austin, TX 78711
(512) 463 5538

Water Development Board
P.O. Box 13231
Austin, TX 78711-3231
(512) 463 7847

UTAH

Health Department
P.O. Box 16700
Salt Lake City, UT 84116-0700
(801) 538 6101

VERMONT

Natural Resources Agency
103 S. Main St.
Waterbury, VT 05676
(802) 244 6916

VIRGINIA

Natural Resources Secretariat
9th St. Office Building, Room 525
Richmond VA 23219
(804) 786 0044

WASHINGTON

Ecology Department
MS PV-11
Olympia, WA 98504
(206) 459 6000

WEST VIRGINIA

Air Pollution Control Commission
1558 Washington St., E.
Charleston, WV 25311-2599
(304) 348 4022

Natural Resources Department
1900 Kanawha Boulevard E.
Charleston, WV 25305
(304) 348 2754

WISCONSIN

Natural Resources Department
P.O. Box 7921
Madison, WI 53707
(608) 266 2621

WYOMING

Environmental Quality
   Department
Herschler Building
122 W. 25th St., 4th Floor
Cheyenne, WY 82002
(307) 777 7937

PUERTO RICO

Environmental Quality Board
P.O. Box 11488
Santurce, PR 00910
(809) 725 5140

APPENDIX E

Educational Organizations

This section has two parts: The first contains a list of colleges and universities with environmental studies programs, emphasizing environmental engineering, at the graduate level. There are some 250 schools that have environmental studies at the undergraduate level; consult a directory such as *Peterson's Guide* or others if you are interested in them. The second part, noncredit ("certificate") programs covers a range of nondegreed programs offered by schools, professional organizations, and private companies for training in the environmental field. Many of these programs are required for workers, managers, or trainers who perform environmental remediation projects such as those at Superfund sites. Typically, an employer will send its staff people to these seminars (some of which run only a couple of days) in order to qualify for bidding on and performing government-funded or -licensed cleanup work. There is nothing that prevents the individual, on his or her own, from taking these courses in anticipation of a job, and they could prove beneficial as an indicator of deep interest in performing environmental work.

SCHOOL/ INSTITUTION	PROGRAM
Credit Programs	
California Institute of Technology Division of Enginering and Applied Science Pasadena, CA 91125 (818) 356 6811	M.S., Ph.D. option in environmental engineering science

California Polytechnic State
  University
Department of Civil and
  Environmental Engineering
San Luis Obispo, CA 93407
(805) 756 0111

M.S. in environmental engineering

Clemson University
Department of Environmental
  Systems Engineering
Clemson, SC 29634
(803) 656 3311

M.Eng., M.S., Ph.D. in
  environmental engineering

Colorado School of Mines
Department of Environmental
  Sciences and Engineering
  Ecology
Golden, CO 80401
(303) 273 3000

M.S. in ecological engineering

Colorado State University
Department of Civil Engineering
Fort Collins, CO 80523
(303) 491 1101

M.S., Ph.D. in environmental
  engineering and water quality

Columbia University
School of Engineering and Applied
  Science
Department of Chemical
  Engineering and Applied
  Chemistry
New York, NY 10027
(212) 854 1754

M.S., Eng.Sci.D., Ph.D. in
  environmental control
  engineering

Cornell University
Graduate Field of Engineering
Field of Civil and Environmental
  Engineering
Ithaca, NY 14853
(607) 255 2000

M.Eng., M.S., Ph.D. in civil and
  environmental engineering or
  water resource systems

Indiana University
School of Public and
  Environmental Affairs
Bloomington, IN 47405
(812) 335 9485

M.S. or Ph.D. in environmental
science

Johns Hopkins University
School of Hygiene and Public
  Health
Department of Environmental
  Health Sciences
615 North Wolfe St.
Baltimore, MD 21205
(301) 955 4712

M.S., Ph.D. in environmental
health sciences, public health

McGill University
Geotechnical Research Centre
817 Sherbrooke Street West
Montreal, Quebec H3A 2K6
(514) 392 4751

M.S., Ph.D. in geotechnical
sciences

Michigan State University
Center for Environmental
  Toxicology
C231 Holden Hall
East Lansing, MI 48824
(517) 353 6469

Ph.D. in environmental toxicology

New Jersey Institute of Technology
Newark College of Engineering
Department of Chemical
  Engineering, Chemical and
  Environmental Science
323 King Blvd.
Newark, NJ 07102
(201) 596 3595

M.S. in environmental science

New York University
Department of Environmental
  Medicine
550 First Ave.
New York, NY 10016
(212) 340 6500

M.S., Ph.D. in environmental
health sciences

Pennsylvania State University
College of Engineering
Department of Civil Engineering
212 Sackett Bldg., Box E
University Park, PA 16802
(814) 865 4700

M.Eng., M.S., Ph.D. in
environmental engineering

Rensselaer Polytechnic Institute
School of Engineering and Science
Department of Environmental
  Engineering and Environmental
  Science
Troy, NY 12180
(518) 276 6000

M.Eng., M.S., Ph.D. in
environmental engineering

Rice University
Department of Environmental
  Science and Engineering
Houston, TX 77251
(713) 527 8101

M.E.E., M.E.S., M.S., Ph.D. in
environmental science or
engineering

Rutgers, The State University of
  New Jersey
Program in Civil and
  Environmental Engineering
New Brunswick, NJ 08093
(201) 932 1766

M.S., Ph.D. in environmental
engineering

State University of New York/
  Syracuse
College of Environmental Science
  and Forestry
Syracuse, NY 13210
(315) 470 6599

M.S., Ph.D. in environmental and
resource engineering

Tulane University
School of Public Health
Department of Environmental
  Health Sciences
1430 Tulane Ave.
New Orleans, LA 70112
(504) 588 5374

M.S. or Ph.D. in environmental
health sciences, public health

University of Alaska/Anchorage
School of Engineering
Program in Environmental Quality
  Engineering and Environmental
  Quality Science
Anchorage, AK 99508
(907) 786 1800

M.S., Ph.D. in science and in
engineering

University of California at Berkeley
School of Engineering and Applied
  Science
Department of Civil Engineering
Los Angeles, CA 94720
(415) 642 6000

M.Eng., M.S., Ph.D. in
earthquake engineering,
geotechnical engineering, water
resources, and environmental
engineering

University of California at Los
  Angeles
School of Public Health
Program in Environmental Science
  and Engineering
Los Angeles, CA 90024
(213) 825 4321

D.Env.

University of California at
  Riverside
Department of Soil and
  Environmental Science
Riverside, CA 92521
(714) 787 5325

M.S. or Ph.D. in soil science

University of Cincinnati
College of Medicine and Division of
  Graduate Studies and Research
Department of Environmental
  Health
(513) 556 6000

M.S., Ph.D. in environmental
hygiene and engineering

University of Colorado at Boulder
College of Engineering and
  Applied Science
Boulder, CO 80309
(303) 492 0111

M.S., Ph.D. in environmental
engineering, geotechnical
engineering, and water resources

University of Florida
College of Engineering
Department of Environmental
  Engineering Sciences
Gainesville, FL 32611
(904) 392 3261

M.E., M.S., Ph.D. in
environmental engineering
science

University of Guelph
Faculty of Graduate Studies
Guelph, Ontario N1G 2WE1
(519) 824 4120

M.S., Ph.D. in ecology, veterinary
sciences, environmental biology

University of Houston
Program in Environmental
  Engineering
Houston, TX 77204
(713) 749 2321

M.S. Env. E., Ph.D. in
environmental engineering

University of Illinois
College of Veterinary Medicine
Department of Veterinary
  Biosciences
2001 South Lincoln Ave.
Urbana, IL 61801
(217) 333 2506

M.S. or Ph.D. in veterinary
biosciences (ecological
toxicology)

University of Illinois at Urbana-
  Champaign
Department of Civil and
  Environmental Engineering
Urbana, IL 61801
(217) 333 1000

M.S., Ph.D. in environmental
engineering and science

University of Kentucky
Graduate Center for Toxicology
204 Funkhouser Building
Lexington, KY 40506
(606) 257 3760

M.S. or Ph.D. in toxicology

University of Lowell
Program in Environmental Studies
1 University Ave.
Lowell, MA 01854
(508) 452 5000

M.Eng. in environmental studies

University of Michigan
School of Public Health
Department of Environmental and
    Industrial Health
109 S. Observatory
Ann Arbor, MI 48109
(313) 764 3108

M.S., Ph.D. in public health,
    environmental health sciences

University of North Carolina at
    Chapel Hill
School of Public Health
Department of Environmental
    Sciences and Engineering
(919) 962 2211

M.S.E.E., M.S., Ph.D. in
    environmental science

University of Oklahoma
School of Civil Engineering and
    Environmental Science
Norman, OK 73019

M.S., Ph.D. in water resources,
    groundwater management,
    environment science,
    occupational safety and health,
    and others

University of Toronto
Institute for Environmental
    Studies
Haultain Building
170 College St.
Toronto, Ontario M5S 1A4
(416) 978 7077

M.S. or Ph.D. degrees in
    environmental chemistry,
    biology and toxicology

University of West Virginia
College of Graduate Studies
Program in Environmental Studies
Institute, WV 25112
(304) 766 2044

M.S., Ph.D. in environmental
    engineering

University of Wisconsin-Madison
Department of Civil and
    Environmental Engineering
Madison, WI 53706

M.S., Ph.D. in environmental
    engineering

Virginia Polytechnic Institute and
State University
Department of Biology/Center for
Environmental and Hazardous
Materials Studies
1020 Derring
Virginia Tech
Blacksburg, VA 24061
(703) 961 5538

M.S., Ph.D. in zoology, botany,
and microbiology

Washington State University
College of Engineering and
Architecture
Department of Civil and
Environmental Engineering
Pullman, WA 99164
(509) 335 3564

M.S., Ph.D. in environmental,
geotechnical, hydraulic, and
other engineering specialties

Wayne State University
Department of Chemical and
Metallurgical Engineering
Detroit, MI 48202
(313) 577 3802

M.S. in hazardous waste
management

Noncredit ("Certificate") Programs

American Conference of
Governmental Industrial
Hygienists
6500 Glenway Ave.
Bldg. D-7
Cincinnati, OH 45211
(513) 661 7881

Industrial hygiene

American Institute of Hazardous
Materials Management
900 Isom Rd., Suite 103
San Antonio, TX 78216
(1-800) 729 6742
(512) 340 7775

RCRA, OSHA compliance,
emergency response, and others

Center for Environmental
  Management
Tufts University
Curtis Hall
474 Boston Ave.
Medford, MA 02155
(617) 381 3531

Asbestos and lead abatement,
environmental management,
and others

Center for Hazardous Materials
  Research
University of Pittsburgh
Applied Research Center
320 William Pitt Way
Pittsburgh, PA 15238
(1-800) 334 2467
(412) 826 5320

Waste site health and safety,
emergency response, industrial
spills, hazardous waste
management, and others

Chemical Safety Associates
9163 Chesapeake Dr.
San Diego, CA 92123
(619) 565 0302

Emergency response, laboratory
procedures

Con-Test Educational Center
Training/Marketing Coordinator
39 Spruce St.
East Longmeadow, MA 01208
(413) 525 1198

OSHA training

Delaware Technical and
  Community College
89 Christiana Rd.
New Castle, DE 19720
(302) 323 9602

Training-the-trainer environmental
courses

Dennison Environmental Training
  Center
74 Commerce Way
Woburn, MA 01801
(617) 932 9400

Asbestos abatement, risk
management, hazards
communications, and others

Energy Support Services, Inc.
P.O. Box 6098
Asheville, NC 28816
(704) 258 8888

Hazardous materials management

The Environmental and
   Occupational Safety and Health
   Education and Training Center
   (EOSHETC)
Brookwood Plaza II
45 Knightsbridge Rd.
Piscataway, NJ 08854
(201) 463 5062

Comprehensive continuing
   education in environmental
   safety and health

The Environmental Institute
350 Franklin Rd.
Suite 300
Marietta, GA 30067
(404) 425 2000

Asbestos, lead abatement,
   environmental assessments, and
   related topics

Georgia Tech Research Institute
Georgia Institute of Technology
Atlanta, GA 30332
(1-800) 325 5007
(404) 894 7430

Environmental audits,
   environmental safety and health,
   and others

Geraghty & Miller, Inc.
c/o American Ecology
   Services, Inc.
127 East 59th St.
New York, NY 10022
(212) 371 1620

OSHA training for hazardous
   wastes

Harvard School of Public Health
Office of Continuing Education
677 Huntington Ave.
Boston, MA 02115
(617) 432 3515

Risk analysis, environmental safety
   and health, and others

Hazardous Materials Control
　Institute
Graduate Program
9300 Columbia Blvd.
Silver Spring, MD 20910
(301) 587 9390

Emergency response, hazardous
　materials and waste manage-
　ment, hydrogeology, and others
　(runs both a certificate and a
　degree program in conjunction
　with Wayne State University)

HAZMAT TISI (Training,
　Information and Services, Inc.)
Columbia Business Center
6480 Dobbin Rd.
Columbia, MD 21045

Hazardous materials training

Institute for Environmental
　Education
208 W. Cummings Park
Boston, MA 01801
(617) 935 7370

Asbestos and lead abatement,
　training-the-trainer, and others

National Environmental Training
　Association
8687 E. Via de Ventura
Suite 214
Scottsdale, AZ 85258
(602) 951 1440

Hazardous materials and waste
　management, safety and health,
　water treatment, emergency
　response, and others

NUS Training Corporation
P.O. Box 6032
910 Clopper Rd.
Gaithersburg, MD 20877
(301) 258 2500

Hazardous communications,
　safety, emergency response,
　hazardous materials handling,
　and others, on video formats

Rocky Mountain Center for
　Occupational and
　Environmental Health
Department of Family &
　Preventive Medicine
Bldg. 512
University of Utah
Salt Lake City, UT 84112
(801) 581 5710

Occupational safety and health,
　industrial ergonomics, asbestos
　sampling, industrial hygiene,
　and others

Texas A&M University System
Texas Engineering Extension
  Service
College Station, TX 77843
(409) 845 6681

OSHA and EPA courses

University of California-Berkeley
  Extension
Programs in Environmental
  Hazard Management (PEHM)
2223 Fulton St.
Berkeley, CA 94720
(415) 643 7143
(Most other locations in the
  University of California system
  offer similar courses.)

Environmental inspection and
  training and others

University of Cincinnati Medical
  Center
Institute of Environmental Health
Kettering Laboratory
3223 Eden Ave.
Cincinnati, OH 45267
(513) 558 1731

Asbestos abatement, training-the-
  trainer, and others

University of Findlay
The Emergency Response Training
  Center
Hazardous Materials Management
  Program
1000 N. Main St.
Findlay, OH 45840
(419) 424 4647

OSHA training, environmental
  management, hazardous
  materials, and others

University of Kansas
Division of Continuing Education
6600 College Blvd., Suite 315
Overland Park, KS 66211
(913) 491 0221

Hazardous waste site training and
  others

University of Texas at Arlington
Center for Environmental
  Research and Training (CERT)
P.O. Box 19021
Arlington, TX 76019
(817) 273 3694

Asbestos abatement, hazardous
wastes, emergency response, and
others

University of Wisconsin-Madison/
  Extension
Department of Engineering
  Professional Development
432 N. Lake St.
Madison, WI 53706
(1-800) 462 0876

Industrial pollution control,
underground storage tank
management, hazardous waste
site remediation, and others

Virginia Commonwealth
  University
Department of Preventive
  Medicine
Box 212 MCV Station
Richmond, VA 23298
(804) 786 9785

Environmental auditing,
inspection, underground storage
tanks, and others

References

CHAPTER ONE

1. Ausubel, J. H., and Sladovich, H. E., eds., *Technology and Environment* (Washington, D.C.: National Academy Press, 1989), p. vi.
2. U.S. Environmental Protection Agency, *Environmental Investments: The Costs of a Clean Environment* (Washington, D.C.: Government Printing Office, 1991).
3. Rennisi, E., "Biodiversity Rides a Popular Wave," *The Scientist*, April 15, 1991, p. 1.
4. Carey, J., "The Next Giant Leap for Mankind May Be Saving Planet Earth," *Business Week*, July 31, 1989, p. 90.
5. Young, J., *Sustaining the Earth* (Cambridge, MA: Harvard University Press, 1990), p. 80.
6. Ibid.
7. For commentary on the Lederman report, see "The Lederman Report and Its Critics," *Issues in Science and Technology*, March 1991, p. 32.

CHAPTER TWO

1. Mann, C., "Lynn Margulis: Science's Unruly Earth Mother," *Science*, April 19, 1991, p. 378.
2. Young, J., *Sustaining the Earth* (Cambridge, MA: Harvard University Press, 1990), p. 88.

3. Holden, C., "Science Career Trends for the '90s," *Science*, May 24, 1991, p. 252.

4. Duga, J. J., and Halder Fisher, W., *Battelle's R&D Forecast, 1991* (Columbus, OH: Battelle Memorial Institute, 1990), p. 4.

5. National Science Board, *Science & Engineering Indicators—1989* (Washington, D.C.: Government Printing Office, 1989), p. 62.

6. National Science Foundation, *Characteristics of Doctoral Scientists and Engineers in the United States—1987*, as cited in ref. [5], National Science Board, p. 246.

7. Snow, C. P., *The Two Cultures and A Second Look* (Cambridge, England: Cambridge University Press, 1980), p. 32.

8. Ibid., p. 33.

9. National Science Board, op. cit., p. 62.

10. Management Information Services, Inc., Washington, D.C., personal communication, 1991.

11. Holmyard, E. J., *Alchemy* (Mineola, NY: Dover Press, 1990).

12. Spitz, P., *Petrochemicals: The Rise of an Industry* (New York: John Wiley & Sons, 1988), p. 235ff.

13. *Chemical Scientists: Supply and Demand in a Changing World*, published by the Marketing Division of the American Chemical Society, prepared by Kline & Co., 1990.

14. Heylin, M., "Recession Raises Joblessness among Chemists; Salaries Post Routine Gains," *Chemical and Engineering News*, July 15, 1991, p. 35.

15. Abbot, S., "Perspective," *Environmental Lab*, February/March 1991, p. 7.

16. U.S. Environmental Protection Agency, *FY-1991 EPA Research Program Guide* (Washington, D.C.: Government Printing Office, 1990) EPA/600/9-90/033.

17. Beck, W., *Modern Science and the Nature of Life* (Garden City, NY: Doubleday & Co., 1961), p. 74ff.

18. Holden, C., "Science Career Trends for the '90s," *Science*, May 24, 1991, p. 1119.

19. U.S. Department of Education, *Digest of Educational Statistics, 1990* (Washington, D.C.: Government Printing Office, 1991), p. 370.

20. "Ecology," *Encyclopedia Brittanica*, 15th ed. (Chicago, IL: Encyclopedia Britannica, Inc., 1974), vol. 6, p. 197.

21. U.S. National Research Council, *Outlook for Science and Technology: The Next Five Years* (Washington, D.C.: National Academy of Sciences Press, 1982), p. 204.

22. Hardin, G., "The Tragedy of the Commons," *Science*, 1968, Vol. 162, pp. 1243–1248.

23. U.S. Office of Technology Assessment, *Bioremediation for Marine Oil Spills* (Washington, D.C.: Government Printing Office, 1991), OTA-BP-O-70.

24. Stevens, W., "Green-Thumbed Ecologists Resurrect Vanished Habitats," *New York Times*, March 19, 1991, p. C1.

25. Pinchot, G., *The Fight for Conservation* (1910), as cited in Nash, R., *The American Environment: Readings in the History of Conservation*, 2nd ed. (New York: Alfred A. Knopf, Inc., 1976), p. 61.

26. Hileman, B., "Alternative Agriculture," *Chemical and Engineering News*, March 5, 1990, p. 28.

27. Pollack, A., "Lumbering in the Age of the Baby Tree," *New York Times*, February 24, 1991, sec. 3, p. 1.

28. University of Maine, *Bulletin* (Orono, ME: University of Maine Department of Public Affairs), vol. 92, p. 297.

29. Hileman, B., op. cit., p. 29.

30. U.S. National Research Council, *Alternative Agriculture* (Washington, D.C.: National Academy of Sciences Press, 1989).

31. Ibid., p. 4.

32. Ibid., p. 14.

33. *Wall Street Journal*, July 31, 1991, p. 1.

34. Kerr, Richard, "NOAA Revived for the Green Decade," *Science*, June 8, 1990, p. 1177.

35. Duffy, John, *The Sanitarians* (Urbana, IL: University of Illinois Press, 1990), pp. 126ff.

36. Corn, Jacqueline Karnell, *Protecting the Health of Workers: The American Conference of Governmental Industrial Hygienists, 1938–1988* (Cincinnati, OH: ACGIH, 1989), pp. 2–6.

37. U.S. Department of Commerce, *Statistical Abstract of the United States, 1990* (Washington, D.C.: Government Printing Office, 1990), Table 684 (p. 416).

38. U.S. Office of Technology Assessment, *Complex Cleanup: The Environmental Legacy of Nuclear Weapons Production* (Washington, D.C.: Government Printing Office, 1991, OTA-O-484), p. 55.

CHAPTER THREE

1. Nash, R., *The American Environment: Readings in the History of Conservation*, 2nd ed. (New York: Alfred A. Knopf, Inc., 1976), p. 92.

2. Layton, Edwin Jr., *The Revolt of the Engineers: Social Responsibility and the American Engineering Profession* (Baltimore, MD: Johns Hopkins University Press, 1971).

3. U.S. Department of Labor, Bureau of Labor Statistics, *Occupations Projections and Training Data, 1990* (Washington, D.C.: Government Printing Office, 1990).

4. *Engineering Degree Statistics and Trends—1990*, Bulletin No. 106 (Washington, D.C.: Engineering Manpower Commission, November 1990).

5. Reynolds, T. S., *75 Years of Progress: A History of the American Institute of Chemical Engineers, 1908–1983* (New York: American Institute of Chemical Engineers, 1983), p. 1.

6. Basta, N., and Irving-Monshaw, S., "1990 Reader Interaction Survey, Salary and Benefits," *Chemical Engineering*, June 1990, p. 55.

7. U.S. National Research Council, *Frontiers in Chemical Engineering* (Washington, D.C.: National Academy of Sciences Press, 1988), p. 105.

8. Hawke, D. F., *Nuts and Bolts of the Past: A History of American Technology, 1776–1860* (New York: Harper & Row Publishers, 1988), p. 31.

9. Varrasi, J., "Environmental Clean-Up is the Job of the Mechanical Engineer," *Mechanical Engineering*, February 1991, p. 66.

10. Samuel Florman, personal communication.

11. U.S. Office of Personnel Management, *Career America* (Washington, D.C.: Government Printing Office, 1990), p. 41.

12. Duffy, J., *The Sanitarians: A History of American Public Health* (Urbana: University of Illinois Press, 1990), p. 129.

13. A good reference on this subject is Melosi, M. V., *Garbage in the Cities: Refuse, Reform and the Environment 1880–1980* (College Station: Texas A&M Press, 1981). See also Rathje, W. L., "Rubbish!," *Atlantic Monthly*, December 1989, p. 99.

14. Melosi, op. cit., p. 89.

15. Rathje, op. cit., p. 102.

16. U.S. Office of Technology Assessment, *Coming Clean: Superfund Problems Can Be Solved* (Washington, D.C.: Government Printing Office, 1989), p. 3.

17. A good source of information on the recycling business today is Bennett, S. J., *Ecopreneuring* (New York: John Wiley & Sons, 1991).

18. *Graduate Programs in Engineering and Applied Sciences 1991* (Princeton, NJ: Peterson's Guides, 1990), p. 1281.

19. "A Perfect Match: Nuclear Energy and the National Energy Strategy," a position paper by the Nuclear Power Oversight Committee, Washington, D.C., 1990, p. 1.

20. U.S. Office of Personnel Management, op. cit., p. 168.

21. Bell, T., "'90s Employment: Some Bad News, But Some Good," *IEEE Spectrum*, December 1990, p. 33.

22. Herman, R., Ardekani, S., and Ausubel, J., "Dematerialization," as published in Ausubel, J. H., and Sladovich, H. E., eds., *Technology and Environment* (Washington, D.C.: National Academy Press, 1989), p. 50.

23. Stewart, R., *Seven Decades That Changed America: A History of the American Society of Agricultural Engineers, 1907–1977*, (St. Joseph, MI: ASAE, 1979), p. 365.

24. Shabecoff, P., "Industrial Pollution Called Startling," *New York Times*, April 13, 1989, p. D21.

25. Meadows, D. H. and D. L., Randers, J., and Behrens, W., *The Limits to Growth* (New York: New American Library, Inc., 1972).

26. See, for example, Tucker, W., *Progress and Privilege* (New York: Anchor Press/Doubleday, 1982), p. 191ff.

Index